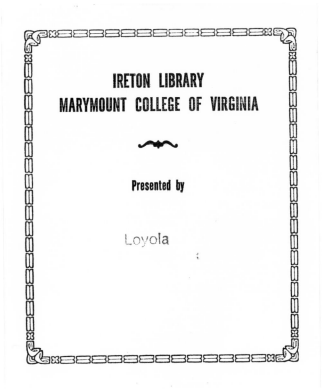

# CORPORATE POLICY, VALUES AND SOCIAL RESPONSIBILITY

# CORPORATE POLICY, VALUES AND SOCIAL RESPONSIBILITY

Anthony F. Buono
Larry Nichols

PRAEGER

PRAEGER SPECIAL STUDIES • PRAEGER SCIENTIFIC

New York • Philadelphia • Eastbourne, UK
Toronto • Hong Kong • Tokyo • Sydney

84841

**Library of Congress Cataloging in Publication Data**

Buono, Anthony F.
  Corporate policy, values and social responsibility.

  Includes index.
  1. Industry—Social aspects.   I. Nichols,
Lawrence T.   II. Title.
HD60.B85   1985          658.4'08          85-6422
ISBN 0-03-063061-4 (alk. paper)

Published in 1985 by Praeger Publishers
CBS Educational and Professional Publishing, a Division of CBS Inc.
521 Fifth Avenue, New York, NY 10175 USA

56789 052 987654321

Printed in the United States of America on acid-free paper

## INTERNATIONAL OFFICES

Orders from outside the United States should be sent to the appropriate address listed below. Orders
from areas not listed below should be placed through CBS International Publishing, 383 Madison Ave..
New York, NY 10175 USA

### Australia, New Zealand
Holt Saunders, Pty, Ltd., 9 Waltham St., Artarmon, N.S.W. 2064, Sydney, Australia

### Canada
Holt, Rinehart & Winston of Canada, 55 Horner Ave., Toronto, Ontario, Canada M8Z 4X6

### Europe, the Middle East, & Africa
Holt Saunders, Ltd., 1 St. Anne's Road, Eastbourne, East Sussex, England BN21 3UN

### Japan
Holt Saunders, Ltd., Ichibancho Central Building, 22-1 Ichibancho, 3rd Floor, Chiyodaku, Tokyo, Japan

### Hong Kong, Southeast Asia
Holt Saunders Asia, Ltd., 10 Fl, Intercontinental Plaza, 94 Granville Road, Tsim Sha Tsui East,
Kowloon, Hong Kong

**Manuscript submissions should be sent to the Editorial Director, Praeger Publishers, 521 Fifth
Avenue, New York, NY 10175 USA**

To Mary Alice and Allison,
who have sustained us

# PREFACE

This volume undertakes an interdisciplinary analysis of business's social role. It represents an effort to integrate the fundamental perspectives of management and sociology, and to bring them to bear upon the issue of corporate social responsibility. In most existing studies, managerial and sociological points of view tend to be mutually exclusive, and are not infrequently regarded as diametrically opposed. While we appreciate some of the reasons for this state of affairs, and respect the work of others within these individual frames of reference, we believe that a more holistic treatment of the problem of the corporate social role is in order. As a step in this direction, it is our goal to build some bridges between management studies and sociology, and to promote further dialogue of an interdisciplinary nature.

We wish to emphasize at the outset the intent and limitations of our discussion, not in a defensive spirit, but merely to clarify our aims and our scope. First, the present work does not seek to be comprehensive, and is much closer to a monograph than to a text. It is therefore probably best used in conjunction with some more general source, whether text, casebook, or reader. Second, although we attempt an interdisciplinary analysis—drawing from business and society studies, business policy, business ethics and sociology—this should not be viewed as a boundary or complete analytic framework. The perspectives of other allied fields—political science, organizational behavior, and psychology among others—have much to offer in furthering our understanding of the complex phenomena in question. Third, the particular cases provided in this book are likewise not exhaustive in character, and are intended primarily to illustrate potential applications of the central conceptual model.

Another concern focuses on the conceptual language used throughout the book. While it is our hope that this language is clear and appropriate to the task, we admit to imperfections in some of the terms selected, especially for the four philosophies of social responsibility. To a considerable degree, such problems are unavoidable, for complex phenomena cannot be forced into the confines of any single word. A variety of alternatives were tested over a period of time, so that the central concepts of productivism, philanthropy, progressivism and ethical idealism seem most appropriate to us despite their shortcomings. In this regard, the term ethical idealism has perhaps remained the most problematic and may not suit the taste of all readers.

In setting out what seem to us the most important perspectives on corporate social responsibility, we have tried to place ourselves in the background rather than inculcate our own beliefs and priorities. Each philosophy of social responsibility has thus been treated with respect, so that it might receive a full and fair hearing from our readers. Our effort to remain relatively non-partisan may be a disappointment to some, while others may dismiss it as an impossibility. Yet it has been our consistent view that a dialogic, rather than militantly ideological, approach best serves the interests of all. Nonetheless, at various points our preferences and commitments may appear between the lines.

The book has developed gradually over a period of several years, many of its chapters and other components being originally a series of papers delivered at social issues sessions of the Academy of Management, and The Institute of Management Science and Operations Research Society of America (TIMS/ORSA). Many of the ideas presented here reflect fuller analysis and discussion of an article entitled "Corporate Responsiveness Policies and the Dynamics of Bank Reinvestment Policy" which appeared in Volume 6 of Research in Corporate Social Policy and Performance (JAI Press, 1984). We found ourselves often surprised as further implications continued to unfold from the conceptual skeleton we had built. At times, the process seemed to have a dynamic of its own, until we unexpectedly reached the point where there seemed to be sufficient material for a book. Our original intent was not to write a book at all, but simply to stimulate a fuller interdisciplinary discussion of business's social role.

As with any work of this nature, there are a number of people to thank for their support and contribution. Many of our academic colleagues, especially Rob Enggist, Mike Hatcher, Ed Marshall, Sev Bruyn, Mike Hoffman, Joe Raelin and Walter Klein have directly or indirectly influenced our thinking in writing this book. Lee Preston provided numerous comments and suggestions on early portions of the manuscript. Gerald Mulligan and Stanley Zoll (Office of the Commissioner of Banks), Frank Dooher, Maureen Ball, and Joanne Schenck (Boston area bankers), John Moynihan (Archdiocese of Boston), David Jones and the staff at the Massachusetts Urban Reinvestment Advisory Group, and the staff at the Industrial Cooperative Association were quite helpful in providing information and insight during the research process. Kathy Kerrigan and Kim Waitkus expertly typed the manuscript, often under considerable time pressure with us looking over their shoulders. Mary Daly, our secretary at Bentley College, oversaw the production process. Finally, our wives, Mary Alice and Allison, to whom this book is dedicated, listened to our ideas and complaints, and undertook more than their share of child rearing responsibilities despite their own career demands during the lengthy process of completing this book.

We sincerely hope that this work will be of benefit to others in their own research. We should succeed if we raise more questions than we answer, and if these questions are sufficiently interesting for others to explore the fruitfulness of the conceptions we propose, modifying or extending them as need be.

AFB
LTN

# CONTENTS

PREFACE      vii

Chapter

1   BUSINESS AND SOCIETY:
    THE GENERAL DEBATE      1

    Corporate Stockholders and Stakeholders      3
    Defining the Issue: From Social Responsibility
      to Social Policy      9
    Conclusion      22

2   AN INTEGRAL CONCEPTUALIZATION      30

    Business and Society      30
    Business Policy      37
    Business Ethics      43
    Social Economy      51
    Conclusion      60

3   PHILOSOPHIES OF CORPORATE SOCIAL
    RESPONSIBILITY      66

    Culture      67
    The Method of Ideal Types      70
    An Ideal Typical Model of Social Responsibility      72
    Summary      104

4   SOCIAL RESPONSIBILITY AND POLICY
    RESPONSES      109

    A Sociocultural View of Policy      110
    From Philosophy to Policy: Crucial Assumptions      111
    Corporate Social Policy: An Integrated Model      113
    The Broader Issue: Organizational Philosophy
      and Policy      120
    Conclusion      123

Chapter                                                           Page

5    THE DYNAMICS OF SOCIAL POLICY I:
     INTERPRETIVE PROCESSES                                        126

     Setting the Terms of Responsiveness: A Brief
        History of the Community Reinvestment Act                 128
     Interpreting the Terms of Responsiveness:
        A Comparative Case Study                                  136
     Conclusion                                                   150

6    THE DYNAMICS OF SOCIAL POLICY II:
     CONFRONTATION AND CONFLICT                                   154

     Conflict Over Reinvestment: Three Cases                      155
     Case Analysis and Interpretation                             163
     Toward a Model of Policy Disputes                            174
     Conclusion                                                   177

7    CORPORATE RESPONSIBILITY AND SOCIAL
     CHANGE                                                       183

     A Theoretical Approach to Change                             187
     An Emergent Movement: Cooperative Corporations               202

8    INVESTIGATING CORPORATE SOCIAL PERFORM-
     ANCE AND POLICY: A RESEARCH NOTE                             211

     Methodological Concerns                                      211
     The Problem of Multiple Realities                            215
     Theoretical, Social, and Empirical Triangulation            218

INDEX                                                             225

# 1

# BUSINESS AND SOCIETY:
# THE GENERAL DEBATE

There was a time, in the not too distant past, when a
U.S. president could declare that, "The business of America
is Business," and feel confident that everyone in his audience
would understand the reference. Today, the circumstances
are quite different. Most people—professionals and lay people—
would probably agree that business is still the dominant social
institution in this country. It has become increasingly difficult,
however, to attain consensus on the specific mission of the
corporate sector. Business organizations and their management
are currently facing many new demands which are based on
changing societal expectations about the appropriate role of
the corporation in the larger social system. This situation has
given rise to a growing literature on "business and society,"
which is now a standard component of managerial training at
the university level. In the political arena, there has simultaneously been vigorous debate over proposals which range
from integrated industrial policies and increased governmental
oversight to the deregulation of entire industries. The question
on everyone's mind seems to be, "What is the proper business
of business?"

Most people would agree with the proposition that social
concerns should be included in the everyday operations of
business firms. These same individuals, however, would tend
to disagree about what concerns to incorporate and how to
implement them.[1] The past two decades have witnessed calls
for corporate reassessment of manufacturing processes in the
light of imminent environmental dangers, for modification of
the racial and sexual composition of our labor force, for improved

product safety, and for more concern about the health and general well-being of employees.[2] And these are only some of the more prominent issues. A recent study, sponsored by the prestigious Business Roundtable,* which focused on these issues from the viewpoints of the general public, relevant interest groups and business executives, revealed a greatly broadened view of the concept of "corporate performance."[4] In addition to the traditional financial and economic-oriented aspects of business activity, significant performance issues ranged from meeting consumer expectations in the marketplace, the appropriate magnitude of business profit and executive compensation, and the usefulness and validity of financial reporting and control, to quality of work life issues, employee citizenship rights, political participation and influence, and ethical and social behavior. While many business executives might attempt to dismiss these expectations as unacceptable or misguided perceptions, such aspects of corporate performance have become the subject of public debate and government action.

Public expectations toward the business sector have evolved to the point where firms are presently evaluated on social and ethical grounds as well as the traditional economic and legalistic performance criteria.[5] However, a consensus on the nature of business's social role has yet to emerge. There is also ample confusion concerning the underlying nature and stability of these broad interpretations of corporate performance.[6] In many instances, the resultant dialogue has been manifested in ongoing controversy between the business sector and an increasing array of claimant groups and public or private "watchdog" agencies.

---

*The Business Roundtable is an organization composed of approximately 190 major U.S. corporations. Membership is composed of the chief executive officers of a wide array of firms—manufacturers, banks, retailers, insurance companies, the extractive industries, and transportation and communication companies. Formed in 1972, the Roundtable is oriented toward more cooperation and less antagonism between the business sector and government. Its basic goals are: 1) to facilitate mutual interaction on various issues by bringing different companies together; and 2) to present the government and the public with knowledgeable and timely information, combined with suggestions for policy and action. In order to accomplish these goals, the Roundtable serves as a vehicle to directly involve CEOs in the public policy decision-making process.[3]

While most business people recognize that there have been various instances of socially unacceptable business decisions and activities, as a group they rarely agree with the proposals suggested by such external groups. This has contributed to the further debate concerning the scope and parameters of corporate performance.[7] Thus, while everyone may agree that we are in the midst of unprecedented social change in our major institutional sectors—educational, political, familial, and economic—not everyone agrees on business's role and responsibilities in this transformation.

## CORPORATE STOCKHOLDERS
## AND STAKEHOLDERS

One way of defining the social function of business is to analyze the relationships between economic firms and the social groups which are affected by their operation. Most immediately relevant for this purpose are groups of owners, employees, customers, suppliers, local communities, and governmental agencies. The social bonds between corporations and these publics, as one would expect, are variable in terms of their intensity, duration, and particular significance. This variability, and the ambiguities inherent in the situation, have given rise to two opposed perspectives—the stockholder and stakeholder models of corporate activity.

### Stockholder Model of Corporate Performance

Through most of American history, the stockholder model has been the norm. According to this view, a corporation is essentially a piece of private property which is owned by the persons who hold stock. These owners elect a board of directors for the corporation, who serve them and guide the corporation in their best financial interests. Future stockholders are eventually attracted by the economic performance of the firm, and decide to invest their money under the expectation that they will receive a fair and reasonable gain in the value of their equity. Such gains are forthcoming when the firm is properly managed under a general policy of profit maximization. Employees are also viewed as servants of the firm, functioning as technical instruments in production, marketing, and sales. The corporation is considered to be a private group of individuals bound by formal contract, which has the freedom to arrange its affairs according to its own preferences, so long as it does not violate any fundamental social norms, such as those prohibiting fraud.

The stockholder model assumes that relations between individual corporations and the groups affected by their operation are best structured as marketplace transactions, based on mutually beneficial exchange. Free markets, responding to and expressing the voluntary choices of individuals and groups, serve several basic functions. They quickly and efficiently store and transmit information relative to supply and demand in the form of adjustable prices. They expand and contract according to the economic realities of the day. And they safeguard all participants against the use and abuse of arbitrary power. For so long as markets include a plurality of buyers and sellers, producers and consumers, employers and employees, none of these individual groups will be controlled by unregulated power centers.[8] The free market, in fact, rather than government, is the great social regulator, and may be said to be as democratic as any social institution is capable of being, when operated under the proper conditions.

As noted above, this stockholder view of the corporation and the economy, in which business firms are regarded as technical instruments for the production of wealth, constituted the dominant, orthodox approach from the end of the eighteenth century into the twentieth. Toward the end of the nineteenth century, certain modifications were added, in the form of antitrust laws intended to prevent the largest corporations from controlling their markets. Early in the present century, other reformist efforts led to federal laws requiring that food and drugs be safely manufactured. Despite such alterations, however, the dominant stockholder view prevailed and seemed unchallengeable.[9] Even the Great Depression of the 1930s seems not to have threatened it in the popular mind. As the Lynds reported in their classic study of Middletown (Muncie, Indiana), there was a widespread desire that economic and political relations return to normal as quickly as possible, which meant that private businesses should be permitted to pursue profit to the extent of their capabilities.[10] Business was considered socially responsible because it produced wealth, permitted free enterprise, and supplied jobs.


Stakeholder Model of Corporate Performance

In contrast to the stockholder view, an emergent perspective referred to as the stakeholder model regards corporations as servants of the larger society. This view indicates that there are increasing demands on business organizations which include a wider variety of publics not traditionally related to the corporation's immediate self-interest.[11] Indeed, as Ackerman and Bauer argue,

> It makes more sense to conceive of the business firm as the central element of a role set in which a new pattern of relationships among the elements is evolving. Each of the parties, either directly or via volunteer spokesmen (e.g., consumerists) is pressing its interests. Presumably, the various elements of the role set are moving toward some state of equilibrium. The firm will have to develop the capacity to manage this demanding set of relationships.[12]

Essentially, this model of corporate activity proposes that each organization has a set of stakeholders who are materially involved with the firm through different transactions and are affected by its performance. Thus, the notion of stakeholders goes beyond the immediate interest of stockholders. It views profit in broader terms, with a longer-term focus that encompasses greater consideration for other groups in the firm's environment. The significant concentrations of resources which businesses control are therefore to be managed in the public interest as a kind of trust. Profit should be pursued within the basic objectives of public policy, such as a pollution-free environment or a racially and sexually integrated work force. Employees are regarded as persons who have a wide range of needs in which the corporation must take an interest. Stockholders continue to occupy a place of prominence, but their interests and desires are no longer absolutely decisive for the determination of corporate conduct.

Inasmuch as the stakeholder model can include an indefinitely large number of groups with some interest in corporate operations, a further distinction is usually made between primary and secondary stakeholders. Primary stakeholders are those individuals and groups who are most directly affected by the activities of the firm, and who make some tangible contribution to its functioning, such as employees, customers, and suppliers. Secondary stakeholders are affected by corporate actions, but do not participate in the ordinary operations of the business. Examples would include consumers as a group, women, ethnic minorities, environmental groups, the press, and competitors.[13] The relationships here are very dynamic,

since the perceptions and demands of any factions can change
without warning. It is also interesting to note in passing that
while many contemporary executives are quite willing to recognize the concept of stakeholders in general, they often resist
the inclusion of what are regarded as adversary groups in the
set of interested parties whose welfare must be considered.

A growing body of evidence indicates that the stakeholder
model of the corporation is becoming the new orthodoxy, especially within large corporations and university schools of
management. A Harvard Business Review survey, for example,
reported that only 2 percent of a sample of 3,453 business
people agreed that the most valid description of a corporation's
duty was primarily to its owners and only to its owners.[14] By
contrast, 61 percent described the most valid role of the corporation as trying to serve as fairly and equitably as possible the
interests of employees, customers, and the public, as well as
the owners of the organization (see Table 1.1). Other surveys
have also indicated that business people feel greater responsibility to their customers than to their stockholders.[15] Such
results suggest that an important component of the professional-
ization of management has been the adoption of a stakeholder
view of corporate operations.

Given this orientation, some of the most critical tradeoffs
facing management today are between the demands of different
constituencies, who each have a stake in some aspect of the
organization's performance.[16] Based on the responses in a
1984 survey of 1,460 executives, middle level managers, and
supervisory managers, for example, stockholders were again
viewed as far less important than customers, internal stakeholders
such as subordinates, co-workers and other employees, and the
general public (see Table 1.2). Even though managers at
different hierarchical levels weighed the importance of these
stakeholders differently, the order of relative importance is
quite similar. Thus, the traditional stereotype of managers
running their organizations for the primary benefit of their
stockholders does not seem to be supported by these studies.

One should not conclude, however, that the stakeholder
view is progressing without significant problems or opposition.
An important stumbling block which has been recognized in
the literature is the allegiance of managers to themselves and
their own career interests. Because job tenure has become
very unstable, even for senior level managers, success for
an executive's career may not coincide with success for the
stockholders or stakeholders of the firm. Statistics show that
the terms of chief executive officers average seven years, and

TABLE 1.1

Managerial Opinions of the Role of the Corporation (in percent)

| Viewpoint | Strongly Agree | Agree | Disagree | Strongly Disagree |
|---|---|---|---|---|
| A corporation's duty is primarily to its owners and only its owners. | 2 | 4 | 20 | 74 |
| A corporation's duty is primarily to its owners and secondarily to employees, customers, and the public. | 20 | 38 | 40 | 2 |
| A corporation's duty is to serve as fairly and equitably as it can the interests of four sometimes competing groups— owners, employees, customers, and the public. | 61 | 24 | 9 | 6 |
| The primary duty of the enterprise is to itself—to ensure its future growth and continued functioning as a profit-making supplier of goods and services. | 28 | 29 | 27 | 16 |

Source: Reprinted with permission of the Harvard Business Review. An exhibit from "Who Wants Corporate Democracy?" by David W. Ewing (September/October 1971). Copyright ©1971 by the President and Fellows of Harvard College; all rights reserved.

TABLE 1.2

The Importance of Various Organizational Stakeholders

| | Supervisory Managers | Middle Managers | Executive Managers |
|---|---|---|---|
| Customers | 5.57 | 6.10 | 6.40 |
| Myself | 6.28 | 6.29 | 6.28 |
| Subordinates | 6.06 | 6.30 | 6.14 |
| Employees | 5.93 | 6.11 | 6.01 |
| Boss(es) | 5.72 | 5.92 | 5.82 |
| Co-workers | 5.87 | 5.82 | 5.81 |
| Colleagues | 5.66 | 5.78 | 5.75 |
| Managers | 5.26 | 5.56 | 5.75 |
| Technical employees | 5.21 | 5.32 | 5.40 |
| White collar employees | 4.96 | 5.25 | 5.40 |
| Owners | 4.07 | 4.51 | 5.30 |
| Craftsmen | 4.14 | 4.75 | 5.01 |
| General public | 4.38 | 4.49 | 4.52 |
| Stockholders | 3.35 | 3.79 | 4.51 |
| Elected public officials | 3.81 | 3.54 | 3.79 |
| Government bureaucrats | 3.09 | 2.05 | 2.90 |

Scaling: 1 = little importance to me; 7 = very important to me.

Source: Copyright © 1984 by the Regents of the University of California. Reprinted from California Management Review XXVI, no. 3, p. 206 by permission of the Regents.

this fact of life may motivate some individuals to place themselves and their career paths above the interests of either stockholders or stakeholders.[17] Moreover, it is important to note that the relatively high rating of "myself" as an important organizational stakeholder in Table 1.2 further reinforces this concern. Posner and Schmidt also found that this high ranking did not change when the data were controlled for gender, age, education level, salary, or years of experience. These findings question the stereotype of younger generations of managers as being more (or less) narcissistic (the so-called "me-generation") than other generations of managers in today's business organizations.

In summary, several analyses have suggested that management of large business organizations in our society has moved from ownership orientations to more of a trusteeship orientation where there is concern for a wider range of claimant groups related to the firm. As the social environment—through many of these critical constituencies—sends messages to business organizations in a number of different forms (for example, social criticism, legislation, media criticism, and so on), such groups are viewed as increasingly operating as "arbiters" of social responsibility.[18]

## DEFINING THE ISSUE: FROM SOCIAL RESPONSIBILITY TO SOCIAL POLICY

While the stakeholder model suggests that business organizations have a broad social role with concomitant responsibilities to a number of relevant publics, the nature of this role and responsibility is still debated. In fact, scholarly examination of these issues has resulted in a variety of conceptual approaches, each defining the business and society field and its agenda of study in a distinctive way. Four general perspectives have become especially prominent for both research and teaching in this area: social responsibility, social responsiveness, social performance, and social policy. These orientations are presented in a chronological and logical sequence, for the earlier concepts dealt more with general ends and moral norms, while the latter have increasingly focused on specific means and technical norms. As part of a foundation for the analysis of current concerns, each of these major conceptualizations will be briefly reviewed.

### Corporate Social Responsibility

Although the idea that business organizations should be socially responsible for their actions has increasingly been placed at the forefront of debate and discussion in today's society, the concept itself is not a contemporary idea. In fact, the rationale for the business sector to assume broader patterns of social awareness and responsibility can be traced back over many centuries.[19] Contemporary usage of the term "social responsibility," however, is usually traced to the 1953 work of Howard Bowen, entitled Social Responsibilities of Businessmen. This volume raised several basic themes which are still reflected in discussions of business and society three decades later.

First was the idea of a purely voluntary commitment on the part of corporate management, the notion that firms would decide to expand their social role without a specific legal obligation to do so. Secondly, the exercise of social responsibility by corporations was to be motivated by a desire to improve the general quality of life in society, rather than by considerations of selfish gain in terms of profit or publicity. As Bowen put it, social responsibility "refers to the idea . . . that voluntary assumption of social responsibility by businessmen is, or might be, a practicable means towards ameliorating economic problems and attaining more fully the economic goals we seek."[20] Finally, the context of corporate action was portrayed as a turbulent social environment, in which business was responding to new demands from a variety of sources, especially labor and government.

In the wake of Bowen's discussion, a large literature quickly appeared, prompting Peter Drucker to remark that, "You might wonder, if you were a conscientious newspaper reader, when the managers of American business had any time for business."[21] By the early 1960s, there seemed to be widespread agreement with the view that "the idea of social responsibility supposes that the corporation has not only legal and economic obligations, but also certain responsibilities to society which extend beyond those obligations."[22] In delineating the essential ingredients of this "new concept" of social responsibility, Clarence Walton pointed to "its degree of voluntarism as opposed to coercion, the indirect linkage of certain other voluntary organizations to the corporation, and the admission that costs are involved for which it may not be possible to gauge any direct measurable economic return."[23]

These perspectives are not to suggest that the topic of social responsibility attracted a unanimous response. On the contrary, one important result of the emerging dialogue was the development of Milton Friedman's well known dissent, most notably in his 1962 work Capitalism and Freedom. Here, Friedman insisted that "there is one and only one social responsibility of business—to use its resources and engage in activities designed to increase its profits so long as it stays within the rules of the game." The other goals referred to by writers about corporate social responsibility would "thoroughly undermine the very foundations of our free society."[24] Many individuals felt profit seeking was not only the indispensable logic of our economy, but that the business sector served the public interest most effectively when it best served its own private interests. Although it was realized that there were nonprofit aspects of business performance, these analyses were emphatic that the focus of corporate attention should remain on profit maximization. In fact, one of the concerns was that it might even be "unethical" to forego profits and, as a result, not live up to the contract with stockholders.[25]

As the decade of the 1970s began, these different views were reflected in at least four versions of social responsibility in the professional literature.[26] Some continued to advocate a position of "fight all the way," meaning that no action other than defensive responses to criticism should be taken by management. Others proposed a more compliant approach, but still argued for minimal departures from traditional practice, under the general guideline of "do only what is required." Proponents of social responsibility often tried to "be progressive," especially by broadening the range of issues to be considered by management. At the end of the continuum were those who argued that corporations, motivated by a sense of social duty, should try to "lead the industry," especially through substantial experimentation and applied research.

Reviewing the situation in 1978, Gerald Keim suggested three major interpretations of the concept.[27] A vocal minority, most notably economists like Friedman and Smith, adhered to a Traditional Viewpoint, which argues for social responsibility in terms of a self-regulating market. Others held a general Popular Viewpoint, a sort of profit-plus philosophy, which taught that corporations had social obligations beyond the narrow goals of profit and earnings. Finally, a growing segment of contemporary managers had adopted an Enlightened Self-Interest Viewpoint, which merged these two interpretations. This approach argued that social responsibility was good business practice, because failure to deal with social concerns in a timely manner often resulted in social criticism and heavy-handed governmental regulation which interfered with corporate operations. Therefore, social responsibility implied a proactive, or even preventive, plan of action.

Thus, over the course of some three decades the concept of corporate social responsibility was explored in considerable depth and detail. In the process, some of the basic themes which seem to consistently emerge from those calling for social responsibility are reflected in moral attitudes and obligations: 1) an emphasis on executive conscience leading to a set of implied standards for behavior; 2) the costs (or foregone profits) of such behaviors to serve social priorities; and 3) the difference between voluntary or discretionary actions and those which are mandated.[28] Many observers, however, began to express the opinion that social responsibility had no clear reference, that it had become, in effect, all things to all people.[29] Dow Votaw summarizes this concern in his argument that the concept of social responsibility is:

> a brilliant one; it means something, but not always
> the same thing to everybody. To some it conveys
> the idea of legal responsibility or liability; to others,
> it means socially responsible <u>behavior</u> in an ethical
> sense; to still others, the meaning transmitted is
> that of 'responsible for,' in a causal mode; many
> simply equate it with a charitable contribution;
> some take it to mean socially conscious; many of
> those who embrace it most fervently see it as a mere
> synonym for 'legitimacy,' in the context of 'belonging'
> or being proper or valid; a few see it as a sort of
> fiduciary duty imposing higher standards of behavior
> on businessmen than on citizens at large.[30]

Informed commentators, therefore, advocated other conceptual approaches.

### Corporate Social Responsiveness

Many critics of the concept of corporate social responsibility argued that while it may have been appropriate initially to focus on moral attitudes and obligations, the emphasis on motivation alone is not sufficient.[31] Since dealing with social concerns is more than simply deciding what to do, the managerial task of implementation—putting these social concerns into practice— becomes critical. This emphasis, which has been referred to as "corporate responsiveness," suggests that as firms become aware of and recognize their responsibility (that is, obligation) to society they begin to react to these concerns. The focus is no longer on social obligations and attitudes per se, but on the adaptation of corporate behaviors.

Sethi, for example, suggests a three-stage framework for classifying corporate response to social concerns: social obligation, social responsibility, and social responsiveness.[32] Social obligation, according to Sethi, is organizational activity in response to market forces or legal constraints. Social responsibility, by contrast, implies bringing corporate response "up to a level where it is congruent with the prevailing social norms, values, and expectations." Such responsibility represents "a step ahead," acting before new social expectations are codified into legal requirements. Finally, social responsiveness focuses on responses which are more "anticipatory and preventive in nature." In this sense, responsiveness places an emphasis on the long-term role of business in our society. Corporations should attempt to:

> minimize the adverse side effects of present or future activities before these side effects assume crisis proportions and become catalysts for another wave of protest against business. [Corporations] should also prepare to accept the challenges that the system may come to consider appropriate for corporations to tackle. [33]

Although much of this distinction may initially appear to be more semantic than substantive, the orientation of many theoretical and empirical works during the early to mid-1970s underscores the shift in study from obligations to the behaviors and process of responding to social concerns. The general pattern which emerged from these efforts suggests that corporate responsiveness involved three basic phases: awareness or identification, commitment, and implementation. [34] The awareness or identification stage reflects the process of identifying existing issues and anticipating the development of potentially significant ones for the organization and the larger society. This is usually accomplished through external public pressures, legal and public policy changes, and internally based environmental monitoring and scanning programs. In terms of the organization's consideration of socially responsible actions, this is where concerns and problems are initially recognized. Although it might be assumed that this is an orderly and rational process, research has indicated that it is much more haphazard and unsystematic than expected. [35]

The commitment stage occurs when questions of how and when the firm will respond begin to emerge. A key aspect of this phase is the selection of issues to which an organization will respond. Although the earlier discussions of social responsibility suggested that such acts should be voluntarily undertaken, empirical investigations have indicated that both the timing and level of commitment are directly related to the intensity of external pressures and concerns. [36] Indeed, many of the issues on which organizations are being asked to respond are matters of law. Thus, the question is not if business will respond, but rather how and when to respond and with what level of commitment.

Finally, the implementation stage focuses on the initiation and execution of social policies and programs at the strategic and operating levels of an organization. While this may appear to be a relatively straightforward process, there are numerous problems associated with implementation which vary according to the structure of the organization, the locus of initiative and execution (for example, in a divisionalized firm where the policy is formulated at the corporate level but carried out at the plant level), and other organizational barriers. Organizational efforts are often hampered by such obstacles as: 1) resistance to undertake actions to which members are not accustomed; 2) perceived violation of managerial autonomy which many managers have come to regard as a right; and 3) potential negative impact on the firm's financial performance which may threaten an individual manager's immediate bonus and "track record."[37]

The emphasis on social responsiveness, therefore, begins to look at managerial concerns and difficulties as well as broader social concerns and obligations. Early research by Robert Ackerman has underscored the fact that this is usually a long and complex process, going through three basic stages.[38] Stage I occurs when a top executive (usually the chief executive officer) recognizes an important issue and becomes committed to doing something about it. Although this commitment is communicated to others in the organization, this "policy development" phase produces little or no organizational change. If the commitment is significant, however, during Stage II a staff specialist (often referred to as a social issue specialist) is appointed. At this point, the issue is dealt with in technical terms as the specialist defines the problem, designs data systems to interpret the environment and "measure" the problem, identifies what needs to be done, and formulates a more explicit policy statement. Despite these efforts, little effective change occurs at the organization's operating level. Stage III, or what Ackerman refers to as the institutionalization phase, is when the issue is defined as a management problem. Operating managers are required to build the implementation of the policy into their business plans: budgets are allocated, objectives are set, personnel are trained, and administrative procedures are designed and put into practice.

The key issues in discussions of social responsiveness, therefore, are the process of responding to these social concerns, and what the long-term role of the organization will be with respect to the issues involved.[39] There is still an emphasis on executive conscience (as in Stage I of Ackerman's model), but the concern is on moral behavior rather than on obligation.

This shift began to orient analyses of business's social role to questions of organizational innovation and strategy. Indeed, as Ackerman and Bauer summarize, the emergent notion of social responsiveness refers to the discharge of organizational responsibility to the larger society on a number of interrelated dimensions:

1. Social demands have strategic implications for organizations which extend beyond the immediate costs of possible responses.
2. Social responsiveness entails the management of a process through which public expectations are identified, placed in the context of other organizational concerns, and woven into the ways of doing business.
3. Management of social responsiveness calls for innovations in performance measurement (e.g., social audits, social accounting systems).
4. Organizations have had to contend with forces that at the outset they did not fully understand.
5. Response to most significant social issues requires the institutionalization of changes in the way decisions are made by operating managers in the field. [40]

Thus, the focus of these examinations moved toward the notion of performance and strategy, and the organizational policies that attempt to protect and improve the welfare of the larger society along with the long-term interests of the organization.


Corporate Social Performance

As investigations and assessments of business's social role moved from an emphasis on moral attitudes and obligations to behaviors, the focus was increasingly placed on outcomes. Part of this process is reflected in both definitions and interpretations of "social responsibility" and in the way in which individual firms were responding to their social role. In an attempt to define social responsibility in this broader framework, for example, Carroll suggested that it encompasses four types of responsibilities:

1. Economic: production of goods and services
2. Legal: compliance with the laws of society
3. Ethical: compliance with those areas that are not embodied by law but in which society expects performance nevertheless; and

4. Discretionary: purely voluntary areas where there is no clear cut message to business.[41]

Carroll is quick to point out that this framework presents a static view of an organization's "total social responsibility." In other words, over time there is a shift from what is viewed as discretionary to ethical to legal (through the incorporation of social controversies into legislation and regulation). For instance, during the early part of this century there were no clear "signals" from society as to what business's position should be with respect to women and racial minorities. During the 1960s, however, this began to emerge as an ethical issue (business organizations should not discriminate) and ultimately became a legal one (through affirmative action laws and equal employment opportunity legislation). The key, however, is that Carroll's definition places its emphasis on performance across these dimensions.

Others have argued that a "more reasonable approach" to defining the social responsibility of business is to identify the specific social programs and activities in which a firm is engaged.[42] A number of studies, for example, have examined managerial perceptions about the types of social issues "which deserved" businesses' priority. The four categories most mentioned were: 1) corporate philanthropy to education and the arts; 2) programs focused on the disadvantaged and racial minorities (e.g., hiring, education, training); 3) local community projects including urban renewal, fund-raising drives and charities; and 4) environmental improvement, pollution control and other ecological concerns.[43]

A significant limitation of this approach, however, is that it takes quite a narrow view of how such performance is evaluated and interpreted by different groups in the organization's environment. Questions which should be raised concern the extent to which an organization's critical constituencies concur about the types of issues which "deserve" business attention. Indeed, is social performance accurately measured by managerial perceptions of what is important and how their organizations are responding? To what extent does such an orientation neglect the larger social processes of evaluation and assessment of such performance by external groups?

In a broad sense, the concept of corporate social performance integrates the notions of social responsibility and social responsiveness. As Archie Carroll has argued, corporate social performance requires that 1) an organization's social responsibilities be assessed; 2) the specific issues it addresses be identified; and 3) a response philosophy be chosen.[44]

## Assessment and Performance

As discussed above, Carroll has suggested that one way to assess a firm's "social responsibilities" is to look at its performance across economic, legal, ethical, and discretionary dimensions. The emphasis on such performance necessitates the development of some system of measurement and reporting which can provide the basis for assessing the performance of individual managers and departments to serve as a basis for internal control and accountability, and measuring the perform- ance of the organization as a whole to serve as a basis for external reporting. Financial accounting and auditing systems have long been the basis for assessing and reporting economic performance. In terms of the other performance dimensions, however, a much broader type of assessment system—often referred to as social accounting or social auditing—is required. In a general sense, a social audit attempts to identify, measure, evaluate, report, and monitor the effects an organization is having on the larger society or on specific stakeholder groups that are not covered by the organization's financial reports.[45] As such a broad definition implies, there are a number of conceptual and technical problems involved in social auditing, which are related to the other concerns of social performance. Identification, for instance, involves some basic decisions con- cerning whether the organization is going to adopt a piecemeal approach to social auditing, measuring only specific programs or areas the company is involved in, or a more broad-based comprehensive approach in assessing the company's overall performance and impact on society. How should these decisions be made? While such concerns as equal employment opportunity, safe and healthful working conditions, and pollution control programs are obvious examples of areas where such a focus is warranted, what about efforts to develop job satisfaction and the quality of work life (as Abt Associates charts), the ethical performance of corporate executives, corporate operations in controversial areas such as South Africa, community and urban redevelopment efforts, and so forth? Once the issues involved are decided upon, how should they be measured? Is it more effective to use single or multiple measures? Should they be input based (for example, reduction in pollution, addition and promotion of women and racial minorities)? How should such measures be evaluated? To whom should the data be reported (specific supervisors and managers, insiders in general, ex- ternal groups)? What type of monitoring system should be used (transitory or continuous, unsystematic or systematic)?[46]

Given these concerns and difficulties, the concept of a process audit seems to best capture the rationale and purpose of these efforts. A process audit consists of four basic inter-related dimensions: 1) an initial description of the social program in terms of its objectives; 2) the proposed course of action; 3) the rationale linking the course of action to the objectives; and finally, 4) a comparison of what was actually accomplished with what was initially planned. Such a process audit, in other words, locates an organization in terms of the actual progress it has made in the several states of implementation which were delineated under social responsiveness.

## Issue Identification

In addition to the nature and assessment of social performance, the specific issues or topical areas to which these performance dimensions are related must also be identified. One approach is to define these concerns in terms of a firm's "public responsibility."[47] Based on the argument that the notion of social responsibility is too vague to be usefully applied, Lee Preston and James Post suggest that a firm's responsibility should be determined by two factors: 1) the organization's primary and secondary areas of involvement; and 2) the public policy process. Primary involvement refers to the "specialized functional role of the organization, the role that defines its nature and social purpose and that provides the basis for exchange relationships with it and the rest of society."[48] Secondary involvement includes "all those relationships, activities, and impacts of the organization that are ancillary or consequential to its primary involvement activities."[49] Based on the principle of public responsibility, corporations should focus on these two levels of activity and should not be charged with "improving social conditions or resolving social problems regardless of their character or cause."[50]

Secondly, the principle of public responsibility proposes that organizations should analyze and evaluate pressures coming from the public policy process, society's decision-making system. Since public policy is the way in which society frames its goals and objectives and directs individuals and organizations to work toward them, this is arguably more appropriate for forming corporate decisions than the individual concerns of particular executives or special interest groups. Thus, as a way of identifying specific issues, Preston and Post point to a firm's primary and secondary areas of involvement, and recognize the public policy process as the main source of noneconomic goals and priorities.

While this approach has substantial appeal in helping to narrow the scope of appropriate organizational social involvement, it has been criticized in terms of its reliance on public policy as its decision-making criterion. Jones, for example, has argued that there are many concerns that are not answered by the doctrine of public responsibility.[51] First, there are a number of issues which confront corporations in social perform- ance areas which are not addressed in our public policy process. Secondly, there are often conflicting statements or expressions of public policy which exist at the same level of government in many areas of corporate social performance. Third, since statements of public policy usually emerge from several levels of government, whose public policy variant should be heeded? Finally, public policy can indeed conflict with "higher ethical or moral codes" as exemplified in the Dow Chemical napalm controversy. Although Dow's actions were in concert with public policy, the company's performance was roundly denounced as highly irresponsible. Accordingly, Jones calls for the idea of social performance to be viewed as more of a process than an outcome per se, considering the difficulties inherent in reaching consensus in a diverse, pluralistic society.

A study by Sandra Holmes exemplifies how such perform- ance considerations are actually made.[52] In a survey of managers in large organizations, she found that the most prominent factors in identifying and selecting areas of social involvement were: 1) matching a social need with corporate needs or its ability to help; 2) the seriousness of a particular social need; 3) interest of top executives; 4) the public relations value of a socially oriented action; and 5) the amount of govern- ment pressure involved. From these various interpretations of how organizations should and actually do decide which issues warrant attention, it is evident that while issue identification is an important component of corporate social performance, there is no clear consensus on what these issues should be.

## Response Philosophy

Response philosophy refers to the basic orientation a particular organization has with respect to the posture it will take on a social issue.[53] As discussed earlier, one framework which has summarized different "social responsibility" philoso- phies reflects the range of alternatives available to industry: 1) "fight all the way"; 2) "do only what is required"; 3) "be progressive"; and 4) "lead the industry."[54] Another model suggests a similar set of options: reaction, defense, accommoda- tion, and proaction.[55] Such a response orientation or philosophy provides the basis on which organizations rationalize and operationalize their perceived responsibilities to societal concerns.

FIGURE 1.1

Carroll's Model of Corporate Social Performance

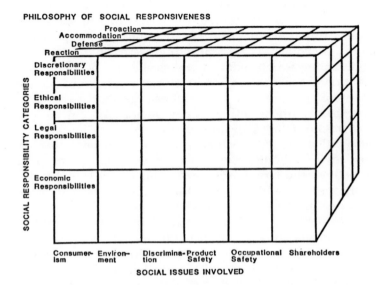

Source: Archie B. Carroll, "A Three-Dimensional Conceptual Model of Corporate Social Performance," Academy of
Management Review, 1979, Vol. 4, No. 4, p. 503. Reprinted
with permission.

Carroll suggests that these three dimensions—assessment
of a firm's social responsibilities, social issue identification,
and response philosophy—should be integrated to illustrate
the issues pertinent to corporate social performance (see Figure
1.1). When conceptualized in this fashion, the discussion of
corporate social performance begins to focus on broader questions
of strategy and organizational policy.

Corporate Social Policy

During the late 1970s and early 1980s, researchers have
increasingly focused on the formulation and implementation of
social policies in different organizations. Although there is no
consensus on the meaning of the phrase "corporate social policy,"
one definition refers to the "attitudes and actions of managers

of business organizations to meet social, as distinct from purely economic, demands and/or expectations of the company's constituents, pressure groups, and governments."[56] Such policies reflect the major decisions made by the top level of management in an organization to be implemented by other organizational members. Social policies may focus on internal as well as external issues facing an organization. Internally, such concerns may focus on ensuring due process in hiring, promotion and termination decisions, establishing day care centers, formulating meaningful career development programs, and so forth. Externally, these policies might concern the production of safe products, minimization of pollution, the effect the company is having on its surrounding community, and so on. Overall, the concept of corporate social policy implies that business organizations do have a social responsibility to their stakeholders, and this responsibility is sufficiently important to warrant integration into the firm's broader strategic considerations.

James Post has analyzed such policies in terms of consistent patterns of response based on three interrelated components: 1) tactics, organizational actions which are immediate in nature and effect, and short-term oriented (for example, public relations statements, bargaining with environmental groups); 2) strategies, concerns which are long-term in nature and imply coherence among different tactics; and finally 3) policy, the overall objectives and goals that identify the direction of the organiza-tion.[57] As Post argues, these three dimensions form a pattern of response which is equivalent to an "operative policy" through which an overall set of organizational actions becomes manifest.

In his research, Post has identified three broad patterns of such response: 1) adaptive, which emphasizes organizational reaction to environmental change; 2) proactive, which empha-sizes organizational action to promote change in the environment; and 3) interactive, which emphasizes simultaneous change in both the organization and the environment. The adaptive model assumes that the environment changes first and is then followed by an organizational reaction. The proactive (or manipulative) model, by contrast, assumes that managers analyze their internal (organizational) interests and then apply "previously successful decision rules" in an attempt to change the environment (through such tactics as lobbying or advocacy advertising) to a state which is favorable for the organization's operations. The inter-active model, however, is based on the assumption that the organization and its environment are both changing simultane-ously, though not at the same rate. Accordingly, Post argues that the most appropriate organizational policies are those which stimulate an ongoing interaction between the firm and its environment. [58]

These views of corporate social policy place an emphasis on environmental analysis and planning. Many organizations, for example, have instituted "public issues scanning" processes designed to obtain, analyze and report information concerning issues in an organization's social and political environment. These data are then used to assist the organization's management in identifying priorities, in developing an awareness of the significance of public and social issues among line managers, and in disseminating this information to managers for incorporation in formulating organizational policy. [59] A good example of this is General Electric's Future Scan system that is used to evaluate environmental threats and opportunities, and demands from various constituencies which the corporation then uses in policy design. [60] While such planning and policy formulation can be quite explicit and focused on specific issues, it can also be quite broad in nature. Steiner, for instance, suggests that the first social policy for a business organization is to "think carefully" about its social responsibilities. [61]

In summary, much of the research on organizational response to social concerns indicates that corporations are increasingly attempting to incorporate the notion of social responsiveness into their organizational structures in a more formalized manner, especially through departments, codes of conduct, the creation of whistle-blowing mechanisms and other structural changes. [62] At the same time, however, it is important to emphasize Post's findings that many organizations still attempt to systematically manipulate their environments and "stonewall" their critics. Thus, although some management scholars argue that "social" policy is being increasingly viewed as part of the corporate policy-making process, others take a more skeptical, sometimes even cynical view of the true commitment and orientation of these policies.

## CONCLUSION

Although initial discussions of business's social role were focused on the social and moral responsibilities involved in business and industry, during the 1970s and early 1980s there was a shift in these assessments towards deeper treatments of the managerial dimensions of these social and ethical issues. As summarized in Figure 1.2, the trend has evolved from dis-

FIGURE 1.2

Conceptualizing Business's Social Role: A Process View

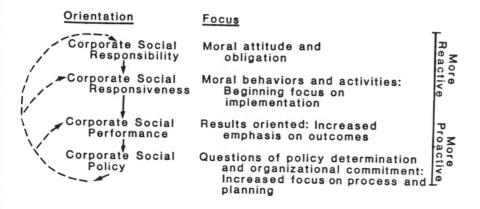

cussions of social responsibilities and social responsiveness to those centered more fully on performance and policy considerations. While previous discussions of responsibility and responsiveness still provide the rationale for corporate activity in this area, the present focus is reflected in the increasing number of companies that are employing a strategic planning horizon of five years or more. Moreover, traditional economic and market-oriented policy concerns have been extended to include social and political trends as part of such environmental analyses.

Thus, on the surface it seems that corporate America is characterized as having increased concerns and actions which reflect specific (e.g., product safety, employee due process) and general (e.g., organizational governance) issues of corporate responsibility. However, there is still significant, and warranted, concern over the definition of, and level of commitment to business's social role. Indeed, while many individuals seem to agree that business organizations do have a responsibility to the larger society, the basic nature of that responsibility and the appropriate manner of response are still being debated. Discussions of (and disagreements over) the "limits of social responsibility" are but one example of the unsettled nature of perceptions of the corporate role.[63]

It should, of course, be emphasized that debates over the appropriate social posture of business and its relationship to the larger society have always existed. Yet, the increased focus on techniques and strategies in the business literature appears to assume that the basic issues and questions which led to the planning and policy efforts in the first place have been resolved. Work by scholars and social observers from other fields, by contrast, indicates that the basic issues underlying business's social responsibilities are re-emerging and are being redefined. Putting the matter in slightly different terms, we may say that even though the events of the past decade seem to constitute a linear trend, we are actually dealing with a much more complex and open-ended dynamic. At any point in time, concerns may shift from the more specific issues of performance and policy back to the broadest questions of the meaning of social responsibility. Indeed, the entire debate on the social role of business which we have been analyzing seems to have been the result of just such an unpredictable circular process. Thus, even though in the near future it is likely that scholarly work will focus heavily on social performance and policy, we should anticipate that all four areas depicted in Figure 1.2 will remain very much alive.

## NOTES

1. Robert W. Ackerman, The Social Challenge to Business (Cambridge, Mass.: Harvard University Press, 1975); and Dow Votaw and S. Prakash Sethi, The Corporate Dilemma: Traditional Values and Contemporary Problems (Englewood Cliffs: Prentice-Hall, 1973).

2. Robert W. Ackerman, "How Companies Respond to Social Demands," Harvard Business Review 51 (July-August 1973):88-98; Ackerman, Social Challenge.

3. Earl A. Molander, Responsive Capitalism: Case Studies in Corporate Social Conduct (New York: McGraw-Hill, 1980), pp. 20-22; Francis W. Steckmest, Corporate Performance: The Key to Public Trust (New York: McGraw-Hill, 1982), pp. ix-xiv.

4. See Steckmest, Corporate Performance.

5. Archie B. Carroll, "A Three-Dimensional Conceptual Model of Corporate Performance," Academy of Management Review 4 (October 1979):497-505; and Henry A. Tombari, "The New Role of Business Management," The Collegiate Forum (Fall 1979):12.

6. Robert W. Ackerman and Raymond A. Bauer, Corporate Social Responsiveness: The Modern Dilemma (Reston, Va.: Reston Publishing, 1976), pp. 37-46.

7. Steckmest, Corporate Performance, p. xvii.

8. See, for example, George Cabot Lodge, "Business and the Changing Society," Harvard Business Review 52 (March-April 1974):59-72.

9. For a succinct discussion of the early legitimation of the role of business see Peter L. Berger, "New Attack on the Legitimacy of Business," Harvard Business Review 59 (September-October 1981):83-85.

10. Robert Lynd and Helen Lynd, Middletown in Transition (New York: Harcourt, Brace and World, 1937).

11. For an in depth discussion of the stakeholder role see E. Merrick Dodd, "For Whom Are Corporate Managers Trustees?" Harvard Law Review 45 (1932):1145-1163; E. Merrick Dodd, "Is Effective Enforcement of the Fiduciary Duties of Corporate Managers Practical?" University of Chicago Law Review 2 (1935):194-207; Russel L. Ackoff, Redesigning The Future (New York: John Wiley & Sons, 1974); R. E. Freeman, Strategic Management: A Stakeholder Approach (Boston: Pitman Publishing, 1983); and R. E. Freeman and D. L. Reed, "Stockholders and Stakeholders: A New Perspective on Corporate Governance," California Management Review 25 (Spring 1983):88-106.

12. Ackerman and Bauer, Corporate Social Responsiveness, p. 16.

13. J. Scott Armstrong, "Social Irresponsibility in Management," Journal of Business Research 5 (1977):185-213.

14. David Ewing, "Who Wants Corporate Democracy?" Harvard Business Review 49 (September-October 1971):146-149.

15. Sandra Holmes, "Executive Perceptions of Corporate Social Responsibility," Business Horizons 19 (June 1976):34-40; Steven Brenner and Earl A. Molander, "Is the Ethics of Business Changing?" Harvard Business Review 55 (January-February 1977):59-69.

16. Barry Posner and Warren H. Schmidt, "Values and the American Manager: An Update," California Management Review 26 (Spring 1984):202-216.

17. Paul Solman and Thomas Friedman, Life and Death on the Corporate Battlefield: How Companies Win, Lose, Survive (New York: Simon and Schuster, 1982).

18. Ronald L. Crawford and Harold A. Gram, "Social Responsibility as Interorganizational Transaction," Academy of Management Review 3, No. 4 (1978):880-888; Rebecca A.

Gould and Eugene J. Kelley, "An Integrated Communications Model of Corporate Adaptation to Social Uncertainty," in The Unstable Ground: Corporate Social Policy in a Dynamic Society, ed., S. Prakash Sethi (Los Angeles: Melville Publishing, 1974), pp. 279-292; and Keith Davis, "Social Responsibility Is Inevitable," California Management Review 19 (Winter 1976):14-20.

19. For an overview of the historical significance of the social responsibility movement see Nicholas N. Eberstadt, "What History Tells Us About Corporate Responsibility," Business and Society Review/Innovation (Spring 1973):91-95; and Clarence C. Walton, Corporate Social Responsibilities (Belmont, Calif.: Wadsworth Publishing, 1967), chaps. 2 and 3.

20. Howard R. Bowen, Social Responsibilities of the Businessman (New York: Harper and Brothers, 1953), p. 6.

21. Peter Drucker, "The Responsibility of Management," Harper's Magazine (November 1954):6.

22. J. W. McGuire, Business and Society (New York: McGraw-Hill, 1963), p. 144.

23. Walton, Corporate Social Responsibilities, p. 18.

24. Milton Friedman, Capitalism and Freedom (Chicago: University of Chicago Press, 1962), p. 133.

25. See Walton, Corporate Social Responsiveness, pp. 54-82; and Ackerman and Bauer, Corporate Social Responsiveness, chap. 1.

26. Terrance W. McAdam, "How to Put Corporate Responsibility into Practice," Business and Society Review (Summer 1973):8-16.

27. Gerald D. Keim, "Managerial Behavior and the Social Responsibility Debate: Goals Versus Constraints," Academy of Management Journal 21 (March 1978):57-69.

28. Ackerman and Bauer, Corporate Social Responsiveness, pp. 6-10.

29. For a good overview of criticisms of the term "social responsibility" see S. Prakash Sethi, "Dimensions of Corporate Social Performance: An Analytic Framework," California Management Review 17 (Winter 1975):58-64; Lee Preston and James Post, Private Management and Public Policy (Reston, Va.: Reston Publishing, 1975), chap. 1; and Carroll, "Three-Dimensional Conceptual Model," pp. 497-500.

30. Dow Votaw, "Genius Becomes Rare," in The Corporate Dilemma: Traditional Values and Contemporary Problems, edited by Dow Votaw and S. Prakash Sethi (Englewood Cliffs: Prentice-Hall, 1973), p. 11.

31. See Ackerman and Bauer, Corporate Social Responsiveness, pp. 6-13; S. Prakash Sethi, "An Analytic Framework for

Making Cross-Cultural Comparisons of Business Responses to Social Pressures," in Research in Corporate Social Performance and Policy, Vol. 1, ed. Lee Preston (Greenwich, Conn.: JAI Press, 1978), pp. 27-54; and Patrick Murphy, "An Evolution: Corporate Social Responsiveness," University of Michigan Business Review (November 1978):20.

 32. Sethi, "Dimensions of Corporate Social Performance," pp. 58-64.

 33. Sethi, "An Analytic Framework," p. 84.

 34. Ackerman, "How Companies Respond to Social Demands"; Ackerman and Bauer, Corporate Social Responsiveness, chap. 4; Votaw and Sethi, The Corporate Dilemma; and Raymond A. Bauer, "The Corporate Response Process," in Research in Corporate Social Performance and Policy, Vol. 1, ed. by Lee E. Preston (Greenwich, Conn.: JAI Press, 1978), pp. 99-122.

 35. Bauer, "Corporate Response Process," pp. 102-106.

 36. Bauer, "Corporate Response Process," pp. 106-107.

 37. J. Collins and C. Ganotis, "Is Corporate Responsibility Sabotaged by the Rank and File?" in Business and Society Review (Autumn 1973):82-88; and Bauer, "The Corporate Response Process," pp. 114-115.

 38. Ackerman, "How Companies Respond to Social Demands," pp. 88-98.

 39. See Sethi, "An Analytic Framework," pp. 33-34; and Archie B. Carroll, Managing Corporate Social Responsibility (Boston: Little, Brown, 1977).

 40. Ackerman and Bauer, Corporate Social Responsiveness, pp. 31-32.

 41. Carroll, "Three-Dimensional Conceptual Model of Corporate Performance," pp. 498-500.

 42. See George A. Steiner, Business and Society, 2nd ed. (New York: Random House, 1975), pp. 159-160.

 43. Arthur M. Louis, "The View from the Pinnacle: What Business Thinks," Fortune (September 1969):92-95; Henry Eilbert and Robert Parket, "The Current Status of Corporate Social Responsibility," Business Horizons 16 (August 1973): 5-14; Jules Cohn, "Is Business Meeting the Challenge of Urban Affairs?," Harvard Business Review 48 (March-April 1, 1970): 68-83; John J. Corson and George A. Steiner, Measuring Business's Social Performance: The Corporate Social Audit (New York: CED, 1974); Harlan C. Van Over and Sam Barone, "An Empirical Study of Responses of Executive Officers of Large Corporations Regarding Corporate Social Responsibility," Proceedings of the Academy of Management, 1975, pp. 339-341;

and Vernon M. Beuhler and Y. K. Shetty, "Managerial Response to the Social Responsibility Challenge," Academy of Management Journal 19 (March 1976):66-78.

44. Carroll, "Three-Dimensional Conceptual Model," p. 504.

45. For a good overview of the issues involved in social auditing see Raymond A. Bauer and Dan H. Fenn, Jr., "What is a Corporate Social Audit?" in Harvard Business Review 51 (January-February 1973):37-48; Clark C. Abt, The Social Audit for Management (New York: Committee for Economic Development, 1974); and Rogene A. Buchholz, Business Environment and Public Policy: Implications for Management (Englewood Cliffs: Prentice-Hall, 1982), chap. 23.

46. Ackerman and Bauer, Corporate Social Responsiveness, pp. 228-229.

47. Lee E. Preston and James E. Post, Private Management and Public Policy (Englewood Cliffs: Prentice-Hall, 1975).

48. Preston and Post, Private Management and Public Policy, p. 95.

49. Ibid., p. 96.

50. Ibid., p. 97.

51. Thomas M. Jones, "Corporate Social Responsibility Revisited, Redefined," California Management Review 22, No. 2 (1980):59-67.

52. Sandra Holmes, "Executive Perceptions of Corporate Social Responsibility," Business Horizons 19 (1976):34-40.

53. Carroll, "Three-Dimensional Conceptual Model," pp. 502-503.

54. McAdam, "How to Put Corporate Responsibility into Practice."

55. Ian Wilson, "What One Company Is Doing About Today's Demands on Business," in Changing Business-Society Interrelationships, edited by George A. Steiner (Berkeley: UCLA Press, 1975).

56. George A. Steiner and John F. Steiner, "Social Policy as Business Policy," in Research in Corporate Social Performance and Policy, Vol. 1, edited by Lee E. Preston (Greenwich, Conn.: JAI Press, 1978), pp. 201-221.

57. James E. Post, Corporate Behavior and Social Change (Reston, Va.: Reston Publishing, 1978), pp. 38-40. See also James E. Post, Risk and Response: Management and Social Change in the American Insurance Industry (Lexington, Mass.: D. C. Heath, 1976).

58. James E. Post, "Research on Patterns of Corporate Response to Social Change," in Research in Corporate Social Performance and Policy, Vol. 1, edited by Lee E. Preston (Greenwich, Conn.: JAI Press, 1978), pp. 55-77.

59. John Fleming, "Public Issues Scanning," in Research in Corporate Social Performance and Policy, Vol. 3, ed. Lee E. Preston (Greenwich, Conn.: JAI Press, 1981), pp. 155-173; and Ian Wilson, "Socio-Political Forecasting: A New Dimension to Strategic Planning," Michigan Business Review 24 (July 1974):15-25.

60. Molander, Responsive Capitalism, case 20.

61. George A. Steiner, "Social Policies for Business," California Management Review 15 (Winter 1972):17-24.

62. Sandra Holmes, "Adapting Corporate Structure for Social Responsiveness," California Management Review 20 (Fall 1978):51. Peter Arlow and Martin J. Gannon, "Social Responsiveness, Corporate Structure, and Economic Performance," Academy of Management Review 7 (April 1982):235-241.

63. Neil Chamberlin, The Limits of Corporate Responsibility (New York: Basic Books, 1973).

# 2

# AN INTEGRAL
# CONCEPTUALIZATION

The summary of conceptual approaches discussed in Chapter 1 should be sufficient to establish that the study of business's social role is quite complex. Considering the nature of this topic and the range of perspectives suggested for analysis, it seems that any future scholarly work in this area should be based on what may be termed an "integral approach." Our rationale is that many academic and professional areas must be continually drawn upon, and their individual contributions synthesized, in the analysis and interpretation of corporate social behavior. While a number of such matrixes are both possible and necessary, our backgrounds and training lead us to distinguish four fields as especially important: business and society, business policy, business ethics, and the social economy.

Such an interdisciplinary approach, which is illustrated in Figure 2.1, reflects our view that a meaningful conceptualization and discussion of business's social role in contemporary society must take these different perspectives into account. Since the organizational and managerial issues which are the focus of this book will be considered within the context of these four perspectives, it is necessary to describe briefly their focuses and orientations. It should be noted, however, that the literature which has been produced by scholars in these different fields is vast, and can only be sketched out here in the most general manner.

## BUSINESS AND SOCIETY

It is no exaggeration to say that for most managers, their main problems, the main obstacles to achieving

FIGURE 2.1

An Integral Approach to the Study of Bussiness's Social Role

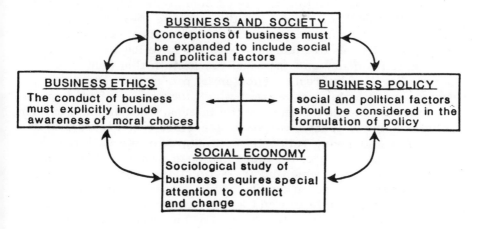

their business objectives are external to the
company . . . the main problems of business
these days are . . . determined in the arena of
public policy. Therefore business managers are
obliged to become students of public affairs. They
must learn to hold their own in public debate, and
know their way around Washington. Today's
managers must take into account public expectations, social and political movements, and moral
obligations that quickly become law if they are
ignored. The present generation of managers is
learning these things the hard way—by experience.

—Reginald Jones[1]
General Electric

The above quote reflects the growing awareness of the
influence that the environment has on business organizations
today. It also focuses on the two main areas of the "business
and society" field: business and its environment, and public
policy. The perspective offered here is that the management
and organization of large companies cannot be adequately understood without an informed analysis of the firm's response to its
social and political environments, which are changing and often
turbulent in nature. Stimulated by the changes and concerns

of the late 1960s, the business and society field was initially based on the conceptualizations of such scholars as John Kenneth Galbraith, Dow Votaw, and Clarence Walton.[2] The main foci of these analyses were the changes taking place in our business system and the changing nature of business's responsibilities within that system. More recently, growing interest by corporate executives and support through the American Assembly of Collegiate Schools of Business (AACSB) have led to significant advances in theory and empirical research in this field.[3] Paralleling this interest, a substantial professional literature has emerged within management which focuses on a broad range of concerns that are related to the internal workings and external relationships of today's corporate structure (see Figure 2.2).[4]

The underlying rationale for this area of study is that over the past two decades there has been dramatic change in the environment in which business functions. As society has increasingly focused on quality of life concerns—pollution control, workplace health and safety, equal opportunity, product quality and safety, and the impacts of business operations on local communities—a number of new roles which emphasize social and political issues have been defined for business organizations. While the principal mission of business is still viewed as economic in nature, such economic functions are perceived as less dominant than they were previously.[5] Indeed, consensus in this field indicates that these economic functions must be assessed in relation to the broader social and political roles and activities that business is being asked to assume.

The idea of a broadened social role for business is typically based on the argument that public attitudes have evolved from the view that large corporations are basically private and accountable to stockholders and market forces, to the emergent perspective that large corporations are "quasi-public."[6] This stakeholder orientation thus suggests that managers are becoming increasingly accountable to the interests of consumers, employees, and other groups. Related discussions of business's social responsibilities focus predominantly on issues of corporate reform. As indicated in the preceding section, the emphasis has been on the various obligations organizations have to the larger society and the methods which can be used to make organizations more responsive to these concerns.

While the business and society field generally takes the position that change is indeed occurring, it is recognized that there is still disagreement in the corporate world concerning this orientation. The social environment, for instance, has quite different impacts on large and small businesses. More-

FIGURE 2.2

The Business and Society Literature: Dimensions and Examples

| | EXTERNAL | INTERNAL |
|---|---|---|
| GENERAL | Systemic Context, Issues<br><br>Historical/institutional framework<br><br>Major social trends<br><br>Culture and ideology | Internal Context, Attitudes<br><br>Corporate governance, participation<br><br>Management ethics (individual, organizational)<br><br>Strategic management |
| TOPICAL | Public Policy Topics<br><br>Economic and social regulation<br><br>Equal employment opportunity, affirmative action<br><br>Environmental protection | Specific Management Policies, Techniques<br><br>Human resource policies<br><br>Issues management<br><br>Environmental scanning and forecasting<br><br>Social reporting |

Source: Copyright © 1983 by the Regents of the University of California. Reprinted from California Management Review, volume XXV, no. 3, p. 160 by permission of the Regents.

over, even in large corporations, not all managers subscribe to this view or even agree that the "rules of the game" have changed all that dramatically. Other executives, while recognizing that the environment has changed, still hold to classical economic views of business and its responsibilities to society.[7]

While some executives may be reluctant to recognize a "true" corporate social role as defined by these commentators, the business and society literature suggests that the idea of a corporate political role is popular among most top level managers.[8] This consensus reflects today's political realities and the recognition that most social controversies are dealt with through the realm of public policy. This process of legislation, regulation, enforcement, and litigation is the dominant way in which significant public concerns are formulated and implemented in our society. The formalization of lobbying efforts through political action committees (PACs), the use of advocacy advertising, and the more visible role played by CEOs and other top level executives in public debate underscore the importance attached to this role.

Paralleling these changing demands and activities, the role of management is also undergoing a transition. While management has traditionally focused on activities and operations within organizational boundaries, managers are increasingly being asked to perform <u>boundary spanning</u> roles between their organizations and a host of external groups and relevant publics. Henry Tombari, for example, describes this new focus as being "politico-economic" in nature.[9] This type of role necessitates that managers become involved in the public policy process in addition to their involvement in the market process. He further suggests that management must transform the corporation into an entity that is politically as well as economically oriented and congruent with society's values and political system. Similarly, a recent study by a task force of the American Assembly of Collegiate Schools of Business (AACSB) reflects this change.[10] Among the attitudes and skills necessary for success most frequently mentioned by managers and executives were: 1) a broadened awareness of the external environment; 2) the ability to integrate basic business concerns with external social and political issues; 3) the development of a political sense that enables the resolution of conflicting interests among different organizational stakeholders; 4) communication skills to articulate effectively an organization's position on various complex issues; 5) and the intellectual ability to analyze and debate difficult public issues with groups outside the traditional business realm.

The notion of macromanagement reflects this broadened awareness and role.[11] Macromanagement refers to the use of systems theory to analyze the relationships of organizations to each other and to the larger society. Modern organizations, for example, are characterized and impacted by functional and divisional units, vertically integrated strategies, rapid social and technological change, government regulation and deregulation, and resource scarcity, to name a few phenomena. To describe any one of these aspects and to analyze a specific organizational problem and response in isolation from other influential elements are relatively easy tasks. The end result, however, will be necessarily fragmented. For instance, although one might understand the strategic decision underlying a more diversified approach to a particular business activity, the systemic effect of this strategy on the rest of the organization and its relevant publics is much more difficult to evaluate.

Although some observers have criticized the business and society field for its lack of a unifying theory or paradigm, arguing that the field may be nothing more than a collection of loosely related topics,[12] it seems that the general framework of open systems theory has become one of the basic, integrating themes.[13] This view proposes that business organizations are part of a larger societal system which can be categorized into four interrelated sectors or subsystems: the economic system, the political-legal system, the technical system, and the social-cultural system. While different theorists define these sectors in different ways, organizational analysis based on systems theory focuses on the interactions between (1) the elements within an organization and (2) the organization and its environment. In the business and society field, the emphasis is placed more fully on external interactions and relationships; however, many analyses also delve inside organizations to assess the effects such interactions have within corporate structures as well.

Preston and Post, for example, have identified different types of systems models that describe the relationship between business and the larger society.[14] Based on the diverse views of such scholars as Adam Smith (market model), Karl Marx (exploitation model), Milton Friedman (legal model), and John Kenneth Galbraith (technostructure), Preston and Post "translated" their key conceptions into systems theory. The basic assumption underlying this approach is that business organizations and society are social systems which are related to each other; the questions that remain concern the nature of this relationship. As illustrated in Figure 2.3, three systems models were identified. The collateral systems framework proposes that systems A, B, and C interact with one another, but have independent identities. As such, a process of exchange—whether the exchange is in terms of market transactions (Smith) or exploitation of one class by another (Marx)—defines the relationship between the firm and the larger society. The dominant suprasystems model, by contrast, proposes that some control authority (dominant suprasystem) has an independent existence and exerts control over systems A, B, and C. Thus, Galbraith's concept of a technostructure dominating social values is suggested to be a suprasystem controlling individual social systems (firms and other organizations). Similarly, the legal model is seen as a process through which the suprasystem (society) establishes the "rules of the game" for the various social units within it.

While these two views seemed to the authors to capture some of the dynamics of contemporary business activity, they argued that no one concept could "explain the 'deviant' situations explained by the other models." Thus, as a way of integrating these different views, Preston and Post used Talcott Parsons's concept of an interpenetrating system. Interpenetration exists when systems interact with respect to a particular event or process, but no system totally contains nor is totally contained

FIGURE 2.3

Basic Social Systems Models

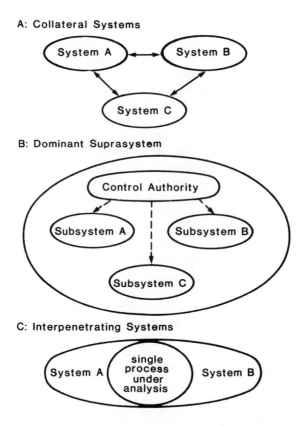

A: Collateral Systems

B: Dominant Suprasystem

C: Interpenetrating Systems

Source: Lee E. Preston, James E. Post, Private Management and Public Policy: The Principle of Public Responsibility, ©1975, p. 17. Reprinted by permission of Prentice-Hall, Inc., Englewood Cliffs, N.J.

by the others. Moreover, while systems influence one another, they also mutually influence the processes through which they continue to interact over time. The authors argue that this approach facilitates analysis of different actions since it can reflect both harmony and conflict, and the various processes underlying the interaction (for example, market and public policy). Organizational activities are thus understood through the examination of the ongoing interpenetration of a business firm, its stakeholders, and the issues that concern them.

Overall, the general viewpoint of the business and society field is that the interrelationships between the emergent social and political components of business activity have created the necessity for social awareness and accountability. This socio-political role is inextricably intertwined with business's economic role and it has become a key for both long-term survival and successful management. As part of this emerging emphasis, students in increasing numbers are being exposed to courses that undertake a broad analysis of business's external environments. Among the topics generally covered in such courses are: business-government relations, environmental analysis (forecasting and planning), the theory and practice of corporate social responsibility, corporate governance, public policy, ethics and values, corporate social policy, and the concerns of key constituencies such as consumers, employees, and other stakeholders groups. Although there is a significant amount of diversity concerning the types of courses offered by schools of business and management in this area, there is an emerging consensus that this is an important part of management education. A 1978 survey of all U.S. business schools listed in the 1977-1978 AACSB membership indicated that the great majority of these programs included study in business and society as part of their curriculum: 85 percent had separate courses and another 14 percent integrated this material into business policy or other business function courses.[15] The general aim of these courses is to develop an awareness among participants about the importance of the external environment and the need to make an effective response to social and political issues emerging out of that environment.

## BUSINESS POLICY

The basic orientation of business policy is the analysis of an organization in its totality—its internal structure, resources and processes, and the constraints and opportunities posed by its environment. Every organization has fundamental needs to define what it is and what it hopes to accomplish; assess what it has to work with; decide how to use its resources within its environment to accomplish its purposes; translate these concerns into specific plans; implement those plans; and measure and evaluate the results.[16] This process, which is referred to as policy, planning, strategy (or the strategic process), implies a broad scope of relationships of the major elements, internal and external, in an organization's situation (see Figure 2.4).

FIGURE 2.4

The Policy Concept

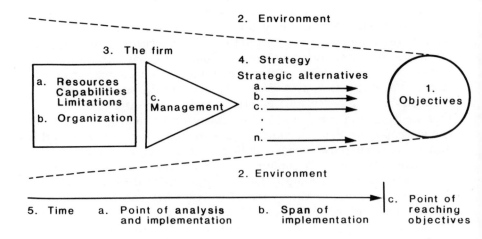

Source: Melvin J. Stanford, Management Policy, 2nd Ed., ©1983, p. 6. Reprinted by permission of Prentice-Hall, Inc., Englewood Cliffs, N.J.

As Table 2.1 indicates, there is no one single approach to this area of study nor even consensus about the meaning of these different terms. What one commentator refers to as policy, another terms strategy. Similarly, there is disagreement concerning the general scope, means, and ends of "policy" analysis. However, paralleling the fundamental concerns mentioned above, the content of this field typically focuses on such topics as the role and responsibilities of the general manager, the strategy determination process, environmental analysis and forecasting, resource auditing (financial, human, and operational capacity), the relationship between organizational strategy and structure, strategic choice, and strategy implementation and assessment. The stress is on a top management perspective rather than that of a functional area manager or that of a specialist.

Initial interest in business policy and strategy began to emerge during the mid-1950s due to product/technology mismatches between companies and their changing markets.[17] These concerns led to thinking about strategy in terms of product/technology/market niches and the environmental analyses necessary for such formulation. During the 1970s, however, this orientation was viewed as too restrictive. As Ansoff has argued,

> The new [policy or strategy] concerns are with the design of the internal environment of the firm, with assuming a new set of responsibilities with respect to the environment, and with establishing a new basis for social legitimacy for the firm. In response to these concerns, concepts of capability strategy, of social responsibility strategy, and of political strategy have begun to emerge . . . the original concept of product/market strategy appears as only one component of a much broader concept.[18]

The main implication of this broader orientation for business planning is illustrated in Figure 2.5. Based on the growing turbulence of the social and political environments, it was argued that the ultimate success of a business firm was increasingly dependent upon its ability to deal with these myriad pressures and changes. Since the primary purpose of business policy and strategy is to improve the "fit" between the organization and its current and future environment, the focus is on an awareness of a firm's different environments—social, political, economic, technological, and international—and an ability to respond to their trends and demands.

Within graduate and undergraduate schools of business and management, business policy has emerged as the integrative, capstone course. It requires a synthesis of the knowledge that the student has acquired in courses concerning management tools and techniques, and the different functional areas of business, combined within a systems perspective. Such courses, which rely heavily on the case method, are structured so that emphasis is placed on the synthesis and application of previous coursework. While the basic orientation of policy courses is focused more fully on market processes and consumer demand, the multi-faceted nature of the planning framework illustrated in Figure 2.5 indicates a broader focus of such analysis.

This situation has led to comparative assessments of the business policy and business and society areas. Since both areas involve matching environmental demands and changes with internal financial, human, and operational resources, the two fields are argued to be intrinsically interwoven.[19] Moreover, both fields focus on the role of the general manager as

TABLE 2.1

Comparison of Business Policy Concepts

| Title | Author(s) | Terms Used for | | | Characteristics |
|---|---|---|---|---|---|
| | | Broad Scope | Ends | Means | |
| Management policy | Stanford | Policy | Objectives | Strategy | Strategy relates firm to objectives within environment; multilateral relationships; alternative sequences. |
| Strategy and organization | Uyterhoeven, Ackerman, and Rosenblum | General management, business policy | Purpose, goals, or objectives | Strategic plans | Strategy external, organization internal; elements and skills; sequential process. |
| Corporate strategy | Andrews | Strategy | Objectives, purposes, or goals | Policies and plans | Formulation and implementation; business strategy: "how"; corporate strategy: "what." |
| Strategic management | Schendel and Hofer | Strategic management process | Goals | Strategy | Achievement of objectives is aim of strategy; hierarchy of strategies at four levels. |
| Administrative policy | Hodgetts and Wortman | Administrative policy science | Purpose or mission | Strategy | Several levels in total policy structure; business one of six components of administrative policy science. |

| | | | | | |
|---|---|---|---|---|---|
| Strategic management | Ansoff | Strategic management | Aspirations | Strategic thrusts | Environment serving organizations (ESOs); multiple power centers; environmental turbulence. |
| Policy formulation and administration | Christensen, Berg, and Salter | Strategy | Purposes, objectives | Policies | Strategy formulation influenced by corporate environment, resources, and management values. |
| A strategy of decision | Braybrooke and Lindblom | Policy making | Objectives, values | Policy | Disjointed incrementalism; sequential and concurrent; objectives and policy considered simultaneously. |
| Strategy and policy | Thompson and Strickland | Policy | Purpose, mission | Strategy | Mission is specified as long-run objectives and short-run goals; relationships rather than sequential flow. |

Source: Melvin J. Stanford, Management Policy, 2nd Ed., ©1983, p. 14. Reprinted by permission of Prentice-Hall, Inc., Englewood Cliffs, N.J.

FIGURE 2.5

Four-Sided Conceptualization of Business Planning

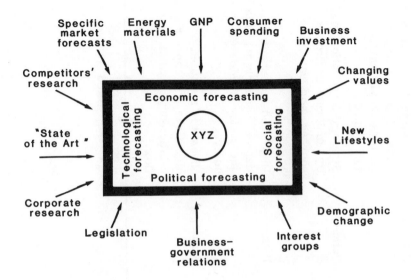

Source: Adapted from Ian H. Wilson, "Socio-Political Fore-casting: A New Dimension to Strategic Planning," Michigan Business Review, 1974 (July) : 163-164. Reprinted with permission.

a problem solver. Since the depth and breadth of the realm of the general manager is so large that no one is expected to be fully knowledgeable in every area, the emphasis in both fields is placed on being informed, sensitive and alert to the various factors, forces, and processes which influence the firm's performance. Thus, within both the business policy and business and society orientations, the general manager is expected to possess or be able to obtain the analytic skills necessary to identify, appraise, and evaluate competing demands and influences.[20]

The main difference between these two approaches is suggested to be a matter of emphasis and perception of the environment. To the business policy analyst, "environment" largely means consumer demand, while to the business and society specialist it reflects broader public issues and interests. As such within business policy, clarification of the legal and social environments, values, ethics, and socially oriented concerns are viewed as secondary constraints to the economic decision process. Corporate actions such as maintaining or enhancing market share, and the operational, financial, and human resources necessary to accomplish such strategies dominate the analysis and subject matter of policy discussions. Courses in business policy typically focus on such topics as planning models, new or start-up ventures, mergers and acquisitions, diversification, consolidation, strategy formulation in different types and sizes of organization, strategy implementation, and social responsibility. As argued in the preceding section, the business and society course more fully emphasizes stakeholder analysis, social planning and forecasting, the regulatory environment, the role of the business firm in society, and the needs and interests of a firm's relevant publics.

Within policy courses, the analysis of social issues has been criticized as being little more than a "gesture to the corporate social responsibility debate of the late 1960s and early 1970s" rather than a true recognition that these concerns have an intimate connection with the overall process of corporate strategy and policy formulation.[21] Yet, while there appears to be some degree of reluctance among policy researchers to actively move toward a conceptualization of policy that incorporates the question of social legitimacy raised by Ansoff, there does seem to be acceptance of the need for expanded environmental analysis. The underlying rationale, however, is oriented more fully toward undertaking a complete analysis of the risks and opportunities confronting a firm's existing strategy rather than an enlightened view of business's social role.


BUSINESS ETHICS

A third perspective which is important for an informed analysis of business's social role focuses on the application of formal structures of ethical thought to management decision making and policy formulation. This study of business ethics, or "what constitutes good and bad human conduct, including related actions and values, in a business context,"[22] was stimulated by a series of business scandals during the late 1950s and early 1960s. These events, which ranged from fixing television game shows and disc jockey payola, to price fixing among 29 major electrical manufacturers and a number of fraudulent business deals, prompted a rise of public opinion about and congressional investigation into such corporate behaviors. During 1962, the U.S. government published its report A Statement on Business Ethics and A Call for Action which revealed widespread confusion and growing concern about ethics in business.[23]

During that same year, William Ruder sponsored a study of the status of teaching business ethics in the AACSB's member colleges and universities. While every respondent argued that ethics instruction should be an important component of management education, most of these institutions did not offer specific courses in this area. Two decades later, however, it is generally accepted in most schools of business and management that it is not only appropriate but necessary to focus on the moral and ethical dimensions of managerial and corporate conduct. Indeed, a recent survey of business and management schools by Hoffman and Moore (at Bentley College's Center for Business Ethics) has documented the significant rise in courses in business ethics and indicates that the area is still gaining momentum.[24] Similar to courses on business and society, these courses delve into the social consequences of corporate policies and decisions. The focus, however, is on the individual in the firm rather than the firm itself. The Hoffman and Moore survey on business ethics curricula, for example, found that the dominant goals of such courses were to provide students with an ethical framework to facilitate the understanding and solving of business problems having moral implications, and to show how ethical theories can be used to analyze such problems.

There are three basic recurring themes which seem to capture a rough consensus by academicians and practicing managers on the emergence of business ethics.[25] First, social acceptance and legitimization of business are crucial to its survival. As shifting expectations and performance criteria complicate the task of management, business must respond in innovative ways. Second, ethical considerations of business activity deal in large part with the implications of economic behavior, the positive and negative consequences caused by such actions. The effects of business activity on organizational stakeholders now and in the future are principal components of society's agenda for justice. Finally, many social critics have observed that both market forces and government intervention have failed to resolve many of the social dilemmas that have emerged from the dynamics of technological and institutional change. Thus, there must also be a change in the process

and structure of business practice to ensure a fuller consideration of ethical issues if we are to achieve true justice in the
corporate sector.

Within this context, there are three general types of
ethical issues which are usually included under the rubric of
business ethics:

1. Moral concerns raised by the external effects organizations have on various stakeholders and the larger society
   such as pollution, plant closings, and "unfair" business
   practices.
2. Moral issues created by internal conflicts business organizations precipitate among their own members such as
   when stockholders complain that corporate officers are
   using company funds for their personal gain, or when
   employees accuse management of being negligent in its
   moral duty to create a safe and healthy work environment.
3. Moral dilemmas which arise out of conflicts between employee aims and values, and the objectives and policies
   of the organization. Examples of these concerns are
   when an organization's management might insist on a
   production schedule which an individual supervisor feels
   could result in a defective or potentially dangerous
   product, or an organization policy concerning the investigation of its employees which an individual manager might
   feel is an invasion of their privacy.[26]

This should not suggest, however, that there is a consensus
on how business ethics should be treated. Recent studies have
indicated that while many institutions are concerned about the
development of moral reasoning and ethical judgment among their
students, they are not clear as to how to meet those objectives
in their curricula.[27] Moreover, there is disagreement as to
how the basic issues themselves should be handled: Do you
treat business as the problem, or do you treat business as a
practice with problems?[28] Obviously, this distinction can readily
influence whether such courses will appear "anti-business."

Some discussions of business ethics appear to locate ethical
concerns about business behavior some distance from the central
and essential activities of business. This is often done on the
assumption that business ethics is no more or less a reflection
of the prevailing moral code of our society. Like all other
citizens, business persons and their institutions are expected
to refrain from engaging in fraudulent practices, polluting the
environment, discriminating against people, and so forth.

Other discussions, by contrast, argue that business ethics is the same as other forms of professional ethics. Historically, professions have always had a moral element, a claim both implicit and explicit that in their professional activities such individuals should be oriented to the well-being of their clients and society. The emphasis should not be primarily placed on the professional's own benefit and self-interest.[29] Thus, just as our society expects certain levels of behavior from doctors and lawyers, high standards of moral behavior should be expected of business professionals as well.

Regardless of the way in which these issues are framed, however, a basic question which often emerges concerns whose morality is to be imposed on business. The underlying assumption is that there are many different moralities and, especially in a highly pluralistic society such as ours, each person may have his or her own moral standards and values which are equally valid. The position that there is no one universal standard or set of standards that can be used to judge the morality of a given act is referred to as moral or ethical relativism.[30] As such, ethical relativists often argue that the same act may be morally right or morally wrong for different societies and even individuals. Yet, although such an argument may initially appear to be persuasive and is tolerant of divergent views, most philosophers reject it for a number of reasons.

First, despite differences in custom and practice from society to society, there is and has been basic agreement on a large number of central issues. Many anthropologists, for instance, claim that all cultures endorse such principles as "senseless killing is wrong," "people should be treated fairly," and "you should not lie or steal." Second, the fact that even if different cultures or subcultures do hold different ethical principles does not mean that there are no correct or "true" principles. Different cultures and individuals obviously hold diverse beliefs concerning a wide range of subjects, but that does not mean that all beliefs on a particular subject are correct, that they are equally worthwhile, or that the final choice is ultimately arbitrary. The main determinant of the worth of any belief is the justification that supports it. Finally, ethical relativism seems to contradict our everyday experiences and beliefs. If ethical relativism is true, no person can disagree with another person about ethics because there is no right or wrong apart from an individual's opinions or beliefs. Yet, this contradicts the ways in which we act in our lives since we continually accuse ourselves and others of making mistakes on ethical issues. In short, there are basic moral or ethical standards that we expect in people's actions, and for our purposes here, in business decisions.

Accordingly, philosophers have applied different ethical theories or principles to business situations. Basically, there are two main classifications or types of these theories: teleological or consequence-based ethics, and deontological or rule-based ethics. Teleological (consequentialist) theories hold that the moral worth of actions or practices is solely determined by the (nonmoral) consequences of those actions or practices. Consequentialists, therefore, determine what is right by considering the ratio of "good to evil" that an act produces. The "right" action is the one that leads to, will probably lead to, or is intended to lead to as great a ratio of "good to evil" as any other course.

The two basic teleological theories applied in business discussions are egoism and utilitarianism. Egoism contends that an act is moral when it promotes an individual's (or firm's) best long-term interests. There is no consensus, however, on what actually constitutes such interests. Different egoists, for example, have focused on such diverse concerns as pleasure and hedonism, to identifying "good" with knowledge, power, rational self-interest, and self-actualization. Thus, different ethical egoists may hold quite different notions of what constitutes good and bad. Utilitarianism, by contrast, holds that an act is moral when it produces the greatest good for the greatest number of people. As initially formulated by Jeremy Bentham and John Stuart Mill in the nineteenth century, utilitarianism has been long associated with social reform or improvement. According to utilitarian theorists, people ought to act in ways which maximize the total balance of good over evil. There are two basic variants of utilitarian ethics. Act utilitarians hold that in every situation individuals should act to maximize total good, even if doing so violates a rule which, if followed, generally produces social welfare. Since these rules are only guidelines, they can and should be broken if the result is in the interest of the "public good." Rule utilitarians, by contrast, apply the basic utilitarian principles to create rules which are firm and publicly advocated, and oriented to promoting the public interest. These rules should thus be followed, even when they do not lead to the greatest good, since the presence of and adherence to the rules ultimately promotes society's general welfare.

In contrast to these consequentialist perspectives, deontological theories maintain that the concept of good is dependent on the concept of duty. Deontologists argue that not all actions

which produce good are necessarily right, and that even "right"
actions may produce unpleasant consequences for different
groups. Thus, an action should not be judged as right or
wrong solely by its consequences, but by the extent to which
it is based on universally accepted principles. Most deontologists
argue that the motives underlying different acts or practices
are also morally relevant. Moral reasoning must focus on the
past as well as the present and the future to fully determine
what is ethical. Immanuel Kant, perhaps the most well known
deontologist, proposed his "categorical imperative" as the
guiding principle: we should act in such a way that we could
wish the maxim (subjective principle) of our action to become
a universal law. Stated in a different way, rational beings can
evaluate their actions, make rules for themselves, and base
their actions on those self-imposed rules; thus, we should
always act so as to treat ourselves and others as ends, and
never as means to ends. [31]

The two deontological or rule-based theories most often
applied in business analysis are the theory of rights and the
theory of justice. A theory of moral rights proposes that
individuals have basic fundamental rights or entitlements that
should be respected in all decisions. [32] Such moral rights are
those which enable individuals to pursue their own interests,
and impose associated requirements and/or prohibitions on
others. In other words, every right or entitlement has a
corresponding duty. Along these lines, advocates of moral
rights have suggested the following ethical norms or guidelines:

1. The Right to Life and Safety: Individuals have the right
   not to have their lives or safety unknowingly and un-
   necessarily endangered.
2. The Right to Truthfulness: Individuals have the right
   not to be intentionally deceived by others, especially
   concerning issues about which the individual has the
   right to know.
3. The Right to Privacy: Individuals have the right to do
   whatever they choose to do outside working hours and
   to control information concerning their personal lives.
4. The Right to Freedom and Conscience: Individuals have
   the right to refrain from carrying out any order which
   violates those commonly accepted moral or religious norms
   to which they adhere.
5. The Right to Free Speech: Individuals have the right to
   criticize conscientiously and truthfully the ethics or
   legality of corporate actions so long as the criticism does

not violate the rights of other individuals in the organization.

6. The Right to Private Property: Individuals have the right to hold private property, especially to the extent that this enables them to be sheltered and to have the basic necessities of life.[33]

Ethical theory dealing with rights, therefore, essentially provides a guide for the decision maker to ensure respect for these rights of the individual.

The theory of justice calls upon the decision maker to be guided by equity, fairness, and impartiality.[34] People should receive differential treatment only when the basis of treatment is directly related to the goals and tasks of the organization. Moreover, all rules should be administered fairly and impartially enforced. This theory calls for fair and evenhanded treatment of people along three types of moral prescriptions: 1) the distribution of the benefits and the burdens of society; 2) the administration of laws and regulations; and 3) the imposition of sanctions and means of compensation for wrongs a person has suffered. Similar to the theory of rights, advocates of the principle of justice have suggested some ethical norms or guidelines for decision makers:

1. Fair Treatment: Individuals who are similar to each other in relevant respects should be treated similarly; those who differ with respect to some relevant aspect of their roles should be treated differently in proportion to the difference between them.

2. Fair Administration of Rules: Rules should be administered consistently, fairly, and impartially.

3. Fair Compensation: People should be compensated for the cost of their injuries by the party that is responsible for those injuries.

4. Fair Blame: Individuals should not be held responsible for matters over which they have no control.

5. Due Process: Individuals have a right to a fair and impartial hearing when they believe that their personal rights are being violated.[35]

Obviously, these different ethical theories conflict with one another and provide ample opportunity for argument and discussion. Indeed, whether these theories are fully incompatible with each other has been the subject of ongoing analysis and debate.[36] Their attractions and weaknesses for business analysis

TABLE 2.2

Application of Ethical Theories in a Business Context

| Theory | Attraction | Weakness |
|--------|-----------|----------|
| **Teleological** | | |
| Egoism | 1. Can serve as the basis for formulating and testing policies.<br>2. Provides the flexibility business often needs in moral decision making. | 1. Ignores blatant wrongs.<br>2. Incompatible with the nature and role of busines<br>3. Cannot resolve conflicts of self interest.<br>4. Introduces inconsistency into moral counseling.<br>5. Undermines the moral point of view. |
| Utilitarianism | 1. Can serve as the basis for formulating and testing policies.<br>2. Provides an objective way of resolving conflicts of self interest.<br>3. Recognizes different stakeholders in business activities.<br>4. Provides the flexibility business often needs in moral decision making. | 1. Ignores actions that appea to be wrong in themselves.<br>2. Potential conflict between principles such as utility and justice.<br>3. Difficult to formulate satisfactory rules. |
| **Deontological** | | |
| Kant's Categorical Imperative | 1. Takes the "guess work" out of moral decision making.<br>2. Introduces a needed humanistic dimension into business decision making.<br>3. Concept of duty implies a moral obligation to act from a respect for rights and a recognition of responsibilities. | 1. Principles provide no clear way to resolve potential conflicts of duties between stakeholders.<br>2. No compelling reason that the prohibition against certain actions should hold without exception. |

Source: Adapted from Vincent Barry, Moral Issues in Business. Belmont, California: Wadsworth Publishing, 1979, pp. 42-55.

are summarized in Table 2.2. The main point for the present
discussion is that concepts of ethics and moral judgment are
being applied to business and management today. Although
there is no comprehensive moral theory that indicates whether
the teleological emphasis on good results or the deontological
focus on rights and duties is the more correct or important,
it is clear that the process of moral reasoning is a central
component in the exploration of business's social role.

## SOCIAL ECONOMY

The social economy refers to a perspective within sociology
which approaches the economy as a fundamental social institution,
and seeks to understand its relations to other institutions, as
well as to society as a whole. Within this viewpoint, economic
units of all sorts and sizes, from simple exchanges through
corporations, occupations, and industries are investigated. In
order to keep the presentation of these various sources relatively
simple and comprehensible, this section divides the social economy
into two broad categories, the analytical and the critical.

### Analytical Variants

Analytical writings on the social economy are distinguished
by procedures which attempt to be "objective" or "value-neutral"
in the sense of the physical sciences. Sociologists operating
within this framework have focused on reporting what is or has
been, rather than what could or should be, and have sought
to keep personal beliefs and loyalties from dictating their findings. Advocates of the analytical approach would refer to
their methods as "empirical" or "scientific," while opponents
would label the attempt as "positivism," "scientism" or "ideology."

Three of the best known and most influential analytical
writers from the late nineteenth and early twentieth centuries
are Herbert Spencer, Emile Durkheim, and Max Weber. The
first two theorists may be discussed together, since they
shared a concern with certain economic issues, especially those
involved in the evolution of modern economies. Spencer viewed
the emergence of economic systems based on free exchange or
contract as an important development in human liberation from
the compulsory, or as he called them "militant" systems of the
past. The relationship characteristic of modern business might
in fact serve as a model for other interpersonal transactions in

familial, political, or religious institutions. Economic contracts could thus provide the prototype for new forms of society, which would naturally develop so long as governments followed laissez-faire or noninterventionist policies.[37] These views were later echoed at Harvard in the socioeconomic teaching of T. N. Carver during the first three decades of this century.[38]

Durkheim agreed with Spencer that economic institutions were becoming more specialized in the course of evolution, much like the complex organs which appeared in the higher animals. He differed, however, from Spencer on the issue of individualism, and on the high value which Spencer accorded to it. New socioeconomic structures, he argued, would still produce a collective unity greater than that of individual economic units, for diversification of structure results in ever increasing interdependence of activity which creates psychological bonds. Such increasing mutual interdependence, in fact, is for Durkheim the most important feature of the emerging socioeconomic order. To be fully effective and successful, however, the evolutionary process, which Durkheim referred to as "the division of labor," would still have to create a further structure, namely, sets of professional ethics to direct the conduct of persons and groups in various occupational spheres. Such a development, in Durkheim's view, was urgently needed, but he was optimistic about its prospects.[39]

Weber, in contrast, combined analysis with personal pessimism. His distinctive angle of approach to economic studies was in terms of the motivational patterns of human participants. In perhaps his most famous study, The Protestant Ethic and the Spirit of Capitalism, Weber argued that modern Western economic systems were the result of attitudinal-motivational transformations which occurred during early modern times in the wake of the Protestant Reformation of the sixteenth century.[40] The crucial change was a redefinition of work as an absolute duty, a calling in the sense of a religious vocation, which demanded a new seriousness and a greatly increased intensity toward labor. Modern workers, under the influence of this new culture, also had to be willing to put off enjoyment of the fruits of their labor, that is, to locate their occupational satisfaction in the future rather than the present. Applied to contemporary practices, Weber's theory helps interpret our willingness to endure long periods of preparation for occupations, as well as our increasingly dominant perspective of unified "careers" spanning several decades. At the same time, it offers an explanation of our detachment during professional transactions.

A further consequence of this line of analysis, developed more fully by Weber in his later works, was the growing "rationalization" of economic activity.[41] Rationalization can be understood here as the trend toward uniformity and impersonality in human activity, especially in terms of standards of efficiency and effectiveness. Such rationalization is seen as the basis of our present concept of technical expertise, and indeed of our view of professionalism in a broad sense. It is readily applied, six decades after Weber, to our increasingly scientific and automated economy. Weber viewed the trend as linear, dominant, and probably irreversible, and brooded over its cost in human terms, since it diminished the value of individuals by turning them into interchangeable cogs in economic machines, while narrowing the realm of spontaneity and emotional expression.

The trend toward greater uniformity and impersonality within industrial structures which precipitated Weber's pessimism also began to raise the concerns of a number of scholars at Harvard University during the 1930s and 1940s. This group, which included Fritz Roethlisberger and Elton Mayo, argued that while firms might seek to standardize skills and methods in the name of organizational effectiveness, businesses could not expect perfectly standard, emotionless behavior from their employees.[42] This perspective, referred to as the human relations school, rejects the views that individuals are (1) essentially rational beings who make decisions strictly in terms of their own interests, or (2) passive beings which can be shaped to meet the needs of organizational efficiency. Based on a series of studies at Western Electric's Hawthorne Plant, they concluded that people were moved primarily by sentiments and emotions (including a desire to gain acceptance and, at times, affection from others). Since the mechanization of work was stripping jobs of their intrinsic meaning, people were seeking meaning in their work through social relationships. Organizations, it was argued, must therefore help people satisfy these natural desires. Rather than being moralistic, however, the arguments were tied to prescriptions for organizational effectiveness and efficiency. If managers did not respond to these socially oriented needs with greater consideration and warmth, lagging work performance and resistance to authority were viewed as likely outcomes.

Despite these warnings, both Roethlisberger and Mayo were not overly optimistic about the outcomes. Roethlisberger, for instance, argued that there was a wide gulf between those who exercise "social skills" (the actual administrators) and those who talk about them. The general concentration on technical problems blinded managers to the importance of the problems of human cooperation and the social skills necessary to create such cooperation.[43] In his discussion of the "seamy side of progress," Mayo was even more critical of our emphasis on the technical and material at the expense of the human and the social. He argued that collaboration in an industrial society cannot be "left to chance—neither in a political nor in an industrial unit can such neglect lead to anything but disruption and catastrophe."[44] He subsequently called for government intervention to ensure that this does not occur.

Given these concerns, Alvin Gouldner proposed that the task of sociologists should be to demonstrate that some administrative options are "better" than others. At this point in his career, Gouldner was careful to maintain an objective, "value-free" position in his work; he still argued, however, that while sociologists might not expound upon what "ought to be," they should focus on the "realm of what can be." Accordingly, Gouldner applied Weber's ideal-type model (see Chapter 3) of bureaucracy to assess the tensions and problems evoked by the process of bureaucratization. Raising the concern that the characteristics of a bureaucracy might differ according to the manner in which rules are initiated (by imposition or agreement), he found three variants on Weber's model (punishment-centered, representative, mock). He thus concluded that patterns of industrial bureaucracy could indeed vary based on such factors as who initiated the organization's rules, whose values legitimate them, the effects the rules have on the status of organization members, and so forth.[45]

In the mid-1950s, Talcott Parsons and Neil J. Smelser approached the social economy from the point of view of functional analysis and its concomitant systems theory. The economy, they argued, should be approached like any other social system, that is, as a complex whole with a tendency toward self-regulation or equilibrium. Its special task, as a differentiated institution, was to enable society to adapt to its environment by producing and making available the maximum possible amount of resources in the form of "wealth." This might then be disposed of according to the preferences of the society, especially as expressed through the political subsystem. In order to accomplish its mission, the economy had to meet the functional imperatives of any social system, namely, to maintain its values, integrate its members, adjust to other social systems in terms of acquiring resources, and formulate goals. Therefore the economy itself had to be seen as internally subdivided into systems devoted to these tasks. Production subsystems met fundamental economic goals; capitalization was especially important in integrating members; and general motivational resources from the culture maintained its basic values, especially productivity and profitability.[46] This conceptualization was the basis for the systems framework discussed earlier under "business and society."

While these analyses focused on the nature of industrial society, over the past decade Daniel Bell has suggested that the study of business and society should be placed in the context of a post-industrial society. In contrast to the agriculturally and industrially based societies of earlier periods, post-industrial society is characterized by quite different dimensions: a basic shift in the orientation of the labor force from goods producing to services rendering/information processing; a gradual and steady rise in the influence of professional and technical occupations; a growing influence and centrality of theoretical knowledge as the source of innovation and policy formulation; an increased need for the planning and control of technology and its growth; and an emergence of mass integrated computer systems that will create a new "intellectual technology."[47] Thus, given such unprecedented change and the various processes it engenders, the work organization as one of the dominant social units of contemporary society must be increasingly prepared to anticipate and to adapt to forces for change—external and internal—if it is to remain an effective and viable institution.

Critical Variants

In contrast to the attempts at "objective" analysis discussed above, those whom we refer to under critical variants readily injected their own values into their assessments of what "ought to be." Perhaps the most famous of the "critical" theorists is Karl Marx, whose protest against capitalist economic institutions is also well known. Marx considered the operation of such organizations to be both unjust and unsatisfying. His verdict of injustice rested upon a particular conception known as the "labor theory of value," which maintains that the value of a product is equal to the sum of the human labor that went into it. Profit, or surplus value, from this point of view, could only be a form of dishonesty or fraud, for it meant that workers were given back in wages and benefits less than the value they had put into the product.

Contemporary work life was condemned by Marx as unfulfilling in terms of what he called "alienation," a feeling of strangeness, of being cut off from and unable to identify with the products of one's own labor. The point is readily illustrated by the case of specialized assembly: If a person stands in one place all day, endlessly repeating a simple operation such as tightening a couple of bolts, without ever participating in or seeing the product as a complete unit, the person is alienated in one sense of the concept. There is a feeling of fragmentation, as well as the feeling that the contribution is of insignificant value. If the person is replaced by a robot, the alienation is not overcome, for an alienating sense of powerlessness remains, which indeed already exists in the large, bureaucratized contexts of industrial activity. Above and beyond these two types of alienation, workers experience a third in terms of lack of creative expression, for they have not designed the forms which their labor shall take.[48]

At some point in time, Marx believed, people would rebel against this organization of economic life. As crisis followed economic crisis, due to the inherent competitiveness and unstable expansionism of capitalism, human workers would band together in a revolutionary movement and transfer power from the wealthy elite to the great majority of average persons who were being exploited. The end result would be a just social system, called communism, which would subordinate economic activity to the humane principle, "From each according to ability; to each according to need."

Ferdinand Toennies analyzed and criticized these economic trends in terms of a loss of intimacy or personalism, which he summarized as the movement from community (Gemeinschaft) to impersonal society (Gesellschaft).[49] Earlier economic arrangements, according to Toennies, rested upon certain natural and stable bases, especially local territory and kinship. As a result, there existed a deep interpersonal bond among the members of the group (for example, farm, craft guild, or village). In the modern period, new economic arrangements were developing on the basis of mutual egotism or self-interest, and consequently involved the participants in temporary transactions that necessitated no deep or genuine merging of identities. Such relations flourished in cities and large markets. One might classify Toennies as an analytical theorist, except for the fact that his interpretation of recent trends motivated him to become active in promoting socialist political policies that were intended to preserve as much as possible such former community elements.

In contrast to these views, a highly individualistic, even eccentric, critique of U.S. economic institutions was expressed by Thorstein Veblen from the 1890s through the 1920s.[50] This approach, which is not as systematic as those of Marx and

Toennies, is perhaps best characterized as a set of recurrent themes. One such theme was the conflict which Veblen perceived between rational and irrational elements in the economies of industrial nations. Under the influence of the evolutionary theory of his day, Veblen conceived of economic progress as the continual improvement of the technical (especially mechanical) means of production, guided by science. Such forward movement, however, was opposed at every point in history by existing economic institutions that benefited from established ways of doing business, and therefore clung to obsolescent arrangements until these became unworkable and unprofitable. The extreme form of such irrationalism was to be found in the "conspicuous consumption" of the very wealthy who were absentee owners of industrial enterprises. Veblen sought to expose and dramatize the injustice and folly of such arrangements, so that institutional change might occur and increase the benefits to average persons. In later years, Veblen became an advocate of socialist ideas, which seemed to him the remedy for abuses of privilege and private ownership. His emphasis on the rational improvement of life also led him to support certain measures for national economic planning. In the wake of the Great Crash on Wall Street, which occurred only a few months after his death, Veblen's writings enjoyed a burst of popularity, and have since retained an appeal for nonconformist economists and others concerned with the issues of economic disparity.

Pitirim Sorokin, like Veblen, approached the social economy from a distinctive angle, one which emphasized culture, historical fluctuations, and the experience of sociocultural crisis. Economic institutions, he noted, occupied very different positions within human cultures: in religiously oriented world views, they were seen as secondary elements, while secular cultures seeking material progress and material comfort granted them a place of honor, often at the very top of the hierarchy of values. The understanding of contemporary American structures therefore required that one recognize both the high status accorded economic institutions, and the relativity of such arrangements. Over long periods of time, Sorokin argued, the place of economic structures could be shown to vary dramatically, as cultural mentalities themselves shifted. In fact, he contended, the time was at hand when the status of modern economic structures must change.

The transformation which Sorokin envisioned would come about, according to his theory, as the result of a severe historical crisis in contemporary culture, society and personality.

The components of the system, which had been built up over several centuries, would begin to malfunction seriously and frustrate the satisfaction of basic human needs, such as the need for happiness, freedom, and security. Ironically, the crisis would result not from the failures of modern institutions, but from their very successes, as when the accumulation of learning and engineering skill in the physical sciences produced nuclear weapons the use of which would destroy the planet. In similar ways, the search for material comfort would degenerate into materialistic accumulation of possessions, the campaign for control of nature would lead to its abuse and the exhaustion of scarce resources, and the emphasis on competition would create a situation of traumatically rapid change that would eliminate security. There would, in short, be a terrible ordeal, a time of intense suffering and confusion, which in fact has already begun. It is observable in the unprecedented warfare, recurrent recessions and depressions, energy shortages, and ecological disasters of the period. If people cannot perceive it, Sorokin concluded, it could only be the result of their conditioning by an obsolescent world view.

Ultimately, however, there was hope. Confronted with crisis, creative human persons would devote their lives to building something better: altruistic rather than selfishly egotistic, and cooperative rather than based on conflict or extreme competition. Many such creative initiatives, in fact, could be identified if one searched for them, despite the fact that those involved would probably be labeled by mainstream groups as unrealistic dreamers and deviants.[51]

Although C. Wright Mills is probably best described as a political theorist concerned with issues of power, portions of his work are sufficiently focused on economic issues to justify his inclusion here. Most relevant for our purposes are two works entitled White Collar and The Power Elite. The first addresses the issue of the emergence of office work on a mass scale in the twentieth century. Such activity is interpreted by Mills as problematic because of its inherent tendency to continually reduce the spontaneity, creativity, and importance of the individual employee, who increasingly becomes a cog in an impersonal machine similar to workers in a factory. Committed to the value of increasing human freedom, Mills set himself against this trend. Echoes of his analysis and interpretation can be found in recent discussions of the "de-skilling" of work in general, even at higher and higher levels of management (what some refer to as the "proletarianization" of managerial activity).[52]

The Power Elite, Mills's best known and most influential work, is a forceful assault on the notion of America as the land of opportunity where people enjoy the freedom to move upward on the social ladder. The reality, Mills asserts, is that of a political-economic dictatorship rather than a democracy. Very small groups, relatively speaking, make more and more of the truly "big decisions" which affect the lives of millions, such as the decision to enter a war or to develop and detonate thermonuclear weapons. This is due to a long-term historical process which concentrates more and more resources in fewer and fewer hands. The economy is thus a pyramid with a rapidly expanding base and a rapidly shrinking top. This arrangement can only be improved through some sort of democratic socialist transformation which would empower average persons and force the economy to serve their real and fundamental needs. At the end of his career, Mills looked to the Cuban Revolution as a model of what might be done.[53]

Over the past few decades, the works of the Frankfurt School of "critical" sociology have further influenced the study of economic institutions. Though originally established in 1923 as a Marxist-oriented center, this group of scholars gradually branched off from the themes of orthodox Marxism and focused on other perceived deficiencies of current socioeconomic systems. The main critical thrust in this body of work is that contemporary institutional arrangements, especially those of "late capitalism," are depersonalizing in their essential character. Private enterprise, science, and technology combine to form a "culture industry" that is highly manipulative in nature, creating wants in those exposed to its relentless, self-interested messages. Oriented to impersonal mass markets, the "culture industry" assaults individualism and nonconformity, while indirectly but effectively undermining such basic human interests and activities as art, poetry, and philosophy. People, in other words, are conditioned to conceive of themselves and to behave as mere consumers of an ever-increasing array of material products which are designed by the scientific, technical, and economic elite. Despite high levels of prosperity, therefore, contemporary economies in countries such as the United States work to continually diminish personhood and freedom, and so to produce "one-dimensional" human beings.[54]

The theories of Mills and the Frankfurt School found echoes in the writings of the New Left in the late 1960s and early 1970s. Some of the best known of these works attempted to demonstrate the existence of elites of wealth and power. Thus, Domhoff in Who Rules America? pointed to a "ruling class" of the super rich who controlled the largest corporations and the highest levels of the federal government.[55] Kolko, in a similar vein, developed statistical data to show that vast economic inequalities have persisted over many decades, and were in fact increasing.[56] In recent years, such analyses have been developed by sociologists connected with the Movement for Economic Democracy, which will be considered in the next chapter. While some of these theories and perspectives may be more familiar than others, the social economy is being increasingly applied to the assessment of business's social role and ways in which this role can be altered.

CONCLUSION

This chapter has proposed that a minimum of four specialized perspectives should be incorporated into the sociological study of business and society. In doing so, we have tried to indicate a manner of thinking, rather than a body of fact or theory. The integral conceptualization advocated here is perhaps best described as dialectical in character, in the general sense that truth emerges from the interaction of opposites. Individual perspectives, that is, cannot simply be combined by addition. Rather, they interpenetrate or reciprocally influence one another at every point in analysis and interpretation. The result is a dialectical matrix or nexus which sensitizes us to the dynamic complexity of any particular case of corporate social policy making.

As this chapter has indicated, the growing body of literature popularly defined as "business and society" takes a relatively positive view of corporate performance and social involvement over time, not simply as a means of justifying or rationalizing business performance, but as a way of delineating growing social awareness and accountability on the part of our large corporations. As discussed in Chapter 1, the emergence of such terms as corporate social responsiveness, social performance, and social policy reflect these analyses. Business ethics, by contrast, refers largely to these phenomena on an individual rather than organizational level. This perspective emphasizes the implications and effects of managerial decision making on organizations, their members and relevant publics. The focus is one of understanding the individual's role within the larger system and, within that context, moral responsibilities and obligations. Business policy takes a broader view of organizations and ways in which they can survive and prosper in their larger social settings. While it is generally agreed that social and political issues should be considered in formulating organizational plans, the focus is on the strategic, operational, financial, and human resource dimensions. Finally, the social economy takes a more critical view of our economic system, pointing out its flaws and contradictions, and suggesting alternative systems which "can" or "ought to be."

The organizational issues which are the focus of this book will be considered within the context of these four perspectives. It is not our intention to suggest that any one of these perspectives has the "right" answer, nor to attempt an even-handed critique using each of these perspectives to look at a particular issue. Rather, our aim is to use these perspectives to add depth and understanding to present criticism of the business sector and its relation to the larger society, and to show how an understanding of these different orientations can lead to a more balanced approach to the study of corporate policy, the values which are a part of this process, and the implications for social responsibility.

NOTES

1. Reported in D. J. Watson, "The New Political Role of Business," in Business Environment/Public Policy: 1979 Conference Papers, ed. Lee E. Preston (St. Louis: American Assembly of Collegiate Schools of Business, 1980), p. 60.

2. John Kenneth Galbraith, American Capitalism (Boston: Houghton Mifflin, 1952); Dow Votaw, Modern Corporations (Englewood Cliffs: Prentice-Hall, 1965); and Clarence C. Walton, Corporate Social Responsibilities (Belmont, Calif.: Wadsworth, 1967).

3. Rogene A. Buchholz, Business Environment/Public Policy: A Study of Teaching and Research in Schools of Business and Management (St. Louis: Center for the Study of American Business, 1979); and Rogene A. Buchholz, Business Environment/Public Policy: Corporate Executive Viewpoints and Educational Implications (St. Louis: Center for the Study of American Business, 1980).

4. For a good summary of texts and research studies in the business and society field see Lee E. Preston, "Teaching Materials in Business and Society," California Management Review 25 (Spring 1983):158-173; Dow Votaw, "Has Corporate Public Affairs Come of Age?" in California Management Review 25 (Summer 1983):160-166; and Michael Useem, "Corporate Social

and Political Action," California Management Review 26 (Winter 1984):141-154.

5. Rogene A. Buchholz, Corporate Executive Viewpoints, pp. 1-2; and Archie B. Carroll, Business and Society: Managing Corporate Social Performance (Boston: Little, Brown, 1981), pp. 33-37.

6. Francis W. Steckmest, Corporate Performance: The Key to Public Trust (New York: McGraw-Hill, 1982), pp. 253-256.

7. Buchholz, Corporate Executive Viewpoints, p. 3.

8. Steckmest, Corporate Performance, pp. 256-257.

9. Henry A. Tombari, "The New Role of Business Management," The Collegiate Forum (Fall 1979):12; and Henry A. Tombari, Business and Society: Strategies for the Environment and Public Policy (Hinsdale, Ill.: Dryden Press, 1984).

10. Buchholz, Corporate Executive Viewpoints, pp. 12-17.

11. Dalton E. McFarland, Management and Society: An Institutional Framework (Englewood Cliffs: Prentice-Hall, 1982), pp. 15-17; and Robert Miles, Macro Organizational Behavior (Santa Monica: Goodyear Publishing, 1980).

12. See Lee E. Preston, "Corporation and Society: The Search for a Paradigm," Journal of Economic Literature 13 (1975):434-453; and Thomas M. Jones, "An Integrating Framework for Research in Business and Society: A Step Toward the Elusive Paradigm?," Academy of Management Review 8 (October 1983):559-564; and Liam Fahey and Richard E. Wokutch, "Business and Society Exchanges: A Framework for Analysis," California Management Review 25 (Summer 1983):128-142.

13. See Lee E. Preston, "Corporate Social Performance and Policy: A Synthetic Framework for Research and Analysis," in Research In Corporate Social Performance and Policy, Vol. 1, ed. Lee E. Preston (Greenwich, Conn.: JAI Press, 1978), pp. 1-26; and James E. Post, "Research on Corporate Response to Social Change," in Research in Corporate Performance and Policy, Vol. 1, edited by Lee E. Preston (Greenwich, Conn.: JAI Press, 1978), pp. 55-79.

14. Lee E. Preston and James E. Post, Private Management and Public Policy (Englewood Cliffs: Prentice-Hall, 1975), chap. 2; and Post, "Patterns of Corporate Response," pp. 58-60.

15. Buchholz, Teaching and Research in Schools of Business; and Rogene Buchholz, Business Environment/Public Policy: Curriculum Development Materials (St. Louis: Center for the Study of American Business: 1980).

16. For an overview of this perspective see Melvin J. Stanford, Management Policy (Englewood Cliffs: Prentice-Hall,

1983); and Hugo R. Uyterhoeven, Robert W. Ackerman, and John W. Rosenblum, Strategy and Organization: Text and Cases in General Management (Homewood, Ill.: Richard D. Irwin, 1977), chap. 1; H. Igor Ansoff, Corporate Strategy: An Analytic Approach to Business Policy for Growth and Expansion (Homewood, Ill.: Richard D. Irwin, 1965); Kenneth R. Andrews, Edmund P. Learned, C. Roland Christensen, and William Guth, Business Policy: Text and Cases (Homewood, Ill.: Dow-Jones-Irwin, 1980).

17. H. Igor Ansoff, "The Changing Shape of the Strategic Problem," in Strategic Management: A New View of Business Policy and Planning, ed. Dan E. Schendel and Charles W. Hofer (Boston: Little, Brown, 1979), pp. 30-38; and Walter H. Klein and Joseph A. Raelin, "Business and Society in the 1980s: From a Business Policy Perspective," paper presented at the Academy of Management National Meeting, August 2-5, 1981, San Diego, Calif.

18. Ansoff, "Changing Shape of the Strategic Problem," pp. 37-38.

19. See Robert Ackerman and Raymond Bauer, Corporate Social Responsiveness: The Modern Dilemma (Reston, Va.: Reston Publishing, 1976), chap. 3; and James E. Post, Corporate Behavior and Social Change (Reston, Va.: Reston Publishing, 1978), p. vi.

20. Michael J. Merenda, "A Comparative Model for Teaching the Business Environment/Public Policy Course," paper presented at the Academy of Management National Meeting, August 15-18, 1982, New York City.

21. Klein and Raelin, "Business and Society in the 1980s," p. 1.

22. Vincent Barry, Moral Issues in Business (Belmont, Calif.: Wadsworth Publishing, 1979), p. 3.

23. Raymond Baumhart, S. J., Ethics in Business (New York: Holt, Rinehart and Winston, 1968), chap. 1; and C. E. Hubner, The Promise and Perils of Business Ethics (Washington, D.C.: Association of American Colleges, 1979), pp. 9-10.

24. W. Michael Hoffman and Jennifer Mills Moore, "Results of a Business Ethics Curriculum Survey Conducted by the Center for Business Ethics," Journal of Business Ethics 1 (May 1982):81-83.

25. Sidney C. Sufrin, Management of Business Ethics (Port Washington, N.Y.: Kennikat Press, 1980).

26. Manuel Velasquez, Business Ethics: Concepts and Cases (Englewood Cliffs: Prentice-Hall, 1982), pp. 2-6.

27. Huber, Promise and Perils; and Charles W. Powers and David Vogel, Ethics in the Education of Business Managers (Hastings-on-Hudson, N.Y.: Hastings Center, 1980).

28. Kristine Hanson and Robert Solomon, "The Real Business Ethics," Business and Society Review (Spring 1982): 58-59.

29. Paul F. Camenisch, "Business Ethics: On Getting to the Heart of the Matter," Business and Professional Ethics Journal 1 (1981):61.

30. Our discussion of ethical theory is drawn from W. Michael Hoffman and Jennifer Mills Moore, "Ethics and Business: From Theory to Practice," in Business Ethics: Readings and Cases in Corporate Morality, ed. W. Michael Hoffman and Jennifer Mills Moore (New York: McGraw-Hill, 1984), pp. 1-11; Richard T. DeGeorge, "Moral Issues in Business," in Ethics, Free Enterprise, and Public Policy: Original Essays on Moral Issues in Business, edited by Richard T. DeGeorge and Joseph A. Pichler (New York: Oxford U. Press, 1978), pp. 3-18; and Barry, Moral Issues in Business, chaps. 1 and 2.

31. For a fuller discussion, see Barry, Moral Issues, pp. 52-55.

32. See Velasquez, Business Ethics, pp. 58-74; Barry, Moral Issues, pp. 13-15; and Gerald F. Cavanagh, American Business Values (Englewood Cliffs: Prentice-Hall, 1984), pp. 142-144.

33. Manuel Velasquez, Gerald Cavanagh, and Dennis Moberg, "Organizational Statesmanship and Dirty Politics: Ethical Guidelines for the Organizational Politician," Organizational Dynamics (Fall 1983):70-71.

34. See Velasquez, Business Ethics, pp. 74-90; Barry, Moral Issues, pp. 59-64; and Cavanagh, American Business Values, pp. 144-145.

35. Velasquez, Cavanagh, and Moberg, "Organizational Statesmanship," pp. 71-72.

36. See Barry, Moral Issues, pp. 40-70; and Velasquez, Business Ethics, chap. 2.

37. Herbert Spencer, The Study of Sociology (New York: Appleton, 1898).

38. See T. N. Carver, Essential Factors of Social Evolution (Cambridge: Harvard University Press, 1934).

39. Emile Durkheim, The Division of Labor in Society (New York: Free Press, 1956).

40. Max Weber, The Protestant Ethic and the Spirit of Capitalism, trans. Talcott Parsons (New York: Oxford University Press, 1931).

41. See Max Weber, The Theory of Social and Economic Organization, trans. Talcott Parsons and A. M. Henderson (New York: Free Press, 1947); and A. Mitzman, The Iron Cage (New York: Knopf, 1970).

42. See Fritz J. Roethlisberger and William J. Dickson, Management and the Worker (Cambridge, Mass.: Harvard University Press, 1939); and Elton Mayo, The Social Problems of an Industrial Civilization (Cambridge, Mass.: Harvard University Press, 1945).

43. Fritz J. Roethlisberger, Management and Morale (Cambridge, Mass.: Harvard University Press, 1942).

44. Elton Mayo, The Social Problems of an Industrial Civilization, preface and chap. 1.

45. Alvin W. Gouldner, Patterns of Industrial Bureaucracy: A Case Study of Modern Factory Administration (New York: Free Press, 1954).

46. Talcott Parsons and Neil J. Smelser, Economy and Society (Glencoe, Ill.: Free Press, 1956).

47. Daniel Bell, The Coming of Post-Industrial Society: A Venture in Social Forecasting (New York: Basic Books, 1973).

48. Karl Marx, Selected Writings in Sociology and Social Philosophy, trans. T. Bottomore (London: McGraw-Hill, 1964).

49. Ferdinand Toennies, Community and Society, trans. C. P. Loomis (East Lansing, Mich.: Michigan State University Press, 1957).

50. Thorstein Veblen, The Portable Veblen, ed. M. Lerner (New York: Viking Press, 1948).

51. Pitirim A. Sorokin, The Crisis of Our Age (New York: Dutton, 1941); and Pitirim A. Sorokin, The Reconstruction of Humanity (Boston: Beacon Press, 1948).

52. C. Wright Mills, White Collar (New York: Oxford University Press, 1953).

53. C. Wright Mills, The Power Elite (New York: Oxford University Press, 1956); and C. Wright Mills, Listen Yankee: The Revolution in Cuba (New York: McGraw-Hill, 1960).

54. A. Arato and E. Gebhardt, eds., The Essential Frankfurt School Reader (New York: Urizen Books, 1978); see also M. Jay, The Dialectical Imagination (Boston: Little, Brown, 1973).

55. G. W. Domhoff, Who Rules America? (Englewood Cliffs: Prentice-Hall, 1967).

56. G. Kolko, Wealth and Power in America (New York: Praeger, 1962); see also R. Dahrendorf, Class and Class Conflict in Industrial Society (Stanford: Stanford University Press, 1959).

# 3

# PHILOSOPHIES OF CORPORATE SOCIAL RESPONSIBILITY

The most fundamental problems of theory and research methodology confront any investigator who attempts to seriously study corporate responses to social concerns.  As indicated in Chapter 1, after nearly two decades of intensive work the central phenomenon remains confusing and defies consensus, even in terms of elementary definitions.  There has been a continuing competition between frameworks and conceptualizations of responsibility and responsiveness which largely stems from their dependence on a particular emphasis or academic discipline.[1]  Moreover, the different perspectives laid out in Chapter 2 suggest very different orientations toward the study of business's social role.  As a result, the masses of empirical data which have been gathered through these approaches and the conclusions that have been drawn often cannot be meaningfully compared.  Thus, many scholars in this area, whether concentrating on theory or empirical research, have expressed frustration at the general state of the field.

The different frameworks and discussions of responsibility and responsiveness which have guided this work have provided much needed synthesis and have prompted ongoing empirical research efforts.[2]  Considering the range of concepts and approaches used to assess business's social role, however, the dissatisfaction expressed by many scholars is understandable.  The next two chapters, therefore, represent our attempt to develop an integrated model for the analysis of organizational responsiveness to social concerns.  Drawing on the integral approach developed in Chapter 2, we shall seek to provide a framework for comparisons across these different perspectives;

explain how and why different interpretations of responsiveness emerge; and facilitate the analysis of how and why different interactions occur between business organizations and their relevant publics.

This chapter introduces the basic analytical and interpretive concepts which will be applied in the remainder of the book. Beginning with a note on culture, the chapter proceeds to a discussion of method and interpretations of general organizational and corporate social responsibility. Chapter 4 then turns to a brief discussion of organizational and public policy, and its application in empirical assessment of corporate responsiveness. Our goal is to link these elements in such a way that they become inseparable components of an integrated theoretical model.

CULTURE

Because the idea of culture plays a prominent part in our discussion of corporate policy and social responsibility, it is necessary to briefly delineate what we understand by the term. Although the fundamental thrust of the concept is simple and clear, its application in research is often difficult and ambiguous. By culture, we understand the specifically meaningful aspect of social life, that is, the set of shared interpretations of reality which enter into the individual and collective experience of human persons. When we focus on the cultural aspect of life, we concentrate on the significance of situations for participants, rather than on their behavioristic action-reactions, or the integration of needs, drives, and events within a personality. Considered as a whole, culture consists of a universe of meanings, expressed in symbols.

Our treatment of culture follows the usage of the well known American sociologist, Pitirim A. Sorokin, especially as set out in his work, Society, Culture, and Personality.[3] Sorokin distinguishes three aspects of culture: ideational, behavioral, and material. This first refers to culture in the pure or abstract sense explained above, while the others denote the embodiment of culture in interaction or in physical objects. In terms of the discussion which follows, most of our attention will be devoted to analysis of the ideational variety, that is, to the conceptions which underlie social interaction and give it structure.[4]

In Sorokin's discussion, ideational culture can be usefully subdivided into three further categories of meanings, values, and norms. Meanings refer to abstractions in the purest sense, as when we have ideas of space, time, number, causation, motion, or color. Values are meanings which have an additional feature: they are ranked according to some criterion of goodness, worth, or desirability. Thus, honesty is not only distinct from dishonesty in an intellectual sense, but is rated as "better" or "higher." In the same way, strength is generally valued more than weakness, kindness more than cruelty, love more than hatred, freedom more than slavery, and wealth more than poverty. Norms, the third element of ideational culture, convert meanings and values into specific rules for conduct. Thus, a group which believes in the existence of a loving God, and values holiness, may teach the norm of "love of God and of neighbor." A society which believes in social order and values democratic control may adopt the norms of "one nation under law," or "government of the people, by the people, and for the people."

In the application of these cultural concepts, Sorokin urged a "logico-meaningful" method of searching for the central unifying premise of a culture. What, he asked, did various groups think of as the essence of reality and its highest value? Our analysis follows a similar procedure. In seeking to understand corporate responsiveness policies, we shall attempt to identify the fundamental ideas and values which underlie interaction. What assumptions are made about the nature of human beings, or the workings of the economy, or the operation of government? What is valued more highly: production or distribution, growth or conservation, freedom or regulation, efficiency or happiness, security or change? Thus, from our point of view, corporate interpretations of social responsibility are comprehensible in terms of cultural systems, that is, in terms of logically integrated ideas and values and norms.[5]

Special emphasis will be placed upon the concept of values as a means of interpreting differences between groups in the area of corporate social responsibility. It is possible for groups to have very similar beliefs, and yet choose to adopt very different values. Over the past decade, for instance, there has been widespread consensus that both inflation and unemployment are urgent social problems. At the same time, however, sharp differences in values have led to conflicts over national policy. Some groups have contended that it is more important in the short run to combat inflation, while others have insisted that providing employment is the higher value. This type of situation appears to characterize the debate on corporate social responsibility: there is intellectual agreement on many issues of fact, but intense disagreement over priorities. What is a primary value for certain groups (for example, growth) remains a secondary, tertiary, or even lesser value for others who operate on a different scale of priorities (as, for example, with holiness the paramount value).

Since the sets of values to be found in any human group may be indefinitely large, it seems useful to suggest some preliminary distinctions. Initially, we can differentiate between the primary or higher, and secondary or lower values in any group's culture. Thus, political freedom and economic prosperity would surely rank among the more important American values, while participation in poetry and philosophy or detachment from material possessions would occupy a place among the lesser values. In suggesting such an approach, of course, we do not wish to imply rigid or absolute application. There will always be shifts in priorities according to the situation, and significant differences in outlook among subgroups or factions.

At the pinnacle of the set of primary values, we propose to use the concept of ideals, the particular qualities which are "best" in members of the group, and which therefore confer upon them the greatest respect and most enduring influence. As an illustration, the American value of "occupational success based on individual initiative" as an important ideal is found widely in our society. Its influence is perhaps greatest in the world of business and management, but the breadth of its impact is reflected even in very different events such as the contemporary women's movement, which promotes occupational success in addition to or even over the fulfillment of duties in automatic marital and parental roles. We do not see on a broad scale in the United States such alternative ideals as Confucian humility, classical Greek moderation, Jewish God-centeredness, or Buddhist enlightenment.

Since the notion of ideals is difficult to translate into precise measurement, it is offered as a "sensitizing" rather than "definitive" concept. It can thus be used to focus on some very important, if elusive, differences in thinking, feeling, and acting of human groups. As will be indicated in forthcoming discussion, the concept plays an important role in the analysis of "ethical idealism" as a philosophy of social responsibility.

It is important to underscore here a basic assumption underlying our analysis of culture: a multiplicity or plurality of cultures can exist, at both the societal and group levels. This approach stands in contrast to the unitary view that for each group or society there is only one culture, to which all members belong. There may indeed be a dominant culture for a particular society, organization or group.[6] In our view, however, a corporation, division, plant, department, committee, office, task force, work team, interest group—or any other policy-making unit—may have a culture (or subculture) which is distinct from the culture of the larger group or society, at least in certain important respects. As a result, a multitude of conflicts over corporate social policy may arise, from disputes on specific issues like employment and the environment, to disagreements on overall corporate philosophy as related to social issues.

## THE METHOD OF IDEAL TYPES

One of the most important steps in theory construction within the social sciences has been the development of ideal types, a variety of conceptual modeling. As defined and popularized by German writers, especially the famous sociologist-economist Max Weber, ideal types have several essential features:

1. The concepts are formed by exaggeration of the distinctive features of the subject being studied;
2. The types facilitate scientific work by improving communication, providing a basis for measurement, and serving as starting points for exploratory study; and
3. The types can capture subjects which may be unique or unrepeated in history (like Western, ascetic Calvinist Protestantism), an achievement beyond the reach of ordinary definitions or quantitative methods of analysis.[7]

To say that the ideal-typical method exaggerates the characteristic features of its subjects means that it overlooks the complexities, interactions, and imperfections of real life. We know, for instance, that it is not completely accurate to refer to corporate policies as either "economic" or "social," for they are simultaneously both. Nor is it valid to divide nations into the familiar categories of "capitalist" and "socialist" because modern economic systems are generally "mixed." Thus, even in such allegedly capitalistic societies as the United States, an enormous number of things are publicly or socially owned, from school systems to welfare programs to wilderness areas. Similarly, in the socialistic Soviet Union important forms of private or quasi-private ownership continue to exist, from private garden plots for workers on collective farms to the secret perquisites enjoyed by the elite members of the Soviet government and Communist Party. Ideal types like capitalism and socialism must therefore be understood as purposeful oversimplifications.

The formulation of ideal types may occur at any phase of the research and theory-building process, as interpretive understanding of the objects of investigation progresses. Our emphasis will be on the usefulness of such abstract models during the earlier stages of work, especially in exploratory study. Again, Weber provides perhaps the best illustration. At the outset of his famous work The Protestant Ethic and The Spirit of Capitalism, Weber admitted a dilemma. He knew there was something "out there" in the social world which could be referred to as "the Protestant ethic," and something else which could be designated as "the spirit of capitalism," but these phenomena could only be properly described after an historical investigation. Therefore he proposed to construct ideal types of each as provisional definitions, which would permit the research to go forward. When the empirical work had been accomplished, the original constructs might be revised or even discarded, much like scaffolding. [8]

Investigators of corporate social responsibility, responsiveness, or performance find themselves in a position similar to Weber's. They know with a considerable degree of certainty that there is something in the social world which corresponds to these terms, and which is so named by the human groups involved, but they also realize that writers in the field have been unable to agree on its precise meaning. By being relatively open-minded and not inclined to circumscribe the object of the study in narrow ideological categories, these individuals will seek to identify a series of reference points that are both clear and sufficiently broad to encompass existing schools of thought. In the discussion that follows, four varieties of responsiveness are developed which capture characteristic tendencies of contemporary corporate thinking and policy making on social issues.

Our intention is that these types will facilitate discussion and even measurement. Because they exaggerate selected features of corporate thought and behavior, they have the virtue of clarity. At the same time, however, we would readily admit that they overlook important empirical complications. It is quite possible, even common, for corporate policies to have a mix of elements from the various types. If the terms were to be applied to particular firms, we would encounter the problem that different sectors or policies might fall under different headings. It might happen, for instance, that a corporation could be referred to as "progressive" overall, even though the label applied more properly to top management than to the middle levels.

Despite these difficulties, the potential use of the types in measurement can again be illustrated by reference to Weber. Having formulated an ideal type of "bureaucracy" with several distinctive characteristics, Weber suggested that the construct might be utilized to gauge the degree of bureaucracy in any particular organization. Thus, in the present analysis, a rough but useful sense of the type of responsiveness in a particular policy or business can be developed by reference to the elements of the conceptual yardstocks. A similar treatment of the issue has been contributed by Sorokin. After detailing three ideal types of social relationships, Sorokin compared them to threads of different color, each of which might be found to some extent in a particular piece of clothing.[9]

## AN IDEAL-TYPICAL MODEL OF
## SOCIAL RESPONSIBILITY

Before proceeding to exposition of our ideal types, it is necessary to examine briefly the basic dimensions underlying these constructs. Within the business and society literature, there are two fundamental, recurring themes: 1) the question of practical self-interest versus moral duty; and 2) the relative emphasis a firm should give to its stockholders and stakeholders.

Max Weber, whose analytic procedure we emulate, devoted considerable attention to the motives underlying social action. Among his basic conceptual tools were the motivational ideal types of technical or instrumental rationality and value rationality. Actions of the former (rational self-interest) are directed toward specific goals and, therefore, have the character of logical, utilitarian calculation. The latter (perceived moral duties) are motivated by some value, taken as an end in itself. These value rational actions are most clearly distinguished when they are undertaken in spite of obstacles which may make them seem illogical, futile, or absurd from a strictly utilitarian standpoint.[10] Both of these motivational types are reflected in the literature on corporate social responsibility. For example, one perspective contends that inherent in the concept of social responsiveness is the duty to abandon the "selfish pursuit" of economic gain as the ultimate objective of corporate activity, exemplified by the often used phrase "human needs before profit" (perceived

moral duty). Others, however, have rebutted this argument
with the contention that any notion of corporate responsiveness
rests upon the premise of corporate survival in a competitive
marketplace, which in turn requires the self-interested pursuit
of economic gain.

In a similar way, a debate has emerged over whether
socially responsive performance requires a departure from the
historical role of serving the corporation's stockholders. As
discussed in Chapter 1, the traditional business gospel has
been that organizations have sacrosanct and inviolable obligations
to their stockholders, the owners of the firm's equity. Thus,
corporate activity should be influenced at all points by the
needs and interests of stockholders. An emerging perspective,
however, argues that there are other groups in society who
have a stake in the actions of the organization. Corporations,
therefore, also have a responsibility to these stakeholder groups
(for example, employees, customers, suppliers, lenders, and
the larger society as well as investors). The key to effective
management is to balance the needs of these, at times, competing
groups. In sociological terms, we may therefore focus on the
primary "reference group" of a corporation or other policy-
making unit.

These two debates provide us with basic organizational
criteria out of which four ideal types of corporate interpretations
of social responsibility may be constructed:

1. Social responsibility refers to corporate behavior which
   is justified in terms of rational self-interest and the
   direct fulfillment of stockholder interests.
2. Social responsibility refers to corporate behavior which
   is justified in terms of moral duty and the direct fulfillment of stockholder interests.
3. Social responsibility refers to corporate behavior which
   is justified in terms of rational self-interest and the
   direct fulfillment of stakeholder interests.
4. Social responsibility refers to corporate behavior which
   is justified in terms of moral duty and the direct fulfillment of stakeholder interests.

When framed in this way, the concept of social responsibility
provides the basis for a comparative classification of corporate
social policy types. The types are respectively referred to as
productivism, philanthropy, progressivism, and ethical idealism.
Their derivations and mutual interrelations are illustrated in
Figure 3.1.

FIGURE 3.1

Responsiveness Types: Motives and Reference Groups

|  |  | REFERENCE GROUPS | |
|---|---|---|---|
|  |  | Private: Stockholder Model | Public: Stakeholder Model |
| MOTIVES | Instrumentally Rational Motives (self–interest) | Productivism | Progressivism |
|  | Value Rational Motives (moral duty) | Philanthropy | Ethical Idealism |

Productivism

Among contemporary interpretations of corporate social responsibility, there is a traditional, or perhaps "fundamentalist" view, which is referred to as productivism. The central doctrine of this school is that business exists in order to fulfill a specialized technical role in society, namely, to produce wealth. This task is critically important for any society, and it is therefore "proper" that people in business should take pride in discharging their mission. When businesses observe safe and sound practices, and maximize profits while minimizing losses, they are serving the common good and behaving in a responsible manner. In fact, our society's standard of living depends on such activities. What may seem selfish and materialistic to some may well be quite altruistic (at least in its effects), if the linkages among the various areas of life are taken into account. How could a nation, for example, enjoy the finest health care, guarantee access to medical technology costing hundreds of thousands of dollars, and have outstanding school systems to provide for the educational needs of all its children, or how could its citizens look forward to a comfortable and secure retirement, if there were not a high level of general prosperity? And how could such prosperity be achieved if safe and sound business practices were not faithfully observed? The notion of corporate social responsibility, therefore, must be rather narrowly interpreted, and cannot include social projects— however well-intentioned—that divert business from its proper activity. The key is to return to the traditional mission of business as understood in early capitalism, which is instrumental and even somewhat mechanistic.

One of the most important theorists of the productivist perspective is Friedrich A. Hayek, winner of the Nobel Prize for Economics in 1974. In a series of works spanning several decades, Hayek articulated the basic psychological, economic, and political elements of this view. Analyzing the role of corporations in democratic society, he argued that only a consistently applied stockholder model would preserve corporate freedom while simultaneously preventing large concentrations of socially undesirable power. Hayek attempted to demonstrate this logically by a process of elimination, as follows. Only four groups might be designated the prime beneficiaries of corporate activity: management, labor, stockholders, and the public at large. If either management or labor assumed the status of specially favored group, however, the corporation would surely fail in the marketplace due to the inefficiency and ineffectiveness of its self-centeredness. The general public, likewise, cannot become the major beneficiary, because it is in reality composed of heterogeneous and conflicting elements which would force corporations to turn their efforts in too many directions. Therefore, the traditional role in which corporations serve the interests of those who provide their capital and equity is the only workable conception.11

This conclusion is reinforced, according to Hayek, when one focuses on the specific issue of power and its use in coercing segments of society to expend their resources in ways that they themselves would not choose. If management were self-consciously to adopt the popular view that corporations have a "social responsibility," a number of centers of uncontrolled power would rapidly emerge. Large quantities of expertise, effort, and money would be rerouted from legitimate uses toward projects which management had arbitrarily designated as worthy. In some cases, recipients might be groups or causes that anyone would support (such as education), but in others the prime beneficiaries might be dangerous ideological factions (like the Nazis who were supported by German business in the 1930s). Therefore, "the old-fashioned conception which regards management as the trustee of the stockholders and leaves to the individual stockholder the decision whether any of the proceeds of the activities of the corporation are to be

used in the service of higher values is the most important safeguard against the acquisition of arbitrary and politically dangerous powers by corporations."[12] Putting the matter another
way, we may say that Hayek is pleading for a kind of economic
objectivity. When social goals begin to be subjectively dictated
by government, society is placed on "the road to serfdom."[13]

These themes have more recently been echoed and expanded
by Milton Friedman, Hayek's colleague at the University of
Chicago, with whom the productivist approach is most often
identified. Friedman has tended to view the concept of "corporate social responsibility" as a poorly defined dream, cham-
pioned by well-meaning but mistaken reformers and self-interested
intellectuals whose careers are based on criticisms of the status
quo. His argument is that because most philanthropic or
charitable activity interferes with the proper functioning of
the specialized role of business, such activities must be opposed
as "fundamentally subversive" of the common good. However
unpopular it may sound in the current climate of opinion, one
must hold to the principle that "the social responsibility of
business is to increase its profits."[14] Against the objection
that this position callously ignores the problem of distribution,
Friedman argues that, "The ethical principle that would directly
justify the distribution of income in a free market society is,
'To each according to what he and the instruments he owns
produces.'"[15] Private individuals can, and should, be generous
in their gifts to worthy causes, but business must retain a
narrower and more "hard-headed" attitude.

Clearly, the central issue is the nature and function of
profit. In Friedman's view, profit is automatically directed
toward socially responsible ends by the mechanism of the free
market, because it can only be obtained by providing goods
or services which are desired by members of society. The
critical inference drawn from this line of reasoning is that,
for practical purposes, the free market is the best guarantee
of good corporate conduct. This can be further demonstrated
by two considerations, which may be referred to as "the worst
case scenario" and "the expanding pie." According to the
former, the measures advocated by Friedman and other producti-
vists will work even in an imperfect world where people are
prone to be greedy, dishonest, and power hungry because
sellers are protected by the presence of many buyers, buyers
are protected by many sellers, and employees are protected
by many employers. The principle of the "expanding pie" is
traced to Adam Smith's observation that "if an exchange between
two parties is voluntary, it will not take place unless both believe

they will benefit from it."[16] In other words, every economic transaction, however microscopic, actually increases the amount of social wealth on both sides if it occurs under free-market conditions. An arrangement that would be more socially responsible can hardly be imagined.

Achievement of Friedman's ideal of corporate responsibility requires the strictest fiscal management within each firm, which necessitates the explicit rejection of corporate philanthropy on principle. Such activity (no matter how highly motivated) introduces uncontrollable and unjustifiable factors into the operation of business. There are two crucial objections against the involvement of management in philanthropic activities: 1) managers lack the specific competence to select appropriate causes, and 2) they exceed their legal authority. On the first point, Friedman argues that managerial personnel are appointed on the basis of limited competencies to function as technicians, not moralists. That so many contemporary managers seek to satisfy public opinion by going beyond their technical tasks seems to "reveal a suicidal impulse." But even if this were not so, one might still object on purely legal grounds, for corporate philanthropy as Friedman sees it, is really "taxation without representation"—an abuse of corporate government to be opposed by all those who believe in true liberty. Because charitable activities are rarely subject to the consent of corporate stockholders or owners, management is wrong to spend "someone else's money for a general social interest" when holding down prices in order to avoid inflation, spending more for pollution control than is required by law, or hiring the hard-core unemployed to combat other social problems. The common good depends upon the smooth operation of a highly complex mechanism, namely, the competitive free market, and charity can only interfere with its efficient functioning. Putting it another way, we may say that Friedman believes corporations cannot "do good" directly, but will accomplish more good than they may realize if they accept the strict discipline of the market and allow it to produce indirect benefits. Concentrate on causes, he argues, and effects will take care of themselves.

Productivism is often portrayed as a relic from the past whose value is merely historical, in the sense that the theory shows us where we are and how far we have come. Galbraith, for example, has referred to Hayek's approach as "the traditional irrelevancy," and considered it to be such even 50 years ago.[17] Many treatments in contemporary management literature do the same. It is important, therefore, to note the resurgence of productivist ideas in recent years and their impact on U.S. economic policies.

Perhaps the best example of contemporary productivist thought is "supply side" economics.[18] In contrast to Keynesian economics which dominated the U.S. economy in the 1960s and 1970s (and which has subsequently been tagged "demand side" economics), supply siders argue that the key to social improvement is through the private sector. Instead of attempting to stimulate the economy by means of continued government expansion and spending, capital formation and corporate investment can most effectively be encouraged through policies focused on the private sector, primarily tax reduction and economic incentives. In its purest form, the philosophy is that the private sector would be capable of creating and delivering— much more efficiently and effectively—its goods and services to consumers if government did not impede the process. Thus, by eliminating, where possible, government intervention through deregulation, and by reducing both the federal budget and the burden of taxation while offering incentives to augment savings and capital formation, the market could once again work as it was originally intended. Through such specific policies as the Kemp-Roth three-year tax cut proposal, "more realistic" depreciation rules, and lower personal tax rates on savings-generated income, the United States could return to its position of industrial dominance in the world.

Proponents of the supply side approach argue that inflation results when an increasing money supply outstrips savings in a deficit economy. Thus, instead of continued government spending on social programs (which is inflationary), tax cuts would provide a stimulus to savings, which in turn would absorb the added financing caused by an unbalanced budget. According to the Laffer Curve, cuts in taxes will stimulate the productive powers of the marketplace and will result in increased productivity, a higher gross national product (GNP), and an improvement in general prosperity. Over time, the higher levels of productivity would reduce inflation, while the added revenues derived from the full employment this process would encourage would eventually eliminate budget deficits.

Other arguments underlying the supply side approach are more ideological in nature. Irving Kristol, for instance, suggests that this orientation encourages individuals to become more involved in the business sector. As people participate fully in the decision-making process of a market economy, Kristol argues, they become "more knowledgeable about it, more expert at it, and more loyal to the institution itself. In short, the spirit of democratic capitalism is, in the longer run, far more important than any year's macroeconomic statistics." He further argues that if the government continues to intervene and to treat the American people as "economic incompetents," they may indeed end up as "conscripted participants in a 'managed' version of capitalism."[19]

In summary, supply side economics relies on the growth of business-oriented incentives to encourage and stimulate the economy. As emphasized by the earlier analyses of Hayek and Friedman, the corporate sector is thought to be responsive when it is allowed to freely perform its basic economic function since the needs of the larger society are most effectively fulfilled in this manner. Thus, as should readily be apparent, the productivist view is not an historical relic of our economic system. The Reagan landslides of 1980 and 1984, and the economic "Reagan Revolution" beginning with the 1981 tax cut, were explicitly related to supply-side productivism.


Philanthropy

A second stockholder-oriented interpretation of corporate responsibility shares most of the assumptions of productivism, but departs from it in the nature and extent of corporate duties. Philanthropy takes into account the obligations that corporations have to society that go beyond considerations of profit and loss. Market forces are therefore not the only factors to be weighed, and businesses must appeal to nonmarket principles that require corporations to engage in some behaviors for their own sake, rather than because the activities adhere to the laws of supply and demand or otherwise facilitate the operation of the economy. The philanthropic interpretation of corporate social responsibility thus constitutes a critique of libertarian capitalism—though a mild one—and offers a vision of corporate life in which private prosperity is combined with an explicit, though limited, emphasis on moral development.

The principles underlying philanthropy have recently been articulated by Harold Lindsell, a well known Christian writer. Lindsell supports private property as divinely ordained, defends competitive free enterprise and denounces socialism, but still rejects what is referred to as productivism. As he sees it, "The Milton Friedman type of free enterprise has all freedom and no adequate controls."[20] More specifically, since productivism lacks a spirit of service and a vision of the common good, he advocates a type of free enterprise guided by two major principles from the Judeo-Christian moral heritage: stewardship and neighbor love.

The rule of stewardship compels us to recognize that all social wealth is in a sense a gift, ultimately from God, which is provided for the common good and not for any irresponsible private use. The earth and its resources must therefore be treasured and carefully tended. Exclusive emphasis on markets and profits distracts from this sense of duty and purpose, so that "today, what measure of free enterprise exists in the West is largely dominated by the secular humanism of this age."[21] Riches are sought for their own sake, and there is great waste and destruction of resources. Lindsell therefore counsels reform, and a return to the ethically responsible ways of stewardship.

Stewardship comes to fulfillment in its social context through the highest norm of neighbor love. This commandment has ancient authority, as exemplified in the many economic controls institutionalized in Israel in the Jubilee Year (every fiftieth year):

> Basically the controls called for altruism as an indispensable component of free enterprise. [Italics added.] The year of Jubilee in which leased land was returned to the owners was altruistic. The release of slaves every seventh year followed the same pattern. In addition the land was to lie fallow every seventh year and whatever grew by itself that year was for the use of the poor and for animals.[22]

Such measures, obviously, would not flow from a completely self-interested, competitive, free-market model of responsibility. Applied to contemporary corporate life, the norm of neighbor love would refer primarily to an active concern for the welfare of all members of a firm, and for that of its customers as well. Therefore, Lindsell argues that "free enterprise boundaried by love of neighbor will concern itself with providing good working conditions, decent hours, and provisions for sickness, old age, and other unexpected accidents."[23] It will not limit itself to the minimum obligations imposed by the letter of the law, but will extend itself beyond the rules in voluntary charity which will give free enterprise a human face.

An interesting example of the philanthropic position is provided by Levi Strauss and Company. Since the company's inception, its founder believed strongly in the principles espoused by Lindsell. As Levi Strauss himself argued during the mid-1880s:

I do not think large fortunes cause happiness to
their owners, for immediately those who possess
them become slaves to their wealth. They must
devote their lives to caring for their possessions.
I don't think money brings friends to its owner.
In fact, often the result is quite the contrary.[24]

Although Strauss felt that his business was his entire life, he
also had a deep interest in the Talmudic admonition of Gemiluth
Chasadim, doing kindly acts. He was a major contributor to
the Pacific Hebrew Orphan Asylum and Home, and the Eureka
Benevolent Society. In 1897, long before any such contributions
were tax deductible, Strauss offered to personally match the
California state legislature's creation of 28 perpetual scholar-
ships, four from each of the state's congressional districts.

As a result of Strauss's personal convictions about "helping
your fellow man," community service was expected of those who
worked for him. Before many other organizations, Levi Strauss
freely integrated its work force, delivered a high quality
product with an honored guarantee ("a new pair free if they
rip"), built a playground for neighborhood children next to
its factory, contributed to the development of the Panama-
Pacific International Exhibition fairgrounds, and sponsored
"Kid's Day," opening the amusement park of the exhibition for
free on the first day of school vacation.

The company's philanthropic position was oriented toward
its employees as well. The organization emphasized its factory
as a clean, good place to work, and made it a company practice
to loan money to its employees at a "very low interest rate . . .
something to keep the borrower's self-respect." During the
late 1940s, the company undertook a plan for widespread stock
ownership among its employees, and later expanded its stock-
option and profit sharing systems.[25] During the mid-1960s,
the organization's position was echoed by its statement, "our
first responsibility is to our employees." With no more reason
than that the firm's board of directors felt that it was "owed,"
retirees of Strauss were granted an 8 percent cost-of-living
adjustment (which is now routinely awarded every two to three
years), and past retirees were raised to the levels of present
retirees.[26]

Analysis by historian Daniel Wren indicates that such
early philanthropy was not unique to Levi Strauss. Wren,
for instance, argues that business philanthropy played a
major role in the development of higher education by filling the
gap between the church-sponsored colleges of our colonial period

and the state college and university system of later years.[27]
Moreover, while business leaders appeared to feel strongly
that it was their <u>duty</u> to support higher education, the pattern
of their philanthropy was quite broad, encompassing such areas
as the founding and support of technical education; the founding,
endowing, and even "rescue" of private education in the
absence of state and church support; the creation of higher
educational opportunities for women and racial minorities; and
the initial attempts to develop a collegiate education for business.

This activity occurred despite the fact that corporate
philanthropy did not receive favorable tax treatment under
nineteenth century law. The main rationale for such a legal
situation is reflected in the productivist orientation discussed
earlier. As Wren argues, an "emerging legal principle regarding
the conduct of corporate affairs held that those who managed
the corporation were bound in a fiduciary relationship of 'sacred
trust' to the stockholder, the owners of the corporation." This
view of management as trustee of the stockholder's property
contributed toward a harsh legal view of philanthropic activity.
In fact, it was not until 1935 that corporations could take
deductions for philanthropic contributions for tax purposes.
Yet, business philanthropy remained quite high during this
earlier period based on such motives as stewardship, the
desire for practical education, memorials, and the creation of
opportunities for disadvantaged groups such as women and
racial minorities.[28] As Wren concludes, despite the various
judgments made about nineteenth century business leaders, it
is clear that they were "generous champions" of our higher
education system.

While Wren's analysis underscores the orientations toward
business philanthropy around the turn of the century, a recent
study by Mutual Benefit Life lends some insight into the views
of executives in large and small businesses today.[29] Mutual's
survey of 300 chief executive officers in $100 million-plus
corporations and 300 executives in smaller businesses indicated
that most executives avidly support the <u>concept</u> of business
philanthropy. The ideal of what actually constitutes philanthropy,
however, varies considerably among these executives. Thirty-
one percent of the sample, for instance, argued that philanthropic concerns are best met by being "good businesspeople
and employers," not by spending time as volunteers on public
boards or donating money. Those executives who felt that
their firms should take more of a proactive philanthropic role
did so mainly through cash contributions rather than donating
nonfinancial support or employee time. Yet, while 69 percent
of these corporate leaders felt that cash donations were both

appropriate and necessary to support public sector efforts,
61 percent added that the recent economic downturn prevented
them from contributing as much as they would have liked.

This survey indicates that while the idea of corporate
philanthropy is supported by most business executives, it is
heavily dependent on favorable economic conditions and profits.
James F. Oates, former chairman of the board and chief executive
officer of the Equitable Life Assurance Society of the United
States, however, criticizes such an "oversimplified" view of
profits and philanthropy. As he suggests, profit optimization
and philanthropy are quite harmonious if profit is viewed in
its proper context, in terms of time (long-term profitability
rather than short-term gain); size (the larger the business
the more it is asked to respond to the problems of society and
to demonstrate its social concern); and the further contributions
that business should make (since corporate success is directly
related to the health of the larger society). Consequently,
business is "compelled to contribute to the welfare of the community by economic as well as moral considerations."[30]

Along these lines, the present concept of corporate philanthropy has been criticized as being too narrow in nature. A
number of corporate executives, for example, have argued
that although formal philanthropy is the most universal social
activity of most corporations, giving money alone is not enough.[31]
The time, effort, and expertise of business leaders are needed
just as much. As Joseph Wilson, chairman and chief executive
officer of Xerox corporation, points out, there are many professional skills in every large company that should be focused on
specific societal problems:

> Too often corporations overlook the fact that manage-
> ment, as a human commodity, is invaluable to those
> who need it and do not have it. Therefore, in
> conjunction with a minority group in Rochester,
> New York, [Xerox] established an inner-city
> factory for production of metal stampings and
> transformers. The plant, which will be owned,
> operated, and staffed by blacks, is guaranteed
> $500,000 in sales by Xerox over the first two years.
> In addition, the corporation provides training and
> technical and management assistance across the
> board.[32]

In closing, it is necessary to emphasize two points concerning the philanthropic orientation since they bear some resemblance
to others which will be discussed in connection with our final two

types of responsiveness. First, while Lindsell encourages a
sense of stewardship and neighbor love in business, he regards
government intervention in the economy as generally harmful,
and absolutely ruinous in cases of "democratic socialism." This
latter approach is condemned as a highly motivated but self-
defeating illusion, which is ultimately tyrannical. There are
important deficiencies in the economy and in current business
practice, but "reformation, not destruction, is the solution to
the problem. Free enterprise is inherently good, not evil, but
when its principles are not fulfilled, evil results come about."[33]

Second, while the initial motives for philanthropy were
largely based on the concept of stewardship, the recent blending
of philanthropy and marketing reflects the orientation of our
next responsiveness type. While the concept of enlightened
self-interest (that is, indirectly improving your own position
by improving the surrounding community or society) is suggested
to have been a part of business philanthropy since the nineteenth century, organizations are currently applying this principle with greatly heightened sophistication. A good example
is American Express Company's campaign to contribute to the
restoration of the Statue of Liberty.[34] During the fourth
quarter in 1983, American Express promised to donate a penny
for each use of its charge card and a dollar for most new cards
issued in the United States. The result was a check for $1.7
million to the Statue of Liberty-Ellis Island Foundation. During
that period, card usage increased 28 percent over the same
period from the year before, new card holders increased 45
percent, and the company had its best fourth quarter ever.
As Jerry Walsh, a senior marketing vice president in the company's Travel Related Services division argued, "The wave of
the future isn't checkbook philanthropy. It's a marriage of
corporate marketing and social responsibility . . . we're saying
to our stockholders: we're giving away money, but we're doing
it in a way that builds business."

Similar examples can be drawn from the highly competitive
computer industry. Both IBM and Digital Equipment Corporation, for example, have recently announced plans to donate
millions of dollars worth of their products to promote the use
of computers in public schools and higher education.[35] While
these programs obviously benefit the schools, colleges, and
universities that are the recipients of the computers and soft-
ware packages, such philanthropy also allows the companies
to reach young computer users and develop brand loyalty among
the next generation of computer purchasers. Such philanthropic-
progressivist strategies are not exclusively a product of the

1980s. When Sears-Roebuck's business was mainly in the rural areas of the country, for instance, the company assisted local farmers. While the farmers benefitted, the rationale was to increase farmer income so that they could buy more from the company—especially since company analysts discovered that there was a direct relationship between farm income and Sears's profits.[36] The main point is that this use of philanthropy reflects a different view of the relationship between business organizations and various groups in their environment.

## Progressivism

A third interpretation of corporate responsibility, referred to as progressivism, builds upon the premise that enlightened self-interest requires business to accept a limited role as an agent of social change, as part of a process of permanent reform. Responsibility means the gradual incorporation of selected new social values and priorities into corporate operations, and their expression in activities necessary to sustain public confidence, even when these are based on nonmarket principles. Specific progressivist policies include aggressive voluntary programs of affirmative action for women and ethnic minorities, as well as investments in urban revitalization or minority-owned firms, energy conservation, environmental protection, and efforts to hire the hard-core unemployed. Sometimes these policies are pursued under the heading of "budgeted, nonfinancial objectives," and the perspective in general is receptive to some form of social auditing, despite the well known difficulties in developing a suitable method to assess social performance.[37]

Progressivism is perhaps the best known and most popular perspective on corporate social responsibility among today's larger corporations and university schools of management. As expressed in a wide series of contemporary writings on "business and society,"* the progressivist orientation develops a number of major propositions which are summarized in Table 3.1.

An impressive effort has recently been made to articulate a systematic ethical basis for the progressivist position. Robert Benne, professor of Church and Society at the Lutheran School of Theology in Chicago, argues that the institutional framework

---

*For a fuller discussion of this literature see Chapters 1 and 2.

TABLE 3.1

Major Elements in Contemporary Progressivism

| Belief | Illustrative Citation |
| --- | --- |
| Business is involved in a contractual relationship with society. | The basic concept of the social contract is that business functions by public consent, and its basic purpose is to serve constructively the needs of society.[a] |
| The terms of this contract are subject to change. | The business institution operates, basically, to serve society's interests as society sees them. . . . The social contract changes continuously.[b] |
| We live in a period of rapid change. | About a decade ago a broad movement, probably of a revolutionary nature, began in the industrialized countries of the world.[c] |
| Business must accept and adapt to these changes. | To effectively survive today and in the future, management must both become aware of the nature and scope of social issues impinging on the organization, and develop mechanisms and modes of response that will best handle these demands.[d] |
| Ultimately, acceptance of a new concept of corporate social responsibility is enlightened self-interest. | Business should be concerned about the quality of life; when that declines, so too do profits.[e] |
| Self-regulation by business is preferable to regulation by the government. | If business fails to evince a higher degree of social responsibility today, it will have much less freedom tomorrow.[f] |

86

Corporate social responsibility
must not be pushed to extremes.

The advocates of the extreme social responsibility
position want a kind of utopian perfection without
understanding the difficulties or considering the
price. . . . Business managers cannot afford to
adopt the more extreme social responsibility position.[g]

---

[a]A. Elkins and D. W. Callaghan, A Managerial Odyssey: Problems in Business and Its Environment (Reading: Addison Wesley, 1981), p. 13.

[b]G. Steiner, Business and Society (New York: Random House, 1975), p. 8.

[c]R. Ackerman and R. Bauer, Corporate Social Responsiveness: The Modern Dilemma (Reston, Va.: Reston Publishing, 1976), p. 3.

[d]Archie B. Carroll, Business and Society: Managing Corporate Social Performance (Boston: Little, Brown, 1981), p. 23.

[e]G. Starling, The Changing Environment of Business (Boston: Kent, 1980), p. 240.

[f]Starling, Changing Environment, p. 240.

[g]Starling, Changing Environment, p. 244.

87

within which corporate activity occurs in this country ("democratic capitalism") conforms to the principles of Judeo-Christian
ethics, and indeed constitutes the best possible context for the
pursuit of corporate responsibility. Democratic capitalism
encourages and protects diversity and freedom, while recognizing the need for growth and increased economic efficiency.
All of these characteristics serve the common good, and as
such are proper objects of corporate social policy.

At the foundation of Benne's analysis is a concern with
the "will-to-power," defined as the desire to place selfish
interests above the good of others, and to realize those interests
at the expense of others. Following Reinhold Neibuhr, the well
known Christian thinker, Benne believes that the "will-to-power"
is much more typical of large groups than of either small groups
or individuals. Therefore, if society is to avoid centralized,
totalitarian rule, it is important to have many private, competing
centers of ownership and initiative. The present corporate
structure in the United States serves this end admirably, and
is to be supported.[38]

This alone does not imply, however, that the current
structure is entirely just, or that it has achieved its full potential. Drawing on the work of American philosopher John Rawls,
Benne goes on to argue that social structures are just only
when they observe the "difference principle," according to
which social arrangements must serve the interests of the
weakest members of society. For this to occur, governments
must assume a strong activist role, both in managing the
economy and in providing for a range of welfare needs. The
state, Benne argues, should compensate for great imbalances
of power by breaking up monopolies and by legitimating the
power of disadvantaged groups—as was done, for example,
when labor unions were legalized in the 1930s. The state should
further cushion the effects of market forces on the most vulnerable elements of the society, through unemployment insurance,
subsidies and loans to marginal farmers, and retraining of
those in declining industries. Above all, the state should
continually increase the value of liberty, by extending civil
rights and ensuring fair equality of opportunity. Corporate
social responsibility requires that business support these
efforts.[39]

Responsiveness in the contemporary world also demands
that business seek growth and improved efficiency. Those
who criticize the American political economy, in Benne's view,
fail to realize the importance of these issues. In less developed

nations, rapid population increases have been exerting tremen-
dous pressure on resources; in more developed nations, a rising
standard of living carries with it accelerating expectations for
more goods and services. Viewing the situation in these terms,
Benne sounds a productivist note, and contends that the problem of production must be solved before the problem of distribution. This conclusion is completely in accord with the perceptions
of policy makers in the larger American corporations, and affirms
their emphasis on profit and continual growth as socially responsible.

In an application of this perspective, Francis Steckmest,
author of the Business Roundtable-sponsored study Corporate
Performance: The Key to Public Trust, proposes the concept
of "voluntary corporate accountability." He argues that
managers must engage in "sensitive interaction" with the
organization's constituent interest groups and participate in
the public policy process in a way that contributes to managerial
attitudes and performance that are consistent with the social,
political, and economic environment; and manifests a sense of
voluntary accountability to the larger society.[40] Among the
specific actions suggested are:

1. Defining the social and political role of a company and
   setting policies and procedures for the management of
   legal and ethical behavior, openness and public disclosure,
   government and political relations, and social performance.
2. Establishing internal financial, legal and administrative
   controls and company codes of business conduct to help
   assure legal and ethical behavior, and publicly acceptable
   conduct.
3. Creating more open and candid relations with shareholders,
   customers, the media, host communities, employees, and
   other relevant publics.
4. Establishing new forms of communication and cooperation
   with employees, from rank-and-file employee participation
   in workplace decisions to involvement of managerial
   employees in government, media, and other constituency
   relations.
5. Meeting with representative community or regional groups
   concerning matters that might be of concern to them.
6. Meeting with consumer, environmental, civil rights, health
   and other interest groups, and with government officials
   to learn of their concerns firsthand and to explain company policy, plans, or actions that they could misunder-
   stand or object to.

7. Seeking or joining ad hoc coalitions with labor unions and selected environmental, consumer, and other non-business interest groups to develop areas of agreement on important public policy questions.

Steckmest's rationale is decidedly based on the concept of enlightened self-interest. As he concludes, "If corporate executives are to avoid ever more burdensome government constraints on their freedom, they will need to innovate and perfect new forms of voluntary accountability to the constituents of their companies while maintaining the large corporation as a private enterprise institution that can continue to generate notable economic, technological, and social achievements."[41] Similarly, Harold Williams, past chairman of the Securities and Exchange Commission, underscores the thesis that such corporate accountability extends beyond short-term growth and profitability. If such accountability is not accepted by our business system, the political process will ultimately substitute another body or structure.[42]

In sum, progressivism, while supporting a significantly expanded role for business in society, and accepting many new welfare functions to a range of corporate stakeholders, still contains a strong element of productivism, which is seen as the basis for such expansion. But where productivism urges a return to traditional "truth," progressivism is committed to permanent reform. These concerns, however, are still clearly linked to the long-term survival of our system of corporate capitalism.

## Ethical Idealism

The final interpretation of corporate social responsiveness, ethical idealism, rests upon the premise that responsiveness requires a complete reassessment of the place of business in society. Putting this in slightly different terms, we may say that the ethical idealist perspective constitutes a radical critique of business theory and practice. Such criticism is produced by means of a comparison of the assumptions of current practice and some set of ethical ideals, adopted as the criterion of what is desirable and necessary. In terms of content, the ideal norms may vary greatly, from the teachings of Christianity or Buddhism to the dogmas of Marxism. Whatever their substance, these standards somehow condemn current arrangements as inadequate on the basis of moral qualities: Contemporary structures are perceived as unacceptable barriers to moral functioning and development, or to realization of the spiritual aspect of business life. Fundamental changes are therefore required in order to initiate a process of moral transformation, which will lift individuals, groups, and society as a whole to a higher ethical level, one that better realizes human potential for seeking and doing good. Ethical idealist approaches are thus "prophetic" in the double sense of proclaiming a message (especially on behalf of someone else, like God or oppressed persons), and pointing toward an alternate future, a "new creation." Overall, this orientation proposes that economic activity requires not only a change of thinking but a "change of heart," a thorough conversion of business attitudes and behavior.

Present American business practices are thought to frustrate moral and spiritual development because the dominant culture conditions individuals and groups to be selfish, materialistic, overly competitive, short-sighted, and extremely wasteful. The results are inevitably destructive: Employees lack security in their jobs; morale is often poor; productivity suffers; the beauty of the natural world is lost; dangerous chemical substances are unleashed; the weaker members of society are neglected; and economies are geared towards warfare rather than peace. Moderate reforms, as proposed by the philanthropists and progressivists, are not sufficient to treat the malaise or to deal with the crisis because our problems are logical outcomes of the fundamental character of the system, in fact, the outcomes of its greatest "successes." The nature of the system must therefore be subjected to a totalizing critique, no matter how impractical or even utopian such an exercise may seem. The problem is moral, not technical, and it is systematic. Corporate activity will not be fully responsible until altruism has transformed business practice, and a new spirit begins to restore a lost sense of community, joy, adequacy, free self-realization, and service.

## Politically-Oriented Varieties

The interpretations below proceed from the premise that corporations are and should be fully "public" organizations, rather than private bodies. On the level of principle, this is considered by proponents to be entirely proper, just, and supportive of the common good. On the factual level, it is seen as historical reality, that is, as something that is evolving or has already come to be.

Galbraith has argued the latter point for some time. In
an article on "the emerging public corporation," for example,
he attacks the belief that large corporations are private entities
governed by market forces. In sharp contrast with the teachings of classical economics, the giant contemporary firm, according to Galbraith, "fixes its prices, controls its costs, integrates
backwards so as to control the supply of its raw materials, and
influences, persuades, and, on occasion, bamboozles its customers."[43] This pattern is most visible in the operation of
firms which conduct their business with the federal government,
such as the major defense contractors. In these cases the
physical plant of the corporation is owned in whole or in part
by the government; the corporation receives working capital
from the government in the form of progress payments; the
goods and services produced by the corporation are consumed
solely by the government; and any cost overruns are absorbed
by the government, and are thus "socialized." Only the earnings of the firm, and the salaries of its personnel remain in
the private sector. Therefore, to Galbraith, it becomes increasingly difficult and thoroughly hypocritical to maintain the
position that corporations of this type are "private." Perhaps
this could be justified if the companies were special cases, and
represented only a small fraction of the economy. The reverse,
however, seems to be true: public corporations are a logical
evolution of twentieth-century economic and political trends,
and they now typify and indeed dominate the economies of
developed industrial nations.[44]

At the threshold of the political ethical-idealist orientation,
we might locate the Nader Group, whose position is articulated
in a broad series of critiques of American business, from attacks
on unsafe products and anti-competitive practices, to indictments of chemical pollution and political manipulation. Most
relevant for our purpose is the recent proposal calling for
"constitutionalizing the corporation." Such a policy would
replace the state chartering of corporations with federal chartering, and define a new "bill of rights" for employees which would
serve as the basis for all internal policies of firms. No employee,
for example, could be dismissed without formal due process,
and the burden of proof would be upon corporations to demonstrate definite grounds for dismissal. Employees would also
be given legal guarantees of freedom of speech (such as "whistle
blowing" against illegal or unethical corporate behavior), con-
fidentiality of personal data, and other rights. This approach
is located at the threshold of ethical idealism because, despite
a strong moral tone, it has a definite legalistic orientation which
would compel corporations to provide certain rights whether

they believed in them or not. Corporate policies based on ethical idealism would generally operate in a more voluntary manner. The Nader approach, however, does seem to go beyond progressivism, because it envisions very significant shifts in power relations between management and labor, whereas progressivism assumes a more traditional management-labor hierarchy.[45]

A second variant of political ethical idealism is found in the movement for economic democracy. Bruyn, for example, argues that corporations are essentially social units, composed of persons of equal human value, with the duty of pursuing social justice. It is therefore important that all members of firms have an opportunity to participate in the formulation of policy, especially in those decisions which have the greatest impact on their work lives. Such participation, however, cannot be accomplished through traditional practices of top-down management; it can only occur after corporations have undergone a process of democratization, which would extend to its employees ownership of a majority of corporate stock. On such a basis, genuine self-determination of corporate policy could be built, without the federal intervention or takeover which is most feared by critics. If the movement were to spread across the nation, the result would be a new "economic republic" which would overcome the alienation of the current socioeconomic order. The new morality of relative equality, full participation, and self-determination would thus create the conditions for personal and social development.[46]

The political variant of ethical idealism also includes a number of writers who have been strongly influenced by Marxist ideas. They accept corporate social responsibility as a principle, but deny its feasibility under current socioeconomic conditions. The premise is that as long as corporations are run from the top down, and the economy is controlled by a small number of giant firms, social responsibility cannot be put into practice. Instead, corporations, driven by the ever intensifying pressure of competitive markets, will continue to: seek maximization of short-term profits; discard people in favor of machines; reduce hard-won social benefits; neglect the natural environment; and even invest in foreign competition while American industry declines. Such policies flow from the very nature of capitalism, its impersonal, rationalized acquisitiveness and class structure. Change will come only when average persons succeed in gaining control of the economy, and socialize its resources for the welfare of all.

An important recent analysis within this perspective is Barry Bluestone and Bennett Harrison's The Deindustrialization of America. Angered by charges that organized labor is to blame for the country's economic ills, the authors develop the thesis that capital is the "real villain." More specifically, they contend that the excessively rapid movement of investment capital, in pursuit of short-term profits, has led to the abandonment of many communities by industry, as well as a host of personal and social sufferings. Some 38 million jobs, they estimate, have been lost as a direct or indirect result of such hypermobility of capital. The crisis can only be resolved by addressing a central ethical issue: "How can we go about the business of constructing a productive economy which produces livelihoods without destroying lives?"[47]

The authors' response is summed up in the phrase "re-industrialization with a human face." The guiding principle here is democratic control of economic development at the local level. In other words, Bluestone and Harrison believe that justice and the common good can only be served by business when corporate policy is closely linked to the needs and desires of communities. In fully developed form, this approach requires measures for advance warning of contemplated plant closings, expanded worker ownership of corporations, government support for "sunrise" industries, as well as programs to minimize the dislocations experienced in "sunset" industries.

The moral outrage of the authors is perhaps best summed up in their discussions of the closing of the Youngstown Sheet and Tube Company in Ohio in 1979. Some 4,100 jobs were directly eliminated, another 12,000 to 13,000 lost as an indirect consequence, and millions of dollars in retail sales deducted from the local economy. In the wake of this massive social damage, the authors point an accusing finger at a corporate conglomerate and at several major banks, arguing that their policies were based on selfish considerations and morally objectionable indifference to the fate of those whose livelihoods disappeared:

> The contractions in the domestic steel industry during the 1970s—including the highly publicized shutdown of the Youngstown Sheet and Tube Company in Ohio—were caused in part by the inability of some of the companies to finance modernization plans. In that case, three of the principal bankers of the conglomerate parent, the Lykes Corporation, began withdrawing their support in the mid-1970s. At the very time they were doing so, these same banks were significantly increasing their investments in the Japanese steel industry. [Italics added.] Between 1975

and 1977 alone, Citibank increased its loans to
Japanese steel from about $59 million to over $230
million. Chase Manhattan's investments in Japanese
steel rose from $59 million to over $204 million.
And the loans from the Chemical Bank of New York
increased more than five times, from $15 million in
1975 to over $82 million just two years later.[48]

To Bluestone and Harrison, such data clearly indicate that
capital and professional business management have abandoned
their social contract with American workers. Therefore,
corporate social responsibility can only be achieved after a
process of political struggle based on a sense of fundamental
human social rights, such as the right to a livelihood, to a
reasonable degree of security in employment, and thus, to
control of economic development.

Martin Carney and Derek Shearer make a similar case for
radical, ethically based transformation of the socioeconomic
order.[49] Under present arrangements, they believe, a fundamental conflict or "contradiction" exists in the United States
between political and economic institutions. The former are
based on the principle of representative democracy, further
supported by checks and balances between branches and
levels of government, while the latter operate on authoritarian,
hierarchical principles of top-down management. The result
is economic government of the few, by the few, and for the
few. Such a contradiction cannot exist indefinitely, but must
eventually give way, the authors hope, to a more just system:

The U.S. economy is faced with a set of economic
problems that appear to be unsolvable by corporate
capitalist development. If changes are to be made,
then the way the economy is governed and the way
things are produced will have to be changed as well.
The essence of such transformation is economic
democracy—the transfer of economic decision making
from the few to the many. The very same arguments
that for two centuries supported the ceding of political choice to the mass of people rather than its
retention by a single individual or a small group,
also provide the rationale for production and investment decision making by workers and consumers,
not by individual capital owners or the managers.[50]

How such change might begin at the corporate level can
be visualized by examining a series of programs currently

operating throughout Europe. One measure is the expansion
of corporate boards to include representatives of employees,
an approach which has been most widely discussed in connection
with its German "codetermination" variant.[51] Workers' councils
are a second structure promoting participatory democracy in
the economy. Over the past decade and a half, such bodies
have been especially active in Italy and France. Other changes
might be introduced by means of legislation that significantly
expands the rights of workers, as was done during the 1970s
in Sweden: the right of health and safety stewards to halt any
processes thought to be dangerous; the right of all employees
to advance notice of termination, and to a hearing on the matter
in a labor court; and the right of unions to negotiate for codetermination in all fundamental policy areas, from hiring and
firing to expansion, mergers, and reorganization.[52]

In fully developed form, the changes advocated by Carney
and Shearer would constitute a system of "democratic socialism."
Against the objection that such proposals are inherently utopian
and unworkable, the authors point to a variety of movements
in the United States over the past 15 years which seem to
indicate that many people are seeking greater control over
their lives, as well as redirection of corporations in the public
interest. Dozens of populist lobbying groups, for example,
sprang up during the period, including such organizations as
Public Interest Research Groups (PIRGs), Common Cause
(national citizens' lobby), Fair Share (Massachusetts), ACORN
(several states), community development corporations, and many
others. At the same time, numerous small businesses began to
organize on the basis of cooperation and worker ownership.
In Texas and California this has led to statewide federations
of cooperatives, which (individually and collectively) now
enjoy the support of the National Consumer Cooperative Bank,
formed in 1978. In view of such developments, Carney and
Shearer argue that there is considerable potential for significant
change in the near future. This does not, however, mean that
the United States is likely to become socialist in the ordinary
sense, for "The roots of a movement for economic democracy
in the United States, if such a movement develops, will not be
in the European socialist tradition, but in the American radical
tradition of populism, whose primary value was always democracy."[53]


Religiously Oriented Varieties

One of the best known proponents of religious ethical
idealism is E. F. Schumacher, who combined the ideals of self-

management with certain economic principles and the standards of Buddhist ethics.[54] Schumacher's basic protest is that the contemporary socioeconomic order, and corporate policies within it, are the result of false priorities. He argues that we have put secondary or tertiary things first, beginning with our pursuit of short-term profits at the expense of the irreplaceable natural environment, whose resources are being squandered at an alarming and unprecedented rate. We have forgotten that people can really be themselves only in small, comprehensible groups. We have lost sight of the ancient wisdom of the world religions, to place spiritual values first, and then to receive what we need for our material well-being. As a result, we are alienated both from our beautiful world, and from our gigantic corporations. According to Schumacher, however, there is a way out. We can begin to develop a "lifestyle designed for permanence," based on restraint and conservation, which will replace maximization of production with optimization of consumption. We can institutionalize the principle of subsidiarity, according to which economic units will be given as much autonomy as possible. And we can forge new forms of economic partnership, up to and including cooperatives and employee-owned firms, such as the Scott-Bader Commonwealth in Britain.

Schumacher's call for a courageous break with past practice is most clearly reflected in his criticism of economics, his own profession. In its present form, he argues, the discipline may be of little genuine worth:

> . . . Is it a matter of goods, or of people? Of course it is a matter of people. . . . If economic thinking cannot grasp this it is useless. If it cannot get beyond its vast abstractions, the national income, the rate of growth, capital/output ratio, input-output analysis, labor mobility, capital accumulation; if it cannot get beyond all of this and make contact with the human realities of poverty, frustration, alienation, despair, breakdown, crime, escapism, stress, congestion, ugliness, and spiritual death, then let us scrap economics and start afresh.[55]

Starting afresh, of course, requires personal involvement, risk, cost, and even suffering:

> How could we even begin to disarm greed and envy? Perhaps by being much less greedy and envious ourselves; perhaps by resisting the temptation of

letting our luxuries become needs; and perhaps by even scrutinizing our needs to see if they cannot be simplified and reduced. If we do not have the strength to do any of this, could we perhaps stop applauding the type of economic "progress" which palpably lacks basis of permanence and give what modest support we can do to those who, unafraid of being denounced as cranks, work for non-violence; as conservationists, ecologists, protectors of wildlife, promoters of organic agriculture, distributists, cottage producers, and so forth? An ounce of practice is generally worth more than a ton of theory.[56]

Catholic Social Justice Teachings. In recent years, one of the world's largest religious bodies, the Catholic Church, has taken an active role in the debate over corporate social responsibility. Particular controversies, like the effect of multinational corporations on the peoples of developing nations, have had much to do with this involvement, but the church's statements during the period spring from a tradition which is a century old.*

Most prominent among the themes of these writings have been the rights and duties of capital and labor; the increasing gap between rich and poor nations; and the spiritual character of work. In the first papal letter in the series, Of New Things, the main focus was on the rights of labor. Employees, it was asserted, must be treated with dignity and justice at all times, not exploited as mere instruments of profit, and their right to organize for collective bargaining must be recognized. In The Fortieth Year devoted itself to the issue of international economic change, expressed concern over the loss of control experienced by developing nations, and declared that the church must speak on behalf of the poor. In the 1960s, The Progress of the Peoples echoed these themes and sought to distinguish between just and unjust patterns of development.

---

*In 1891, for example, the very influential papal letter of Pope Leo XIII, Of New Things appeared (Rerum Novarum). Similar authoritative statements followed at irregular intervals: In The Fortieth Year (Quadragesimo Anno, 1931), Mother and Teacher (Mater et Magistra, 1952), Peace on Earth (Pacem in Terris, by Pope John XXIII in 1963), The Progress of the Peoples (Populorum Progressio, by Pope Paul VI in 1967), and On Human Labor (Laborem Exercens, by Pope John Paul II in 1981).

The most recent papal letter seeks to relate earlier teachings to the issue of the proper nature of work. Its basic thesis is that human beings were intended by God to participate in the activity of creation through their own work. Therefore, work ought to be something which is inherently personal and beneficial. Work is for human beings, not human beings for work. If this principle is to be realized in practice, however, people must exercise control over the contexts of their work, something which they cannot accomplish under either materialistic capitalism or bureaucratic socialism. New arrangements must therefore be sought that elevate workers to their proper place and allow work to express their creative freedom. A major proposal to be considered in this context is cooperative self-management, where "On the basis of his work each person is fully entitled to consider himself a part-owner of the great workbench at which he is working with everyone else."[57]

These papal teachings have recently been given further expression by certain Catholic economists, such as Kenneth Jameson and Charles Wilber of the University of Notre Dame. In a series of articles over the past several years, these writers have attempted to apply the general themes of the encyclicals to the specific economic issues of the day. At the heart of their interpretation is the superiority of nonmarket over market principles. As they argue, public policy must "subordinate markets to the attainment of individuals' and society's moral values and goals, while using them in the process."[58] Three moral values are identified as primary: stewardship, subsidiarity, and jubilee. As indicated under the discussion of philanthropy, stewardship states that private use of property must not detract from the common good. Subsidiarity safeguards the dignity and autonomy of average persons and small groups by requiring that policies be implemented at the lowest possible levels. Finally, jubilee recalls the Old Testament practice of celebration and redistribution of economic resources every 50 years. At the present time, an ethic of jubilee would entail "the adoption of policies that provide, with dignity, a full employment policy for all who can work. In addition, basic goods, especially housing, should be ensured to all."[59]

Other Variants. Catholic principles of economic and social justice have been taken in more radical directions by numerous contemporary authors. Most influential among such critics are partisans of "liberation theology." This perspective seeks to blend the dogmas of Marxism (discussed under Politically Oriented Varieties) and Christianity (outlined above). Since these orientations have already been touched upon, they will not be developed further here.

A different sort of Catholic radicalism is found in John Kavanaugh's repudiation of the contemporary socioeconomic order for the sake of Christian discipleship.[60] Kavanaugh argues that contemporary capitalism is by its very nature idolatrous, elevating material objects above persons made in the "true image of God." Advertising and marketing manipulate people, and urge them to seek their happiness in acquisition, competition, and possession, rather than in the sharing of love. Individualism and perpetual dissatisfaction are systematically promoted by corporations, which thus pit themselves against the values of joy and community. From Kavanaugh's perspective, therefore, those who would be true Christian disciples must become "a people apart" within the contemporary economic order, withholding their loyalty from traditional corporations, and practicing a "revolutionary holiness" based on a liberation from materialism, which seeks to personalize the world. The conflicts between persons (personal form) and things (commodity form) referred to by Kavanaugh are summarized in Table 3.2.

The relevance of these broad teachings for contemporary business practice is perhaps best demonstrated by the recent Pastoral Letter on Catholic Social Teaching and the U.S. Economy.[61] Released by the bishops of the United States in November of 1984, this document quickly gathered headlines and provoked a spirited debate. Indeed, one group of concerned Catholics went so far as to publish a rejoinder to the statement a week before it was actually issued. The authors of the pastoral letter (which is a first draft) planned for approximately one year of dialogue with interested parties, to be followed by a final statement of the American church's position.

Although the pastoral letter does not condemn the U.S. economic system, and indeed expresses high praise for it in terms of several of its essentials, the document sustains a tone of criticism and concern. According to the bishops, much more can and should be done to ensure that the economy safeguards and enhances the dignity of all persons. The attainment of this objective requires three conditions: that the economic system enable persons to find significant self-realization in their labor; that it provide adequate wages and benefits; and that it promote unity within the family, the nation, and the world community.[62]

Such principles might seem relatively obvious and free from controversy. What injects passion into the issue is the bishops' perception that the American system works against

the weakest and most vulnerable members of society. The
church, therefore, to be faithful to its distinctive mission,
must identify with those who are suffering and exercise a
"preferential option for the poor," who have no one to speak
for them.[63] From the point of view of Judeo-Christian ethics,
an economic system must first of all be just; this is far more
important than its productivity or efficiency, although it is
recognized that these latter aspects of the system are certainly
important. Moreover, the most fundamental measure or test of
justice is the effect of policies on the weakest and poorest.
Judged from this perspective, the U.S. economic system falls
short.

New policies are therefore urgently needed and must be
rooted in a conversion of the heart. A major effort should be
made to seek full employment, or at least to reduce unemployment to about 3 or 4 percent, with government programs for
the structurally unemployed, private sector programs, and
expanded job placement services. Tax reform should reduce
the burden of the poor, while welfare reform would provide
more adequate levels of support. Ultimately, the objective
should be the creation of a cooperative economy based on democratic principles, including worker participation in fundamental
policy decisions, employee ownership, and self-management.[64]
The pastoral letter, therefore, represents a challenge to initiate
a deep and broad process of change for the sake of greater
personalism and solidarity, under the guidance of a particular
ideal of justice.

Overall, our discussion of ethical idealism may give some
the impression that this orientation is a fringe phenomenon,
essentially utopian in character, and not to be taken very
seriously by practical investigators of corporate social responsibility and performance. It is relevant to note in closing,
therefore, that ethical idealist themes have recently been
sounded in mainstream business publications. A good example
is Collier's Harvard Business Review article which proposes
that it is time for a new species of corporation, termed the
"co-corp," whose objective would be to provide services rather
than to maximize profits and pursue growth.[65] Joseph Kennedy's
oil-shipping organization, which provides elderly and low-income
groups heating oil at below market prices is an example of such
a "co-corp." Along the way, Collier seeks to debunk the profit
motive, which has generally been accepted by members of our
productivist, philanthropic, and progressivist orientations.
Moreover, as will be discussed more fully in the following chapters, many of the stakeholders which business must contend

TABLE 3.2

Comparison of Kavanaugh's Commodity and Personal Forms

| The Commodity Form | The Personal Form | The Commodity Form | The Personal Form |
|---|---|---|---|
| Value grounded in thinghood | Value grounded in personhood | Thing-like affectivity | Personal affectivity |
| Marketability of the person | Intrinsic value of person | Sexuality as mechanics | Sexuality as sign of person |
| Production: worth as what you do | Worth as who you are | Body as machine | Body as temple— sacral presence |
| Consumption | Self-Gift | Fear/threat | Fear not |
| Thing knowledge | Personal knowledge | Noncommitment | Covenant-committed devotedness |
| Observation and description | Faith: self-consciousness and interiority | Retention of self | Self-donation |
| Measurement and control | Understanding and trust | Technique | Telos |
| Quality as quantity | Human quality as non-measurable | Externality | Interiority |
| Emphasis on derived knowledge | Immediate experience | Replaceability | Uniqueness |
| How questions | Why questions | Coolness | Tenderness |
| | | Hardness | Compassion |
| | | Accumulation | Detachment |
| | | Invulnerability | Vulnerability |
| | | Exchange | Prodigal love |
| | | Hedonism: immediate self-gratification | Generosity: suffering love |

| Thing willing | Personal willing |
|---|---|
| Determinism | Limited freedom |
| Escape | Self-investment |
| Noncommitment | Convenant |

| Thing behavior | Person behavior |
|---|---|
| Violence: | Peace: |
| Domination | Acceptance of weakness |
| Manipulation | Respect of freedom |
| Retaliation | Forgiveness |
| Punishment | Healing |
| Defense | Defenselessness |
| Devaluation of Life | Exaltation of least person |
| Demand | Invitation |
| Competition | Sharing |
| Retention | Giving |

| Thing reality | Person reality |
|---|---|
| Having | Being |
| What is | What we can be |
| Human skepticism | Faith and fidelity |
| Human paralysis and doubt | Hope and trust |
| Individual isolation | Love |
| Unfreedom as final condition | Freedom as final condition |
| Death | Life |

Source: John Kavanaugh, Following Christ in a Consumer Society. Maryknoll, N.Y.: Orbis Books, 1981, pp. 96-97. Reprinted with permission.

with today hold ethical idealist interpretations of corporate social responsibility.

From one point of view, at least, the appearance of such articles in traditional business forums should not come as a surprise. Observers and sociologists like Daniel Bell have long argued that we are moving into a "post-industrial" economic order based on services rather than manufactured goods.[66] If so, an ethical idealist approach to corporate social responsibility, based on a morality of service and self-sacrifice, would seem to be a natural component—however large or small its ultimate place.

### SUMMARY

This chapter has outlined four basic interpretations of corporate social responsibility. Our discussion of the background and views of these ideal types was meant to exemplify the underlying differences that exist in various analyses of business's social role. The philosophy and criteria used to depict socially responsible behavior are deeply rooted in the values of the observer and, depending on the individual's orientation, can vary quite considerably. It should be readily apparent, therefore, that the concept of social responsibility is highly subjective in nature.

Each of these orientations was presented as an analytic type. We did not wish to suggest a preference for any particular perspective; rather the discussion has attempted to portray the rationale underlying the different interpretations of social responsibility as objectively as possible.

The discussion of ethical idealism is, perhaps, a bit longer and more fully developed than the analysis of productivism, philanthropy, or progressivism, and the reason is two-fold. First, this particular orientation is the least well known of our four types; thus we felt it necessary to provide a clear delineation. Second, while there are differences of viewpoint in each of the types, they are more extreme in ethical idealism. It was necessary, therefore, to represent both the politically and religiously oriented variants.

These four types capture some of the tension of the contemporary debate over the reassessment of corporate social responsibility. The main implication for our present purposes is that, based on these various orientations, different groups— whether they be profit or nonprofit in nature—can hold quite different perceptions and expectations concerning business responsibility.

NOTES

1. For an overview of these criticisms see Liam Fahey and Richard E. Wokutch, "Business and Society Exchanges: A Framework for Analysis," California Management Review 25 (Summer 1983):128-142; Lee E. Preston, "Corporate Social Performance and Policy: A Synthetic Framework for Research and Analysis," in Research in Corporate Social Performance and Policy, Vol. 1, ed. Lee E. Preston (Greenwich, Conn.: JAI Press, 1978), pp. 1-26; and Robert J. DeFillippi, "Conceptual Frameworks and Strategies for Corporate Social Involvement Research," in Research in Corporate Social Performance and Policy, Vol. 4, ed. Lee E. Preston (Greenwich, Conn.: JAI Press, 1982), pp. 35-56.

2. See Archie B. Carroll, "A Three-Dimensional Model of Corporate Social Performance," Academy of Management Review 4 (October 1979):497-506; Lee E. Preston and James E. Post, Private Management and Public Policy (Englewood Cliffs: Prentice-Hall, 1975); S. Prakash Sethi, "Dimensions of Corporate Social Performance: An Analytic Framework," California Management Review 17 (1975):58-64; and T. Zenisek, "Corporate Social Responsibility: A Conceptualization Based on Organizational Literature," Academy of Management Review 4 (October 1979):359-368.

3. Pitirim A. Sorokin, Society, Culture, and Personality (New York: Harper & Row, 1947).

4. See also Peter Berger and Thomas Luckmann, The Social Construction of Reality (Garden City, N.Y.: Doubleday, 1966).

5. Pitirim A. Sorokin, Social and Cultural Dynamics, Vol. 1 (New York: American Book Co., 1937), chaps. 1 and 2.

6. E. B. Tylor, Primitive Culture: Researches Into the Development of Mythology, Philosophy, Religion, Language, Art and Customs, Vol. 1 (New York: Henry Holt, 1871); Terrance E. Deal and Alan A. Kennedy, Corporate Cultures: The Rights and Rituals of Corporate Life (Reading, Mass.: Addison-Wesley, 1982); and James L. Bowditch, Anthony F. Buono, and John W. Lewis, "When Cultures Collide: The Anatomy of a Merger," paper presented at The Academy of Management National Meeting, August 14-17, 1983, Dallas, Texas.

7. On ideal types, see Rolf E. Rogers, Max Weber's Ideal Type Theory (New York: Philosophical Library, 1969); and S. M. Miller, ed., Max Weber: Selections from His Work (New York: Crowell, 1963).

8. Max Weber, The Theory of Social and Economic Organization, trans. by Talcott Parsons and A. M. Henderson (New York: Oxford University Press, 1947), Part I.

9. Sorokin, Society, Culture, and Personality, chap. 5.

10. Weber, Theory of Social and Economic Organization, Part I.

11. Friedrich A. Hayek, "The Corporation in a Democratic Society," in Studies in Philosophy, Politics, and Economics, ed. Friedrich A. Hayek (Chicago: University of Chicago Press, 1967), pp. 300-312.

12. Hayek, "Corporation in a Democratic Society," p. 301.

13. Friedrich A. Hayek, The Road to Serfdom (Chicago: University of Chicago Press, 1944). For a scathing rebuttal, see Herman Finer, Road to Reaction (Chicago: Quadrangle Books, 1963).

14. Milton Friedman, "The Social Responsibility of Business Is to Increase Its Profits," New York Times Magazine, September 13, 1970, pp. 122-126.

15. Milton Friedman, Capitalism and Freedom (Chicago: University of Chicago Press, 1962).

16. Milton Friedman and Rose Friedman, Free to Choose (New York: Avon Books, 1979), p. 5.

17. See John Kenneth Galbraith, A Life in Our Time (New York: Ballantine Books, 1981), p. 50.

18. The discussion of supply side economics was drawn from George F. Gilder, Wealth and Poverty (New York: Basic Books, 1981); Martin Feldstein, "Inflation and Supply Side Economics," Wall Street Journal, May 20, 1980, p. 22; and Irving Kristol, "Economics and 'Eco-Mania'," Wall Street Journal, September 19, 1980, p. 28. For a critical appraisal of the supply side position see Lester Thurow, The Zero-Sum Society (New York: Basic Books, 1980); Herbert Stein, "Some 'Supply-Side' Propositions," Wall Street Journal, March 19, 1980, p. 24; and Sidney Blumenthal, "A Nice Theory Runs Up Against Reality," Boston Globe, February 14, 1981, p. 11.

19. Kristol, "Of Economics," p. 28.

20. Harold Lindsell, Free Enterprise: A Judeo-Christian Defense (Wheaton, Ill.: Tyndale House, 1982).

21. Ibid., p. 25.

22. Ibid., p. 69.

23. Ibid., p. 120.

24. Ed Cray, Levi's (Boston: Houghton Mifflin, 1978), p. 40. The discussion of Levi Strauss' philanthropic posture which follows is drawn from Cray's analysis.

25. Ibid., pp. 54-107, 132-140.

26. Ibid., pp. 172-180.

27. Daniel A. Wren, "American Business Philanthropy and Higher Education in the Nineteenth Century," Business History Review 57 (August 1983):321-346.

28. Ibid., pp. 340-343.

29. Mutual Benefit Life's survey is reported in "Research Spotlight: Corporate Philanthropy, circa 1983," Management Review (September 1983):54.

30. James F. Oates, "The Corporation and the Community," in The Corporation and the Campus, edited by Robert H. Connery (New York: Praeger, 1970), pp. 153-154.

31. See Edgar F. Kaiser, "Problems as Opportunities," in The Corporation and the Campus, pp. 137-147; and Joseph C. Wilson, "Technology and Society," in The Corporation and the Campus, p. 158-165.

32. Wilson, "Technology and Society," p. 163.

33. Lindsell, Free Enterprise, p. 54.

34. The discussion of American Express Company's strategy and the quote by Jerry Walsh are based on Wendy L. Wall, "Helping Hands: Companies Change the Ways They Make Charitable Donations," Wall Street Journal, June 21, 1984, pp. 1, 21; and Nancy Josephson, "AmEx raises corporate giving to marketing art," Advertising Age, January 23, 1984, pp. M-10, M-14.

35. Charles Stein, "Digital plans $45m education project," Boston Globe, June 23, 1984, p. 20; and Ronald Rosenberg, "Boston schools to use IBM plan," Boston Globe, August 1, 1984, pp. 1, 9.

36. Wilson, "Technology and Society," p. 164.

37. Conference Board, Business Credibility: The Critical Factor (New York: Conference Board, 1976); Clark Abt, The Social Audit for Management (New York: AMACOM, 1977).

38. Robert Benne, The Ethic of Democratic Capitalism: A Moral Reassessment (Philadelphia: Fortress Press, 1981), pp. 152-154.

39. Ibid., chapter 4.

40. Francis W. Steckmest, Corporate Performance: The Key to Public Trust (New York: McGraw-Hill, 1982), pp. 259-262.

41. Ibid., p. 271.

42. Harold Williams, "Corporate Accountability—One Year Later," paper presented at the Sixth Annual Securities Regulation Institute, January 19, 1979, San Diego, California, reported in Robert H. Bok, "Modern Values and Corporate Social Responsibility," MSU Business Topics 28 (Spring 1980):5-17.

43. John Kenneth Galbraith, "The Emerging Public Corporation," in Issues in Business and Society, edited by G. Steiner and J. Steiner (New York: Random House, 1977), pp. 530-533.

44. See John Kenneth Galbraith, The New Industrial State (Boston: Houghton Mifflin, 1967).

45. Ralph Nader, Mark Green, and Joel Seligman, eds., Taming the Giant Corporation (New York: Norton, 1976).

46. Severyn Bruyn, The Social Economy: People Transforming Modern Business (New York: Wiley, 1978).

47. Barry Bluestone and Bennett Harrison, The Deindustrialization of America (New York: Basic Books, 1982), p. 21.

48. Ibid., p. 145.

49. Martin Carney and Derek Shearer, Economic Democracy, The Challenge of the 1980s (Armonk, New York: M. E. Sharpe, 1980).

50. Ibid., p. 3.

51. For an interesting critique of codetermination, suggesting that the changes brought about have been far more cosmetic than substantial, see Alfred L. Thimm, The False Promise of Codetermination (Lexington, Mass.: D. C. Heath, 1981).

52. Carney and Shearer, Economic Democracy, see chap. 9.

53. Ibid., p. 375.

54. E. F. Schumacher, Small Is Beautiful: Economics as if People Mattered (New York: Harper & Row, 1973). See also E. F. Schumacher, Good Work (New York: Harper & Row, 1979).

55. Ibid., p. 75.

56. Ibid., p. 39.

57. Pope John Paul II, On Human Work (Washington, D.C.: U.S. Catholic Conference, 1982), p. 45.

58. K. Jameson and C. Wilbur, "Negotiating Society's New Social Contract," in The Moral Dimensions of Economics (National Catholic Reporter, 1983), pp. 6-7.

59. Ibid.

60. John F. Kavanaugh, Following Christ in a Consumer Society (Maryknoll, N.Y.: Orbis Books, 1981).

61. National Conference of Catholic Bishops, Pastoral Letter on Catholic Social Teaching and the U.S. Economy: First Draft (Washington, D.C.: National Conference of Catholic Bishops, 1984).

62. Ibid., p. 27.

63. Ibid., p. 19.

64. Ibid., pp. i-vii.

65. A. Collier, "The Co-Corp: Big Business Can Re-Form Itself," Harvard Business Review 57 (November-December 1979): 121-134.

66. Daniel Bell, The Coming of Post-Industrial Society (New York: Basic Books, 1973).

# 4

# SOCIAL RESPONSIBILITY
# AND POLICY RESPONSES

Corporate social responsibility can be investigated at many
levels—from the most limited actions of individuals and small
groups, to the totality of corporate behavior in a given society—
since any act which conforms to legal and moral criteria within
a business context may properly qualify as being "responsible."
The concern of loading dock employees for cleanliness in their
immediate environment has as much claim to the title of responsiveness as that displayed by top executives in the planning
of a multi-million-dollar campaign of pollution abatement. Whenever persons at any corporate level accept women and minorities
in positions previously closed to them, they are living out the
ideals of social responsibility. The same is true of individual
workers attempting to conserve small amounts of energy,
exercising vigilance over product safety, or simply being
conscientious about putting in a full day's work.

From a research standpoint, however, such a broad
behavioral conceptualization is unworkable. If one is interested
in conducting manageable research in this area, and in comparing
the findings with those of other investigators, then researches
of the most microscopic or macroscopic sort become problematic.
Very small studies may be difficult to compare, while very
large investigations may be simply impractical. In conceptualizing corporate social activities, however, the notion of policy
lends itself to manageable research within a broad middle range
and, if the elements of policy are clearly defined, facilitates
comparative analysis. Since policy, that is, the group action
which results from a collective process of planning and decision
making, is sufficiently distinct from the infinitude of individual

actions, it can serve as a useful starting point for empirical investigation.

## A SOCIOCULTURAL VIEW OF POLICY

Within the business literature, the concept of policy has a number of meanings, and the underlying process is referred to by various names such as policy, strategy, strategic management, or the planning process. As discussed in Chapter 2, the perspective of business policy focuses on an organization in its totality, its internal structure and external posture, and includes such concerns as the role and responsibilities of the general manager, the strategy-determination process, environmental analysis and forecasting, resource structure, and strategy implementation. In distilling the various uses of the concept, policy analysts suggest three main points: 1) the outcomes of processes rather than the processes themselves; 2) a framework of rules and values, rather than detailed choices within a particular framework; and 3) various kinds of behavior which are goal-oriented. Thus, if organizational policies are to serve as the basis for empirical investigation, two central research issues are: 1) the observation and measurement of policy data, and 2) the classification and categorization of these data for the purpose of building empirical theory.[1]

In order to pursue these objectives and as a necessary preliminary to our research work, we have formulated an ideal-typical, sociocultural model of policy. The starting point for this effort is Kerr's analytical definition of policy, in which its essential features are an agent, who carries out the policy; a rule of action, or "conditional imperative," which guides the actors' behavior; the actors' intention to follow the rule of action; a situation, which is likely to recur; discretion to modify the rule of action; and relevant publics who are affected by the policy.[2] Within this conceptualization, Kerr further differentiates between public and private types of policy, a distinction quite valuable for research purposes. Those policies which are announced to relevant publics are referred to as public; those which are not so announced, and may very well be the guiding force underlying organizational actions, are termed private. Relevant publics are seen as composed of two groups: those who help bring about the situation in which the policy response is activated; and those who have an interest in or are affected by the policy. In the present context, members of relevant publics would include employees, consumers, clients, community residents, government agencies, and others who come under the headings of both stockholders and stakeholders. While our research interest might begin with the public policies of corporations, it would also extend to private or unannounced policies, especially where these conflict with publicly declared programs.

Among the important variants of these policy types are the general and the specific. Corporations may, for example, have a single overall policy in the area of social responsibility. Most corporate policies, however, are obviously more limited in nature, as when there is one policy on hiring, another on product development, a third on investments, and so forth.[3] Such programs take place in a broad middle range between the isolated behavior of individuals and the most general response of the corporation as a whole. Not surprisingly, middle-level policies often conflict with one another, with the result that the corporate posture is neither homogeneous nor completely consistent. Such conflicts should be a major item on the agenda of those who investigate responsiveness.

The related notion of formal and informal policies leads to many well known sociological issues: the official organization chart versus the real functioning of the firm; stated versus actual goals; varying degrees of organizational participation, and so forth.[4] Based on such concerns, a number of questions may be raised. In relation to the policy process, which levels have what sort of input? Is policy merely a series of directives from on high, or the product of a gradual organizational consensus? How do corporations deal with the problem of multiple organizational cultures? We know, for example, that subsystems and subcultures sometimes formulate covert policies of resistance to management programs, as when efforts to increase productivity or instill responsiveness are subverted by a myriad of conflicting pressures and narrow perceptions of job-related activities.[5]

Drawing on the business policy concerns outlined in Chapter 2, we have condensed these conceptualizations into a set of key variables and research questions which focus on the agents, rule of action and consequences of the policies. The resulting model is presented in Table 4.1.


## FROM PHILOSOPHY TO POLICY: CRUCIAL ASSUMPTIONS

In Chapter 3 we presented four philosophies of corporate social responsibility as if they were separate entities. This was done for purposes of clarity. Similar to the integral approach

TABLE 4.1

Key Policy Variables and Research Questions

| Policy Variable | Research Questions |
|---|---|
| Agents | |
|   Designers | Who participates in the formulation of the policy?  How do they participate? |
|   Executors | Who is involved in the implementation of the policy?  What are the forms of such implementation? |
| Rule of action | |
|   Rationale | What general justification or explanation is provided for the policy?  Does this change over time? |
|   Operations | Which organizational functions are directly and indirectly affected by the policy? |
|   Services | What specific goods and services are provided under the policy? |
| Consequences | |
|   Relevant publics | Whose interests are directly and indirectly affected by the policy?  Are such groups informed about the policy?  How? |
|   Monitors | Who assesses the performance of policy agents, and the overall success or failure of the policy from within the organization?  What specific oversight procedures are used in evaluating the policy? |
|   Assessment standards | What norms or performance guidelines are used in evaluating the policy?  How clear are they?  Do they fluctuate? |
|   Rewards/penalties | What are the consequences for policy agents, in terms of incentives, recognition, advancement or demotion, payments or punishments, which follow from observance or nonobservance of the policy? |
|   Frequency of assessment | How often is the policy reviewed?  What determines the timing of the reviews? |
|   Organizational changes | What structural and procedural modifications occur in the policy-making organization, as a result of the policy? |

developed in Chapter 2, however, these types represent an interactive, dialectical matrix since they are all present, to varying degrees, in contemporary thinking about social responsibility. This point will become more apparent as we shift the focus of discussion from philosophies about what constitutes the social responsibility of business, to the different assumptions underlying these views, to the actual interpretation, formulation and assessment of responsiveness policies.

If the four philosophies of corporate social responsibility developed in Chapter 3 are to be useful to a discussion of policy, it is necessary to isolate their premises and underlying assumptions, and translate them into elements which can serve as the basis for action. Table 4.2 outlines the basic assumptions—psychological, social, economic, political, and ethical—for each of the philosophies of responsibility. As indicated by the similarities and differences of the domain assumptions, these four models capture much of the tension of the contemporary debate over and reassessment of the appropriate social role of business in our society. These underlying assumptions and conflicts range from the extent to which we should base our actions on an individualistic or systemic conception of society, and whether self-regulating "free markets" are more appropriate than markets subjected to governmental regulations, to the extent to which human beings are essentially self-interested or altruistic by nature. As such, this foundation provides a useful conceptualization which can serve as a guide for empirical investigation since these assumptions influence the nature of specific organizational policy responses.


CORPORATE SOCIAL POLICY:
AN INTEGRATED MODEL

Thus far, our discussion of corporate social responsibility has been split into two models: 1) an ideal-typical depiction of four different orientations to socially oriented activities, and 2) a set of key policy variables and related research questions. These philosophy types and policy variables may now be drawn together in an integrated model of social policies. A fully developed ideal-typical model illustrating what these policy types might look like in practice is presented in Table 4.3. As this table indicates, "socially responsible" policies range from those which involve little or no change from traditional business practice to those which require extensive change.

Productivist policies are typically formed from above, usually at the highest corporate levels. Few structural or procedural

TABLE 4.2

Crucial Assumptions of Social Philosophies

| | Productivism | Philanthropy | Progressivism | Ethical Idealism |
|---|---|---|---|---|
| Psychological | Human beings are naturally self-interested. | Human beings are naturally self-interested, but should share. | Human will-to-power is a constant danger. | Human beings need to be altruistic. |
| Social | Individualistic conception of society. Society is a free contract. | Individualistic conception of society. Society is a free contract. | Systemic conception of society. Society is a contract, which should contain significant familistic elements. | Systemic conception of society. Society should become as familistic as possible. |
| Economic | Self-regulating free markets are best mechanism for both production and distribution. Free enterprise. | Self-regulating free markets are best mechanism, but cannot meet all human needs. Free enterprise. | Free markets must be guided by limited governmental regulation. Democratic capitalism. | Free markets must be subject to government regulation, because they work against the weak. Democratic socialism/economic republic. |

114

| | | | | |
|---|---|---|---|---|
| | Socioeconomic imperative: Need for continuous growth. | | | Socioeconomic imperative: Limit to growth. |
| | Centralized government planning does not work. | Planning does not work. | Some planning must be accepted. | Some planning must be accepted. |
| | Corporations are material entities. | Corporations are material, with social elements. | Corporations are social-material. | Corporations are social-material. |
| Political | Government has an unhealthy tendency to expand. | Government has an unhealthy tendency to expand. | Government has naturally expanded as society has. | Government has naturally expanded as society has. |
| | Legal reform: Return to control stockholders. | | | Legal reform: Federal chartering of corporations. |
| Ethical | Freedom is highest value. | Freedom must be tempered by stewardship. | Freedom must include social duties. | Freedom means liberation from economic and political domination. |
| | Corporate philanthropy can be unethical. | Neighbor love. | Utilitarianism; pragmatism. | Altruism; revolutionary holiness. |

TABLE 4.3

An Integrated Model of Corporate Social Policies

| | Productivism | Philanthropy | Progressivism | Ethical Idealism |
|---|---|---|---|---|
| **Agents** | | | | |
| Designers | Internal: exclusive | Internal: consultative | Internal-external: accountable | Internal-external: participatory |
| Executors | Public relations office | Top management | Top/middle management | Organization-wide |
| **Rule of action** | | | | |
| Rationale | Education/image management | Community-mindedness | Corporate citizenship | Discipleship/moral transformation |
| Operations | Publicity | Charity | Target areas | Total business |
| Services | Information | Gifts | Specific projects | General organizational behavior |
| **Consequences** | | | | |
| Relevant publics | Corporation/small groups | Corporation/small groups | Corporation/interest groups | Corporation/society |
| Monitors | Top management | Top management | Top/middle management | Organization-wide |
| Assessment standards | Public relations norms | Charity norms | Specific policy norms | Moral code |
| Rewards/penalties | Honorific: internal recognition | Honorific: publicity recognition | Incentives: promotion, compensation | Incentives and punishments |
| Frequency of assessment | Intermittent | Intermittent | Intermittent to continuous | Continuous |
| Organizational changes | Publicity staff | Committees | Special offices | Centralized procedures |

changes are required, perhaps simply those involved in gearing
up for a publicity drive to emphasize what is already being
done by the organization. Relevant publics are quite limited
in type of size, sometimes extending only to the corporation
itself, its customers and various small groups. Monitoring is
transitory and guided largely by concerns for effective image
management. Examples of such responsiveness policies are
legion. Corporations have demonstrated this approach in such
efforts as campaigns extolling the benefits of the American
economic system, as well as advocacy advertising programs
which detail the ways in which the organization is fighting
various social problems such as inflation, or already fulfilling
the mandate of specific public policy initiatives. Many corporations have also sent out free booklets emphasizing their central
role in the community, and have even sponsored such evangelical
efforts as "free enterprise days."

The initiatives behind philanthropic policies still largely
come from above, but relevant publics are extended to include
specific beneficiary groups which begin to play a limited role
in the policy-planning process. Since few structural or procedural changes are required, however, rewards are largely
honorific with little bearing on performance evaluation. Excellent
examples of such philanthropic policies are provided by the life
and health insurance industry which annually contributes
millions of dollars to a broad range of projects in such areas
as urban and civic affairs, federated charitable drives, health
and safety programs, education and cultural events.[6] Other
corporations have developed policies to facilitate volunteerism
among their employees in the form of tutorial assistance, blood
donations, and a variety of community involvements. There
have also been instances of programs to dispose of corporate
resources with community needs in mind, as when obsolete
equipment and even whole buildings are donated to particular
causes.

Outside groups begin to take on more importance in progressivist policies as both beneficiaries and limited planners.
The extent of personnel involved in policy implementation is
also expanded to mid-level managers and supervisors. Extensive
structural and procedural changes are often required, usually
in targeted areas such as affirmative action offices or social
responsibility committees which review investments. Rewards
and sanctions may also figure prominently in job performance
reviews and promotion decisions. Specific types of policies in
this sphere include active programs of affirmative action for
women and minorities, as well as efforts to invest in minority-

owned enterprises or troubled inner-city areas. Similarly, progressivist programs focus on such areas as energy conservation, environmental protection, and efforts to hire and train the hard-core unemployed. Within this policy type, a variety of related efforts attempt to meet specific "budgeted non-financial objectives."[7]

Finally, ethical idealist policies are strongly value-oriented and reflect an ambitious philosophy rather than a pragmatic economic strategy. Initiatives often come from lower levels of organizational members. Many structural and procedural changes are necessary since virtually all organizational operations and functions are affected. Monitoring focuses on all employees, and rewards and sanctions are closely related to adherence to activities specified by policy principles. Examples of ethical idealist policies range from efforts to "constitutionalize" the corporation, to the movement toward economic democracy and collective employee ownership with democratic participation in the policy formulation process, to specific policies to engage in extensive profit sharing by organizational members, or to even create an organizational form which stresses rendering services to a given group or community rather than maximizing profits.[8]

As suggested by this brief discussion, these specific policy types reflect the various assumptions underlying different philosophies of social responsibility which are fully discussed in Chapter 3 and summarized in Table 4.2. The model developed here, however, rests on two further assumptions which should be made explicit. First, we are taking the individual corporation as the policy-making unit. This is an arbitrary simplification since many larger and smaller units must be considered in empirical research. Corporations offer many such examples, from the distinct cultures of upper management and blue-collar workers, to the contrasts between the subcultures of marketing sectors, technical research and development departments, and human resource offices. As suggested by the framework illustrated in Table 4.4, this could create a situation where one level or sector would favor a particular policy type, while a different policy type could be favored and even followed by another organizational sector.

A second assumption concerns the nature of the corporation's interpretation of its responsibility toward a range of issues which, in this model, is treated as unitary and consistent. Corporations may, indeed, have a single overall policy in the area of social responsibility. Most corporate policies, however,

TABLE 4.4

Social Policy by Levels and Sectors

| Organizational Sector | Policy Type | | | |
| --- | --- | --- | --- | --- |
| | Productivism | Philanthropy | Progressivism | Ethical Idealism |
| Top management | | | | |
| Middle management | | | | |
| White collar employees | | | | |
| Blue collar employees | | | | |
| Formal sub-systems (e.g., marketing, finance) | | | | |
| Informal sub-systems (e.g., work groups) | | | | |
| Unions Professional associations | | | | |

would tend to be more restrictive, as when there is one policy on hiring, another on product development, a third on investments, and so forth. Thus, as illustrated by the matrix in Table 4.5, complete analysis of a particular organization should focus on the relationships between its general social policy, which is usually public and formally announced, and specific policies which focus on individual social issues and are often private and unannounced. These interpretations may also differ by organizational sector and level. Similarly, an organization's relevant publics might expect uniform behaviors across all sectors of the organization, or different responses from different functions in terms of their actual degree of "responsibility." Thus, to appreciate fully the complexity of the responsiveness dynamic—how such policies are formulated, modified, implemented, and even subverted—it is important to consider the different levels and variables presented in Tables 4.4 and 4.5.

TABLE 4.5

Social Policy by Specific Issues

| Responsiveness Type | General Corporate Policy | Specific Social Policy Issues | | |
|---|---|---|---|---|
| | | Issue A | Issue B | Issue C |
| Productivism | | | | |
| Philanthropy | | | | |
| Progressivism | | | | |
| Ethical idealism | | | | |

## THE BROADER ISSUE: ORGANIZATIONAL PHILOSOPHY AND POLICY

In order to comprehend fully the question of the social responsibility of economic organizations discussed thus far, it is useful to link it to the larger theme of the social responsibility of any group or organization. Each legitimate group operates with some sense of its "proper" place in society, that is, with a conception of its formal and informal rights and duties. Some organizations explore such issues extensively, and develop complex statements of the relationships involved, while others conduct themselves on more of a "common-sense" basis. When organizational behavior accords with the interpretation of social responsibility shared by its members, a sense of doing justice, of duty fulfilled, is often experienced.

As suggested by the conceptualization presented in Chapter 3, we believe that four broad, generic types of organizational responsibility can be theoretically identified and subsequently applied as a guide to case study. These interpretive constructs are achieved by expanding the dimensions of reference groups and motives (see Figure 3.1) used in Chapter 3 to an internal or external orientation, and a technical or moral emphasis respectively. As illustrated by Table 4.6, when the internal and technical criteria are combined (A), the most specialized or "strict constructionist" philosophy emerges. Here, the discharge of a mission to the organization's members, with maximum freedom and privacy, is thought to be sufficient to satisfy an overall sense of social responsibility. A second variant retains the generally private orientation of the first, but recognizes certain moral duties beyond its ordinary mission, especially in cases of exceptional external suffering or need (B). A third view of such social responsibility combines a technical emphasis with a broad orientation to social groups and public issues (C). Finally, a fourth philosophy rests on the primacy of moral duties toward a wide range of external groups (D), and a willingness to completely rethink the fundamentals of the organization's social mission.

An example of the range over which this model may be applied can be obtained by linking these concepts to religious groups. Some churches hold a very specialized view of their relation to society, interpreting their social responsibility as service to their members only (A). In addressing the spiritual welfare of these persons, such groups believe they are discharging their obligations to society as a whole. Other religious groups share this membership orientation, but believe that the church should be more community-minded, especially in times of emergency (B). The third model of organizational responsibility and policy is found in churches that reach out on a regular basis to a wide array of groups beyond their membership (C). This might be termed the "ecumenical" variant, after the well known interfaith movement of the past several decades. Finally, there is an externally focused, very demanding interpretation of the social responsibility of religious groups. This is the "prophetic church," which seeks the most intense life of discipleship, to the point of explicitly challenging mainstream churches or other social institutions and building alternate religious structures (D).

TABLE 4.6

Organizational Policy Types

| | Orientation | |
| | Internal Orientation (Private) | External Orientation (Public) |
|---|---|---|
| Emphasis Technical emphasis | A (Productivism) | C (Progressivism) |
| Moral emphasis | B (Philanthropy) | D (Ethical idealism) |

A second application can be found in the social philosophy and social policy of science. Traditional views of the social role of science dating back to the nineteenth century defined its proper function as the production of knowledge through precise methods of research (A). As a result, it was held that scientists and scientific organizations could not permit themselves to become preoccupied with the potential external effects of their discoveries Edward Teller, father of the hydrogen bomb, once asserted, for example, that scientists, as scientists, should not accept blame for the misuse of nuclear weapons. He would feel, he said, no more guilt than would a manufacturer of tin cans who learned that one of his cans had been thrown through a window.

More recently, sharply contrasting perspectives have been advanced. Some, while strongly defending the traditional social mission of science, call for much greater awareness of the social, psychological, environmental, and other consequences of its activity (B and C). In the medical field, for example, they advocate increased sensitivity in the use of technology, as well as greater participation by both patients and their families, especially in the extreme situations of death and dying. Patients are now allowed to refuse in advance having their lives prolonged by extraordinary measures, and enjoy expanded rights to be informed of the exact nature of their illnesses. In a similar manner, medications are better explained, and potential side effects are listed on packages. Some professional organizations have gone on record with (progressivist) calls for increased self-regulation, popular participation and even some legislative controls.

Other observers dissent quite sharply, contending that science is directly or indirectly responsible for some of the most severe problems and catastrophes of the times (D). Specific indictments include the immorality of modern weapons, from the poison gases of World War I to current forms of chemical and bacterial warfare (napalm, Agent Orange, yellow rain, and others), to the indiscriminate nuclear weapons that threaten all life on earth. Even if such devices are never used in war, critics charge that their development has already caused widespread environmental and psychological damage. Thus, Dr. Helen Caldicott asserts that,

> Thousands of tons of radioactive materials, released by nuclear explosions and reactor spills, are now dispensing through the environment. Nonbiodegradable, and some potent virtually forever, these toxic nuclear materials will continue to accumulate, and

eventually their effects on the biosphere and
human beings will be grave: many people will
begin to develop and die of cancer; or their repro-
ductive genes will mutate, resulting in an increased
incidence of congenitally deformed and diseased
offspring—not just in the next generation, but for
the rest of time. [9]

Consequently, from this (ethical idealist) perspective, a socially
responsible science requires a radical critique of contemporary
scientific institutions, and the creation of a nonviolent, pro-life
and personalized alternative under democratic control.

Further parallels could be drawn from a broad range of
social groups. Medical organizations, for example, run the
gamut from for-profit institutions (A), through those that
accept occasional charity patients (B), and those that engage
in social outreach (C), to facilities that commit themselves to
an alternate vision of community-based, democratically controlled
health care (D). Educational organizations likewise exhibit a
similar range of variation. The above examples, however,
should be sufficient to establish our general conception of
social responsibility. Thus, although the following discussion
of policy and policy responsiveness focuses on economic institutions, the orientation presented in this chapter could be adapted
and applied to a wider range of groups and organizations, not
simply those which are business corporations.

CONCLUSION

In presenting our typology of responsiveness policies, we
have spoken as though each corporation had a single posture.
This was done in the interest of clarity and comprehensibility.
It would be inaccurate, of course, to claim that any of the
discussed types of response can be applied to all of the activities
of any corporation or any industry. Some activities would
naturally fall in one category, while others would have to be
classified differently. Thus, the typology is, to some extent,
an oversimplification. All classifications are, especially those
based on conceptual dichotomies. Nevertheless, the model
presented in this chapter helps to capture the connectedness
between these different concepts, and indicates that the types
are neither arbitrary nor isolated cases. They are also, evi-
dently, related in other ways as well. One might argue, for
example, that the elements of the private (stockholder) and

public (stakeholder) conceptualizations of the role of business actually form continua. Philanthropy can slip over into productivism, while extensive progressivism may approach ethical idealism. Even so, the responsiveness model is useful for exploring and testing the concepts.

It seems, therefore, that despite the limitations of this approach, this conceptualization of responsiveness policies is sufficiently clear and grounded in actual behavior to serve as a useful tool for comparative analysis. Indeed, as Weber has argued:

> The more sharply and precisely the ideal type has been constructed, thus the more abstract and unrealistic in this sense it is, the better it is able to perform its methodological function in formulating the clarification of terminology, and in the formulation of classifications, and of hypotheses.[10]

This model will thus serve as the basic guide for the exploration of corporate responsiveness discussed in the remainder of this book.

## NOTES

1. James E. Post and Edward Baer, "Analyzing Complex Policy Problems: The Social Performance of the International Infant Formula Industry," in Research in Corporate Social Performance and Policy, Vol. 2, ed. Lee E. Preston (Greenwich, Conn.: JAI Press, 1980), pp. 157-158.

2. D. Kerr, "The Logic of 'Policy' and Successful Policies," Policy Sciences 7 (1976):351-363.

3. See Robert Ackerman and Raymond Bauer, Corporate Responsiveness: The Modern Dilemma (Reston, Va.: Reston Publishing, 1976); and Donald W. Kelly and R. Terrance McTaggant, "Guidelines for Social Performance Case Studies," in Research in Corporate Social Performance and Policy, Vol. 1, ed. by Lee E. Preston (Greenwich, Conn.: JAI Press, 1978), pp. 287-291.

4. For a good overview of these issues see Charles Perrow, Organizational Analysis: A Sociological View (Belmont, Calif.: Brooks/Cole, 1970).

5. See J. Collins and C. Ganotis, "Is Corporate Responsibility Sabotaged by the Rank and File?" Business and Society Review (Autumn 1973):82-88.

6. For a good example of the range of these activities see the "Social Report" put out by the Clearinghouse on Corporate Social Responsibility, located in Washington, D.C.

7. Conference Board, Business Credibility: The Critical Factor (New York: Conference Board, 1976).

8. See, for example, Severyn Bruyn, The Social Economy (New York: John Wiley, 1977); and A. Collier, "The Co-Corp: Big Business Can Re-Form Itself," Harvard Business Review 57 (November/December 1979):121-134.

9. Helen Caldicott, Nuclear Madness (New York: Bantam Books, 1978), p. 3.

10. Max Weber, Theory of Social and Economic Organization, trans. A. M. Henderson and T. Parsons (New York: Oxford U. Press, 1947), p. 111.

# 5

# THE DYNAMICS
# OF SOCIAL POLICY I:
# INTERPRETIVE PROCESSES

It has long been recognized that corporate social policy making requires an interpretive process. This process, which has been designated by a variety of terms, seems to fall under the general rubric of policy development, organizational learning, and institutional commitment.[1] Yet, while scholars in the area of business and society may have reached agreement on the general nature of this dynamic, the identification of its more specific features must emerge gradually from comparative research. Accordingly, using the conceptions of responsibility types, policy, and responsiveness policies developed in Chapters 3 and 4, this chapter undertakes such exploration by focusing on organizational response patterns in reaction to a specific public policy initiative.

During the late 1970s and early 1980s, a significant amount of attention was being focused on the social performance of banks, especially in relation to the issue of community disinvestment. Within the Boston metropolitan area, a spirited, and at times heated, consideration of this issue was encouraged both by the location of the city (as a center of policy for the state) and by the presence of a skillful and active community advocacy group known as the Massachusetts Urban Reinvestment Advisory Group (MURAG). The organizations which form the basis of this analysis were reacting to legislation recently passed by the U.S. Congress, the Community Reinvestment Act of 1977. This law reflected the idea that banks were "quasi-public" rather than entirely private institutions, and therefore duty bound to serve the larger public interest, and imposed an "affirmative obligation" on banks to meet the credit needs of their communities, as defined by local "convenience and needs." Financial institutions, in other words, would be required to reach out to their communities rather than simply react to demand, and to cultivate an attitude of responsibility for their immediate environment. The particular focus of the CRA was on the low- and moderate-income communities surrounding urban banks. In order to ensure the effectiveness of these norms in the framing of organizational policy, the CRA provided for enforcement within the context of certain regulatory decisions, most importantly those governing bank expansion through branches, mergers, and acquisitions.

These provisions were largely unacceptable to the majority of bankers. The critical issue concerned the meaning of the CRA in practice, in particular the definitions which would be adopted by regulatory agencies and by citizen groups. Would the new obligations result in confusion, and create unreasonable expectations? Would they eventuate in any significant changes at all? At this point, no one seemed to be in a position to provide a definitive answer.

The ambiguities of this situation led us to a broad sociological tradition referred to as "interpretive sociology." This approach, often traced to the seminal work of Max Weber, begins its study of social phenomena with the question of <u>what particular events mean to the actors involved</u>. Behavior, in other words, is social insofar as it is meaningful to the participants, or insofar as these individuals are able to define the terms of their interaction. Within American sociology, this premise has been developed most systematically by the school of thought referred to as symbolic interactionism. The conceptual and empirical writings of this approach have attempted to focus on how definitions are established in social settings, and how they are subsequently interpreted and re-defined in a continuous process of interaction.[2] The process as a whole has been synthesized in Robert MacIver's concept of "dynamic assessment."[3] In MacIver's formulation, this refers to an on-going process of selective perception and a continuous modified valuation of social and cultural elements which are themselves in constant flux.

To explore these issues, this chapter will examine the interpretive process of policy formulation of three Boston-area banks as part of their reaction to the Community Reinvestment Act (CRA). In order to provide the context of these decisions, the discussion focuses initially on the development and passage of this legislative mandate. Using the responsiveness policy model (Table 4.3) developed in the preceding chapter as the basic research guide, the chapter examines the CRA-related policies of the three banks. In delving into the assessment of the CRA and the development of related policies, the responses of these institutions provide a good starting point for the study of the "definition of the situation" of responsiveness.


SETTING THE TERMS OF RESPONSIVENESS:
A BRIEF HISTORY OF THE COMMUNITY
REINVESTMENT ACT

A decade-long controversy involving lending institutions, urban neighborhood groups, and government agencies reached a significant point on November 6, 1978 when the federal Community Reinvestment Act went into effect.[4] Although there had been growing concern that banks must serve their entire communities, from a social as well as financial perspective, the extent to which this was actually being done was the subject of much debate. While banks had been given a clear mandate to meet community needs in their charters, many traditional banking procedures were increasingly being questioned by an array of external groups. There was a growing feeling— expressed by neighborhood groups, citizen lobbies, and other relevant publics—that bankers must exercise more leadership in community problems, particularly in the areas of urban renewal, community reinvestment, racial inequities, and municipal debt.[5] Such concerns were prominent among the precipitating events which led to the passage of the Community Reinvestment Act (CRA).

In his opening statement during the hearings for the CRA, Senator William Proxmire, chairman of the Senate Committee on Banking, Housing and Urban Affairs, argued that the bill he was promoting would underscore that bank charters carry with them the obligation that banks must serve the credit needs of the area they are chartered to service:

> The bill (CRA) is based on two widely shared assumptions. First: Government through tax revenues and public debt cannot and should not provide more than a limited part of the capital required for local housing and economic development needs. Financial institutions in our free economic system must play a leading role.
> Second: A public charter for a bank or savings institution conveys numerous benefits and it is

fair for the public to ask something in return.
In theory, and in law, banks and savings institutions are charged to serve local convenience and
needs. In practice, the regulatory agencies look
only to the capital adequacy of the applicant, his
character and reputation, and whether the proposed
service area contains sufficient deposit potential to
support another new bank or branch. The Community Reinvestment Act would provide that 'the
convenience and needs' of communities includes
the need for credit service, and further, that
regulated financial institutions have a continuing
and affirmative obligation to help meet the credit
needs of the local communities in which they are
chartered.[6]

The premise that financial institutions have certain responsibilities to their surrounding communities that exceed their
economic obligation to maintain solvency and profitability reflects
the gradual evolution of change in the way in which our society
views the role of business in general and our banking industry
in particular. If we are to appreciate fully the significance of
these proposed guidelines, we must consider the life cycle of
such concerns as a social issue.


Stockholder View

Historically, the United States has been served by a
"decentralized, entrepreneurial" banking system which was
loosely regulated in the interests of preventing excessive
competition and guaranteeing sound operating procedures.
The main public purposes of banking regulation were focused
on such fiduciary concerns as protecting deposits and stockholder investments, and maintaining a national network of
dependable financial intermediaries. Virtually all of the post-
Depression laws which define our banking system emerged from
this perspective.
As early as 1935, the concept that banks must meet the
"convenience and needs" of local communities was codified in
legislation, in an amendment to the Federal Reserve Act of
1933. This action, however, can be traced to events which
occurred 25 years earlier, when New York stipulated that
banks within the state should only be chartered on the condition
that they promote "public convenience and advantage." This

mandate was passed in the wake of the panic of 1907, when many banks had failed. During this period, a number of states had passed similar laws that focused on whether the amount of business in a community was sufficient to justify the establishment of additional banks. The main concern was that too many banks in a given area could create a situation which could weaken the system and render all of the banks unsafe. Thus, when codifying this concept in the 1935 legislation, it appears that Congress was relying on well-established regulatory procedures and was primarily addressing the community's ability to support the bank to be chartered.[7] While this is obviously quite a different interpretation of the phrase compared to its use today, it reflects the symbolic interactionist premise that social definitions are continuously interpreted and redefined in an ongoing process of interaction.

Stakeholder View

Over the past two decades, our society has taken an increasingly broader view of banking's role in our economy. During this period, Congress enacted a number of consumer protection and civil rights measures which placed definite responsibilities on banking institutions that went well beyond their basic obligation to operate safely and soundly. The Equal Credit Opportunity Act (ECOA), for example, placed far-reaching obligations on lenders and their regulators and had a direct impact on the substantive underwriting decisions made by lenders.[8]

A specific concern of citizen groups around the country was the disinvestment in and redlining of particular communities. Many neighborhood residents, especially those living in racially mixed, inner-city areas, alleged that banks, as well as savings and loan institutions, would not give them mortgages or home improvement loans despite their needs and a strong demand for such monies. These groups felt that banks were "exporting" funds deposited by local residents in their neighborhood institutions to investments outside that particular neighborhood, investments that would not have any benefits, either directly (through rehabilitation loans and mortgages) or indirectly (through neighborhood-based development loans), for the neighborhood and its residents.[9] The frustration experienced by these local groups was intensified by the absence of any legal requirements that banks disclose information on the geographical distribution of their loans and mortgages.

Citizen pressures, however, led to a series of initiatives at the state level—in Massachusetts, California, Illinois, and New York—which attacked redlining through administrative regulations aimed at the state legislative banking committees, which essentially represented banking interests. In 1975, for example, Illinois Governor Dan Walker signed a bill focused on outlawing the "evil practice of redlining" by requiring public disclosure of mortgage information by geographic area.[10] With such actions as precedent, Senator Proxmire's Home Mortgage Disclosure Act (HMDA) of 1975 was enacted by Congress. In effect, this required banks to publicly disclose their patterns of mortgage lending by census tract and zip code. Although the HMDA did not offer any direct solution to the redlining issue, it did require disclosure of relevant data. The Act strongly suggested that redlining was "unfair"; however, it did not make the practice illegal. Yet, passage of the HMDA was a precipitating event in the eventual enactment of CRA.

While the law required that banks forward this information to the Federal Reserve Board for examination, the Board required instead that computer printouts summarizing these lending patterns be kept where community groups could study them. Although this initially seemed to be focused on the needs of these local groups, the decision was criticized because there would not be any federal study of lending practices. In Boston during this period, the state Banking Department hired its first résearch director and, staffed largely by college student volunteers, undertook an analysis of the lending patterns of Boston banks. Based on data provided under the HMDA, the findings documented that for every dollar Boston residents deposited in their savings bank, an average of only 13 cents was reinvested in mortgages in the neighborhood. In Boston's outer suburbs, by contrast, for every dollar deposited the banks invested $1.12 in mortgage funds and in some communities this investment exceeded $3.00 invested for every dollar deposited by local residents.[11] Thus, the initial fears that city banks were "exporting" neighborhood funds for investments outside that neighborhood were finally supported.

Although the banking industry was opposed to the passage of the HMDA, in several large cities bankers realized that they had to respond to public criticism of their lending policies. A number of voluntary action plans were initiated, often after arduous and heated debates concerning the role of banks in inner-city development. In such cities as Los Angeles, San Francisco, and Pittsburgh mortgage review boards, voluntary groups of savings bankers and other community lenders, re-

viewed rejected mortgage loans if the applicants who were
denied these monies alleged redlining.  In Boston, under
Carol Greenwald's administration as commissioner of banks,
such a mortgage review board was created.  As Greenwald
explains:

> As commissioner, I had originally proposed an
> assigned-risk pool for mortgages in redlined areas,
> as was done, for example, in Massachusetts's
> "FAIR" plan for insurance in certain districts.
> Membership in a Massachusetts mortgage agency
> would have been mandatory for all financial insti-
> tutions.  These would have been assessed up to
> 2.5 percent of their capital and surplus accounts
> to support the agency.  But the proposed plan for
> mortgages would have required legislation.  Savings
> bankers confidently told me they could defeat any
> such measure introduced in the legislature.  I
> agreed that no bill would pass if introduced that
> year, 1975; new concepts very rarely win passage
> the first time they are broached.  But I challenged
> the bankers to bet on the odds of passage by the
> fourth year the legislation was introduced.  The
> bankers were not willing to gamble.[12]

Thus, by threatening an extended battle which would likely
damage the images of some of the banks, Greenwald persuaded
the industry to form a "voluntary" mortgage review board with
community participation.  Although bankers subsequently
stonewalled the creation of this group—insisting on assurance
that it was not in violation of antitrust laws and on surveys
which documented public opinion that banks should be involved
in community programs—the board was finally created the
following year.

Commissioner Greenwald, however, became quite critical
of the performance of the board, arguing that bankers had
come to welcome the Mortgage Review Board as a "way of de-
fusing the redlining issue," and that the Board was only
"marginally effective."  Yet, through the existence of such
boards, growing public pressure from community advocacy
groups, and the realization by many bankers that their lending
decisions would be held up to scrutiny and potential public
challenge, the percentage of home sales in Boston which were
financed with bank mortgages rose from 55 percent to 64 percent
over a two-year period, with impressive gains in neighborhoods

with large minority populations.[13]  Some change was therefore
beginning to emerge.

While HMDA disclosures documented similar disinvestment
patterns in other major U.S. cities, there was still nothing
illegal about such geographic discrimination.  In February 1976,
however, a landmark decision in Cincinnati held that redlining
practices were in fact not only unfair but illegal as well.  Citing
the 1968 Fair Housing Act (FHA) as its basis, a federal court
ruled that banks could not refuse to lend money for home
purchases in racially mixed communities.  Any such practices
were in violation of the FHA.  This decision was further reinforced in 1977 when the American Institute of Real Estate
Appraisers was informed through court decision that any
appraisal standards which scaled down the value of homes
because of racial composition of the surrounding community
were also in violation of the FHA.  Subsequent criticism of the
inactivity of the federal regulators* to ensure that bankers
were responding to these concerns set the final stage for the
passage of the CRA.

The Community Reinvestment Act

Similar to the Home Mortgage Disclosure Act, The Community Reinvestment Act reflects a concerted congressional
effort to move toward our national policy goal of providing
sufficient housing for all Americans, as set fourth by the
Fair Housing Act.  Since deposit interest-rate controls are
supposed to guarantee a sufficient supply of funds for housing
loans by attracting deposits for thrift institutions, which are
then supposed to be re-lent in the local mortgage market, the
CRA was designed to ensure that the flow of funds through
these institutions met the needs of local residents.  While it
might seem that such obligation could be met by continuing to
offer the loans and other credit services for which these financial institutions originally were created, the complexities of

---

*These regulatory agencies are the Comptroller of the
Currency (for national banks), the Federal Reserve Board
(for member state-chartered banks), the Federal Deposit
Insurance Corporation (for nonmember state-chartered banks
and mutual savings banks), and the Federal Home Loan Bank
Board (for savings and loan associations).

today's urban economies make such a perspective overly simplistic. The changing economic, social, and demographic conditions of these areas have, in many instances, rendered the banking industry's policies and programs of yesterday ineffective for the needs of their present communities.[14]

Passed in 1977, the essential guidelines of the CRA are relatively clear: Banks are regarded as quasi-public institutions whose charters require them to act in the public interest. Such action is understood as going beyond the traditional requirements of "safe and sound" banking practices to encompass the "legitimate" credit demands of their communities as defined by local "convenience and needs." While there is nothing in the CRA that states that banks must make unsound or unsafe loans, it is clear that banks must make every effort to ensure that low- and moderate-income groups are treated fairly and equitably. Thus, with the CRA setting overall public policy guidelines, banks were called upon to play a critical role in the urban renewal process, by working toward the revitalization of declining neighborhoods through an aggressive, affirmative action program of local housing and small business lending. Success in these efforts is thought to depend primarily upon improving communication between banks and their local communities, in which process the CRA requires the financial institutions to take the initiative. In order to ensure the effectiveness of its norms in the framing of practical policy, the CRA provides for enforcement within the context of certain regulatory decisions, most importantly those governing bank expansion through branches, mergers, and acquisitions. Community groups can challenge any proposed bank expansions on the basis of insufficient CRA activities, thereby initiating an examination by the appropriate regulatory body.*

------------

*Introduced under S.406 in the Senate, the act which eventually passed reads in full as follows (Community Reinvestment Act, 12 U.S.C. 2901-2905; Title 12 of the U.S. Code, Section 2901):

  (a) The Congress finds that—
      (1) regulated financial institutions are required by law to demonstrate that their deposit facilities serve the convenience and needs of the communities in which they are chartered to do business;
      (2) the convenience and needs of communities include the need for credit services as well as deposit services; and

As suggested by the preceding discussion, the CRA has gone through three distinct phases as part of its life cycle: 1) during the 1920s and 1930s when it was initially recognized that banking consideration of community needs was an important component of regulatory decisions; 2) during the mid-1960s to mid-1970s when a number of acts were passed concerning housing policy and mortgage disclosure; and finally 3) the late 1970s when it was mandated that community involvement and investment be a generic part of banking policy and practice.

From this brief synopsis, we can see what is meant by the symbolic interactionist premise that rules of interaction arise gradually out of a social process. Although it may seem that such a sequence of events is unpredictable, most social issues follow a course that, in retrospect, appears to be quite predictable. As Ackerman and Bauer have argued, with respect to any social controversy,

> There was generally a time when the issue was un-
> thought of or unthinkable. In fact, social and
> economic sanctions are regularly applied to those
> fostering causes of some consequence that have no
> public support. However, should interest develop

---

    ( 3) regulated financial institutions have continuing and affirmative obligation to help meet the credit needs of local communities in which they are chartered.
 (b) It is the purpose of this chapter to require each appropriate financial supervisory agency to use its authority when examining financial institutions, to encourage such institutions to help meet the credit needs of the local communities in which they are chartered consistent with the safe and sound operation of such institutions.

Title 12 of the U.S. Code, Section 203 continues:

In connection with its examination of a financial institution, the appropriate Federal financial supervisory agency shall—
    (1) assess the institution's record of meeting the credit needs of its entire community, including low- and moderate-income neighborhoods, consistent with the safe and sound operation of such institutions; and
    (2) take such record into account in its evaluations of an application for a deposit facility by such institution.

and be sustained, the issue enjoys a period of increasing awareness, expectations, demands for action and ultimately enforcement. At the end of this period, possibly measured in decades, it may cease to be a matter of active public concern. New standards may then have become so ingrained in the normal conduct of affairs that to behave otherwise would bring the social and economic sanctions formerly reserved for the contrary behavior. Thus, like the product life cycle, there is an analogous social issue life cycle.[15]

## INTERPRETING THE TERMS OF RESPONSIVENESS: A COMPARATIVE CASE STUDY

While the major contribution of the CRA and similar state regulations which have been subsequently passed* is suggested to lie in the requirement that lending institutions become aware of and consider plans for helping to meet the credit needs of their entire community, the act is not a panacea for the ills of urban areas.[16] Despite many of the criticisms by bankers that the CRA is a "time bomb" and a "credit allocation policy,"[17] the act is not an income-redistribution measure. Although the intent of the CRA is to encourage banks to lend in low- and moderate-income areas, it does not require them to relax "safe and sound" credit standards.

This can create difficult decisions for local bankers. At a recent forum on the implications of the CRA, for example, this issue was among those debated:

---

*In Massachusetts, a state version of the CRA was passed in 1982 as part of the Bank Reform Act (Brennan Bill). This act which is quite broad and represents the most substantial change in Massachusetts banking law since the 1930s, will permit all Massachusetts banks—thrift and commercial—to offer the same services by April 1, 1986. It also contains a state CRA which parallels the federal act and specifies that on an annual basis the Bank Commissioner must assess a bank's performance in meeting those needs and that such assessment could be the basis for denying a bank's application for branching, merger, or acquisition.

To take just one example, rapid inflation has eroded
the savings of many depositors who, at a previous
time, would have constituted a sizable market for
mortgage loans. Devalued savings often translate
into an inability to place a sufficient down payment
on a home, in spite of the depositor's income. These
people, who comprise part of the lender's community,
still have credit needs. But can they be met if the
lender merely does business as usually, offering
its standard loan terms?

To ask the question is to answer it. New programs are needed, new approaches are called for,
if the CRA is to have more than symbolic significance.[18]

While application of the CRA made it clearer that the primary
intent of the Act is to improve communication between banks
and their surrounding low- and moderate-income communities
and to promote community development,[19] arguments that these
geographic areas do not have sufficient funds to warrant such
investment do not excuse financial institutions from their
responsibilities under this public policy mandate.

Whenever "new programs" and "new approaches" are
called for, however, there is a wide managerial zone of discretion, a variety of options available for approaching the problem.[20]
As a result, one of the key concepts, that banks have an
"affirmative obligation" to serve the legitimate credit needs of
their local communities has ranged in practice from a mere
absence of overt discrimination to a positive record of active
reinvestment. The internal administration of CRA-related
programs, for example, could vary from a "business as usual"
stance, to the creation of community reinvestment staff positions,
"social issue" specialists who are in charge of overseeing CRA
activities, to the involvement of senior bank personnel who
report directly to the board of directors, or the creation of
new community investment departments, and housing and urban
affairs divisions.

As a result of such actions, a number of banking institutions have been commended for their community involvement
and redevelopment.[21] Not all banks, however, have been
judged as "responsive." In April 1979, for example, the
Federal Deposit Insurance Corporation (FDIC) denied a suburban
branch extension application from a New York mutual savings
bank due to "insufficient community action."[22] In 1980, a

Boston-based savings bank had a similar expansion request denied. Since regulatory agencies must now consider a bank's reinvestment record when evaluating applications for mergers or new facilities, the threat of such adverse regulatory activity has prompted many banking organizations to more fully assess their community investment policies and procedures. Yet, since many banks are also faced with numerous financial pressures (for example, volatile interest rates, disintermediation, economic deregulation, increased competition) and the potential impact on their ability to meet their community responsibilities,[23] as well as different philosophies of social responsibility, a range of response strategies are observable.

## The Response to the CRA: Three Cases

As suggested by the preceding discussion, a number of critical issues emerged concerning the meaning of the CRA in practice. Given the ambiguities of the situation during the period after the law went into effect (late 1970s and early 1980s), it appeared that individual banks interpreted the meanings of their "affirmative obligation" and the "convenience and needs" of their communities in different ways. In other words, considering the zone of discretion which surrounded organizational reaction to this public policy, our research efforts focused initially on potential variations in the interpretation of the CRA and their implications for the responsiveness policies of different banks. Thus, using the responsiveness policy model developed in Chapter 4 (Table 4.3) as the basic research guide, the CRA-related policies of three Boston area banks were examined.

### Case A

One of the first policies developed by banks to deal with the CRA was an informationally oriented strategy: the communication of present activities and services the bank offers. Bank A, however, appeared to interpret the mandate of the CRA solely in such terms—as access to information. Accordingly, it formulated a policy of providing more extensive and detailed information to customers and relevant publics concerning its present activities. A series of documents were printed, advertised, and made available in the lobby of the bank or upon request. Special emphasis was placed on publication of the particulars of the bank's loan portfolio, and a general effort was made to educate the community about the many benefits of the services offered at the bank. At the same time, the materials were intended to communicate the bank's sincere interest in, and historical commitment to, its surrounding community. The policy fit smoothly into the normal flow of operations at the bank, and required changes primarily in the activities of its community relations staff.

Thus, while the organization made a systematic effort to publicize all the services it offered to its community, the policy had virtually no impact on the normal operation of the bank. The claim was advanced explicitly that the bank was, in fact, meeting the needs of its community. Little request for dialogue was evident. Accordingly, the decision-making component focused solely on internal operations and traditional fiduciary matters with virtually no community input.

## Case B

Bank B interpreted the demands of the CRA somewhat more broadly, taking the position that the law envisioned a new relationship between banks and their surrounding communities in addition to fuller disclosure of information. Therefore, in the materials that it printed, advertised, and made available, the bank explicitly requested community feedback. Its policy aimed to initiate a dialogue with some of its relevant publics, who had not previously played a significant role in the formulation of bank policy. As the institution proposed in its CRA statement after presenting a compilation of its "community" loan services,

> We encourage you to respond and give us your input
> on how well you think we are doing. We think we
> are doing a good job, but unless you tell us your
> thoughts, we will never really know.

Thus, in this instance the Act initiated the opening of a potential dialogue and a more detailed delineation of banking services. Although the decision-making process was still internally focused, it began to take on a consultative orientation.

Bank B pursued a cautious but open-ended course which accepted some risks and introduced an element of unpredictability, since there was no guarantee that individuals or groups in the area would not utilize the opportunity to raise petty grievances, or even to provoke confrontation. Bank B also differed slightly from Bank A in that it attempted to reflect a philanthropic concern for its local community by allowing certain community groups to use its facilities for meetings, and by listing in its

publications the various service organizations supported by
the bank and its members (for example, Kiwanis, Lions, Rotary,
and others). However, a simple listing of such service organizations to which individual members of the bank belong as an
indication of the bank's involvement in community activities
might be considered highly questionable. Indeed, the rationale
for the policy may be criticized in terms of overt and covert
perspectives. Overtly, the bank may be arguing that it is
opening the lines of communication with its community and that
the individual actions of its members also reflect this interaction.
From a covert perspective, on the other hand, it may simply
be a matter of image management, a public relations posture
to protect its position from potential regulatory intervention.
Similar to Bank A, this bank delegated most of the CRA-policy
work to its existing community relations department, so that
the mandates of the new law were implemented without alterations
in organizational structure.

## Case C

In contrast to the above policy responses, Bank C developed
an activist interpretation of the demands of the CRA, formulating
a dramatically different policy in several phases. During the
first phase, the bank, through an existing urban subcommittee
at the board of directors level, began a dialogue with its neighborhood. This laid the groundwork for a second stage, in
which a series of meetings were held between bank personnel
and local residents. On the basis of these interactions, which
defined community renovation as a key concern, a third phase
was initiated in which the bank undertook to rehabilitate one
unit of local housing as a pilot project for a possibly expanded
effort, and facilitated the processing of home improvement loans.
In a final policy phase, the bank sought a response from governmental agencies to its housing effort, and explored the possibility
of subsidies to support further renovations.

The first stage of this process was largely internal, dealing
with the bank's initial interpretation of the CRA. From the
institution's perspective, the new law required considerable
initiative on the bank's part. Earlier, the bank had established
an urban subcommittee to its board of directors, which acted
as an outreach mechanism to specific inner-city branch areas.
Now, drawing upon the experience of this subcommittee, the
institution opened a dialogue with its neighboring communities.

The second phase consisted of a series of meetings in which
community residents expressed their concerns and bank personnel
communicated the views and plans of the organization. Data ob-

tained at the meetings indicated that citizen concerns fell into three major categories: 1) the general image of the community, 2) home improvement loans, and 3) abandoned housing stock in the area. The institution learned at the same time that there was a good deal of skepticism and suspicion in the neighborhoods concerning the bank's intentions and behavior.

The third phase of the dynamic assessment was the most intensive, as the organization moved to implement specific policy objectives. Since the impact of the abandoned housing was directly related to the community's overall image, bank officials decided to initially address this issue. Specifically, the bank chose to select and rehabilitate one unit of housing as a pilot test of a projected program of housing renewal. In order to meet both the needs of the community and the organization, several guidelines were drafted. To be eligible for the program, a housing unit would have to be near one of the branch offices; be located on a relatively stable street, with no more than one or two structures in poor condition; be on a street where neighbors were receptive to the rehabilitation; be in the private sector and unoccupied (since the bank did not wish to compete in this project with the private market); and have a three-decker structure, which was characteristic of homes in the area.

Implementation of this course of action was facilitated by the existence within Bank C of two structures not found in its counterpart institutions. The first was the urban subcommittee already referred to. The second was a small construction firm, set up under a 1970 amendment to the banking laws, known as the Leeway Provision, which permitted savings banks to invest between 1 and 3 percent of deposit funds in real estate or personal property. Referred to by bank executives as an "innovative application" of this provision, the initial role of this firm was to oversee the construction of bank extensions and upgrading of facilities. In the context of the CRA, it was decided that by expanding the role of this subsystem, it was possible to undertake the housing renovation policy.

Before work could begin, however, the bank had to engage in a new round of negotiations pursuant to acquisition of a suitable property. Because the institution had targeted abandoned housing stock, the concurrence of both the federal department of Housing and Urban Development and the city of Boston was needed. As events unfolded, the support of these agencies posed new problems because the housing unit which the bank selected had been the object of a citizen petition. Due to persistent vandalism and a recent fire, residents in the

area had asked that the structure be demolished. It was some
six months before the agencies and community members agreed,
the owner was located, and a purchase agreement was formalized.

At this point, the institution still faced a series of choices.
It was known from the start that the costs of rehabilitation would
exceed the eventual sale price of the property. Thus, the
question arose as to how much of the difference the organization
should absorb, and how this should be done. The bank decided
to fix the sale price at the level of direct costs, and to absorb
the indirect costs of design and administration. The institution
recognized at the same time that implementation of its responsiveness policy required that restrictions be placed on the sale of
the property. It was important that the unit be sold to residents
of the community, who would be willing to make a commitment
to living there for at least a moderate period of time. Sale to
outsiders or speculators would defeat the purpose of the initiative.

To oversee the implementation process, a new structure
was created, the position of "project coordinator" whose duties
included participation in property selection and purchase;
participation in the legal aspects of acquisition where an attorney
is not necessary; presentations to bank staff and neighborhood
residents; liaison with local groups; negotiation with relevant
agencies; maintenance of cost control standards; inspection
work; documentation of progress; and participation in marketing
and sales of the rehabilitated stock.

As the renovations neared completion, the bank sponsored
two open houses for prospective buyers. The first produced
mainly curiosity seekers, but the second netted some serious
customers. Consistent with the general goals of the project,
the open houses and the property itself were advertised only
within the immediate community. It appears to have been only
at this point that the interpretation of the project held by many
residents changed, from the perception that there must be some
sort of "hidden agenda" for the institution, to the sense that
the organization was sincere in its efforts to improve the quality
of life in the area. The unit, which was subdivided into condo-
miniums, was sold to three local families (mortgage support was
provided by the bank). Successful completion of the pilot
project led to a fourth phase in this dynamic assessment, in
which the bank sought out the views of government agencies.
In these negotiations, the organization's objective was to determine the feasibility of expanding its efforts. Since the bank
had decided that sales must at least cover depositors' funds,
however, future work would be contingent upon subsidies of

some kind. The dynamic underlying this interaction is illustrated in Figure 5.1.

## Interpretations and Implications

The above cases, which have necessarily been compressed, lend themselves to analysis in terms of the conceptual framework. Based on this model, it seems that Banks A and B exhibit a productivist and productivist-philanthropic stance respectively, while the policy of Bank C has the features of progressivism (see Tables 5.1 and 5.2). The former institutions made no significant departures from conventional concepts (market model) of corporate social responsibility, and did not pursue an activist role as willing agents of social change. They seem, however, to have met the letter of the law, understood in a relatively narrow way. Bank C, by contrast, sought new areas of activity and decided to explore an unusual avenue which directly addressed unmet (and expressed) needs of its local community. It absorbed the cost of a new internal position, and took the financial risks involved in selling the renovated residence. Moreover, it facilitated the processing of home improvement loans in the area to encourage further development of the neighborhood. This policy might not make sense within

FIGURE 5.1

The Dynamic Assessment of Bank C

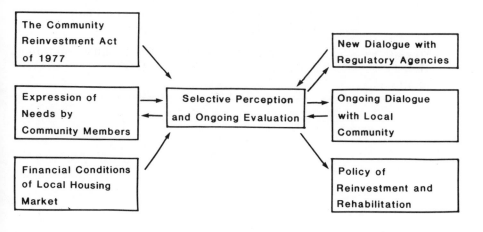

TABLE 5.1

Responses of Banks A and B

| Selected Variables | Bank A Productivism | Bank B Mixed: Productivism-Philanthropy |
|---|---|---|
| **Agents** | | |
| Designers | Internal: exclusive no community input | Internal: exclusive/ consultative beginnings of community input |
| Executors | Community relations department | Community relations department |
| **Rule of action** | | |
| Operations | Publicity: loan portfolio | Publicity: loan portfolio |
| Services | Information: List of services; defense of position | Information: List of services Gifts: Sharing of facilities |
| **Consequences** | | |
| Relevant publics | Bank, regulatory agencies | Bank, individuals taking advantage of potential services listed regulatory agencies. |
| Rewards/ penalties | Honorific: No direct relationship to performance appraisal | Honorific: No direct relationship to performance appraisal |
| Organizational changes | Community relations staff | Community relations staff |

a market model of responsiveness (productivism) because the activity appears to go beyond sound banking practice and does not conform to the principles of profit maximization. However, the departures of Bank C do make sense in terms of its progressivist assumption that the contract between banking and the larger society is undergoing important change.

There are two intriguing footnotes concerning Bank C's response to the CRA: 1) the response of the institution's employee population, and 2) the vulnerability of such programs to organizational change. First, although the concept of relevant publics typically focuses on groups external to the organization (for example, public interest groups, consumer groups, citizen lobbies, regulatory agencies), a firm's employee population should also be considered in such analysis. The classic Collins and Ganotis study, for example, found that social responsiveness efforts were often thwarted by the organization's middle managers who perceive a sense of futility concerning their ability to effect corporate social policy and believe that social goals can be best fulfilled by those outside their companies.[24] Yet, despite the growing body of evidence concerning the importance of employee perceptions in the implementation of responsiveness programs,[25] these individuals are often overlooked in business and society case analyses.

In an attempt to assess the reactions of this critical constituency, employee opinions about the community involvement program of Bank C were gathered as part of a general Quality of Work Life survey in the organization.[26] In contrast to the findings of the Collins and Ganotis study, most employees expressed favorable attitudes about the institution's responsiveness policy (52 percent favorable, 38 percent neutral, 10 percent unfavorable). There were also modest positive correlations between employee evaluations of the bank's reinvestment policy and commitment to the organization ($r = .19$), a sense of doing something worthwhile and important ($r = .20$), and overall job satisfaction ($r = .12$). Moreover, there were no significant differences by job classification or salary level. Finally, most of those who expressed an unfavorable attitude toward the renovation project felt that the bank should do more rather than less in this area. Such findings tend to lend credence to the argument that responsive policies are in the best interests of the organization as well as society in general.

The second point concerns the institutionalization of responsiveness programs over time. Although Bank C entered into negotiations with a number of government agencies in an effort to expand its program to the extent of 12 to 15 renovations

TABLE 5.2

The Emergent Progressivist Policy of Bank C

| Research Variables | Phase 1: Reaction | Phase 2: Dialogue | Phase 3: Implementation | Phase 4: Continuation |
|---|---|---|---|---|
| Agents Designers | Top mgt. | Community input | Internal-external: accountable and participatory | Internal-external: accountable and participatory |
| Executors | CEO, VP personnel | Community input | CEO, VP personnel, urban subcommittee, Leeway Corp., project coordinator, community group | CEO, VP personnel, urban subcommittee, Leeway Corp., project coordinator, community group |
| Rule of action Rationale | "Responsible" neighboring institution | "Responsible" neighboring institution | "Responsible" neighboring institution | "Responsible" neighboring institution |
| Operations | Public relations | Public relations | Investment policy, community redevelopment, urban renovation, fiduciary services | Investment policy, community redevelopment, urban renovation, fiduciary services |
| Services | Information | Information | Housing renovation, community financing | Possible: same as Phase 3 |

Consequences

| | | | | |
|---|---|---|---|---|
| Relevant publics | Bank officials, urban sub-committee, local communities | Bank officials, urban sub-committee, local communities | Bank, residents of renovated unit, community, banking industry, regulatory agencies | Bank employees, state and federal agencies |
| Monitors | Top mgt., urban sub-committee | Top mgt., urban sub-committee | Primary: project coordinator, CEO, VP personnel, urban sub-committee; secondary: community reps, regulatory agencies | Possible: state and federal agencies |
| Assessment standards | Successful communication | Successful communication | Quality of work on project; success in meeting initial objectives | Undetermined |
| Rewards/penalties | Honorific: local goodwill | Honorific: local goodwill | For bank employees, honorific; for project coordinator, performance evaluation | Undetermined |
| Organizational changes | Expanded role of urban sub-committee | Expanded role of urban sub-committee | Creation of project coordinator, expanded role of Leeway Corp. | Undecided |

annually, the reaction from these groups was far from favorable. While many of those in the bank wanted to continue the project nevertheless, on a much smaller scale of one to two renovations per year, the plan was scrapped following a merger of the organization with another savings bank in the area. While there was an initial attempt to institutionalize the program as part of the bank's operating policy, the reality is that such programs are based on the support of the chief executive officer and other upper level managers. The vulnerability of the policy was under-scored when many of these individuals were assigned different job responsibilities or let go after the merger. Since Bank C's merger partner ultimately became the dominant force in the merged institution, the resultant responsiveness policies reflected quite different interpretations of social responsibility and per-formance.[27] While many of Bank C's employees expressed concern that the renovation policy was being terminated, the anxiety precipitated by the merger and significant concern about the possibility of their own employment termination quickly made this a nonissue. Thus, while it is often suggested that once such programs become institutionalized they are an ongoing part of the organization's operating policy, it seems that such social programs are more vulnerable to organizational changes than other functionally oriented policies.

## Variations Among the Types

The preceding discussion raises the issue of types and subtypes of responsiveness. While the general framework developed in Chapters 3 and 4 is useful as an initial guide for empirical research, should the policies of Banks A and B be placed in the same category? Or are there sufficient grounds for viewing them as different species of productivism? Although Bank B did have overtones of philanthropy in its decisions ("mixed" type), was its orientation truly philanthropic in nature? In a similar way, does the policy of Bank C have the characteristics which would be expected in any progressivist course of action?

Based on these questions and the policy responses in the above cases, it seems that there is justification to sketch out some subtypes of responsiveness, at least in a tentative way. Productivism, for example, could range from a highly cynical view of business's social role, to a basically fundamentalist view of such a role as economically oriented, to one of image management where the organization attempts to slightly modify its actions to minimize external criticism.  Philanthropy could range from those efforts which are more educational in nature (underscoring what the organization has done), to monetary donations to actual organizational volunteerism and involvement. Similarly, progressivism could involve relatively passive attempts to adapt to a changing environment, or more active and ongoing efforts toward affirmative compliance with public expectations and new public policy initiatives.  As suggested by the range of views underlying what we have termed ethical idealism (see Chapter 3), some subtypes of this interpretation of social responsibility would also be expected.  These subtypes and their relation to the basic types are summarized in Figure 5.2.

In terms of the cases in this chapter, Bank A's policy was defensive in tone, seeking to justify its past performance, and at the same time exclusionary with respect to community partici- pation.  Bank B, by contrast, adopted a more neutral tone, and invited limited participation by outsiders.  As such, the first posture may be referred to as "fundamentalism," and the second as "image management."  Bank C's policy, because of its proactive character and its eagerness to explore the new terms of the social contract, is designated as "affirmative compliance."  The reader is once again referred to Tables 5.1 and 5.2 for the specific features of these approaches, as related to the set of policy variables discussed in Chapter 4.

FIGURE 5.2

Corporate Response Policy Subtypes

| | REFERENCE GROUPS | |
| | Private: Stockholder model | Public: Stakeholder model |
|---|---|---|
| **Instrumentally Rational** | Productivism<br>Cynicism<br>Fundamentalism<br>Image Management | Progressivism<br>Adaptation<br>Affirmative Compliance |
| **Value Rational** | Philanthropy<br>Education<br>Monetary Gifts<br>Volunteerism | Ethical Idealism<br>Legalistic Reform<br>Cooperativism<br>Utopianism |

MOTIVES

CONCLUSION

As a way of illustrating the interpretive process which underlies the formation of organizational responsiveness policy, this chapter examined the responses of three banks to the Community Reinvestment Act (CRA). Using the research framework developed in Chapter 4, we focused on potential variations in the interpretations of the mandate of the CRA. One bank responded with an information-oriented strategy, by publicizing the services being provided to the local community. This approach had virtually no impact on the normal operation of the bank, especially since the information was already available at the institution by request. A second bank developed a similar policy, but went somewhat further and encouraged community feedback. Thus, a dialogue was initiated, and with it the potential for a changed relationship between the institution and its public. In terms of our variables, the first policy was almost entirely internal in character, while the second began to acquire a consultative orientation.

The policy response of a third bank provided a dramatic contrast. Interpreting the directives of the CRA in a much broader fashion, the bank developed an innovative strategy and used its subsidiary corporation to rehabilitate vacant housing stock in the area. Open discussions were held with local residents as the project was being designed. A new position was created within the bank to oversee the housing program, and operational services were expanded to meet the specific needs of the redevelopment effort. In our terms, this progressivist response is systematically distinguished from the productivist stances above.

The analysis indicates that the responsiveness policy conceptualization developed in earlier chapters provides a useful way of differentiating organizational response patterns to social concerns. As suggested by the discussion, however, research in this area should be extended in two directions. First, each of the original types of responsiveness seems to be more properly conceptualized as a range, and there may be significant overlaps or mixed types in actual response patterns. Second, the analysis highlights the importance of going beyond the organizational structure to consider the responses of the firm's relevant publics. The community affected by the redevelopment program, for example, was initially quite skeptical of Bank C's motives and feared a hidden agenda. Only after the housing project was completed did this hesitation and doubt turn into acceptance. Especially considering the different philosophies of social responsibility discussed in Chapter 3, difficulties can arise when different groups hold different perceptions and expectations concerning what constitutes "responsive" performance. While corporate actions may be justified on the basis of internal assessments and discussions, the ultimate validation of those actions depends on the assessments and interpretations of external groups. Chapter 6 turns to an exploration of these issues, and the related processes of conflict and its resolution.

## NOTES

1. Robert Ackerman, "How Companies Respond to Social Demands," Harvard Business Review 51 (July-August 1973): 88-98; Robert Ackerman and Raymond Bauer, Corporate Responsiveness: The Modern Dilemma (Reston, Va.: Reston Publishing, 1976); and E. Murray, "The Social Response Process in Commercial Banks: An Empirical Investigation," Academy of Management Review 1 (January 1976):5-15.

2. See Herbert Blumer, Symbolic Interactionism: Perspective and Method (New York: Free Press, 1969).

3. Robert MacIver, Social Causation (New York: Ginn and Co., 1942).

4. The following discussion of the development of the Community Reinvestment Act is drawn in part from Warren L. Dennis, "The Community Reinvestment Act of 1977: Defining 'Convenience and Needs of the Community'," Banking Law Journal 95 (1978):693-717; Carol Greenwald, Banks Are Dangerous to Your Wealth (Englewood Cliffs: Prentice-Hall, 1980); and Nathan Weber, Banks, Neighborhoods and the Community Reinvestment Act (New York: The Conference Board, 1981).

5. See Richard E. Ratcliff, Mary Elizabeth Gallagher, and Kathryn Strother Ratcliff, "The Civic Involvement of Bankers: An Analysis of the Influence of Economic Power and Social Prominence in the Command of Civic Policy Positions," Social Problems 26 (February 1979):298-313; Richard E. Ratcliff, "Banks and the Command of Capital Flows: An Analysis of Capitalist Class Structure and Mortgage Disinvestment in a Metropolitan Area," in Classes, Class Conflict and the State, ed. Maurice Zeitlin (Cambridge, Mass.: Winthrop Publishers, 1979).

6. Hearings before the Committee of Banking, Housing and Urban Affairs, United States Senate, 95th Congress, first session on S. 406, March 23-25, 1977, p. 1.

7. Dennis, "Community Reinvestment Act," pp. 694-695, 704-707.

8. Ibid., p. 696.

9. For a fuller discussion on the redlining issue see Donald T. Savage, "CRA and Community Credit Needs," in Bank Management: Concept and Issues, ed. John R. Brick (Richmond, Va.: Robert F. Dame, 1980), pp. 499-501; and Greenwald, Banks Are Dangerous, chap. 5.

10. Greenwald, Banks Are Dangerous, pp. 149-150.

11. Department of Banking, "Home Mortgage Lending Patterns in Metropolitan Boston," 1977, reported in ibid., pp. 150-151.

12. Ibid., pp. 153-154.

13. Ibid., pp. 155-156.

14. See Weber, Banks, Neighborhoods, and the CRA, pp. 4-5.

15. Ackerman and Bauer, Corporate Responsiveness, p. 37.

16. Savage, "CRA and Community," pp. 501-503.

17. See ABA Banking Journal, "Action, Not Reaction, Will Defuse CRA," ABA Banking Journal 71 (October 1979): 126.

18. Weber, Banks, Neighborhoods, and the CRA, p. 4.

19. See Banking, "New CRA Regs Go Into Effect Nov. 6," Banking: Journal of the American Banker's Association 70 (November 1978):74; G. E. Bozcar, "What to Expect When the Bank Examiners Come—And Turn Their Attention to Your CRA Record," ABA Banking Journal 71 (April 1979):35-40, 104; and J. Brown, "Will the New Law Rub Out Bank Redlining?" Business and Society Review (Fall 1978):38-43.

20. Ackerman and Bauer, Corporate Responsiveness, pp. 38-39.

21. ABA Banking Journal, "BHC Steps Up Its Role in Inner-City Renewal," ABA.

22. ABA Banking Journal, "Action, Not Reaction," p. 126.

23. C. A. Bruning, C.A. (1979) "In Difficult Times, How Does a Community Banker Meet All His Responsibilities?" ABA Banking Journal 71 (February 1979):22-29, 93-94.

24. J. W. Collins and C. G. Ganotis, "Is Corporate Responsibility Sabotaged by the Rank and File?" Business and Society Review (Autumn 1973):82-88.

25. For a discussion of the importance of employee perceptions, especially in service-oriented individuals see B. Schneider, "The Service Organization: Climate Is Crucial," Organizational Dynamics (Spring 1980):52-65; and B. Schneider, "Employee

and Customer Perceptions of Service in Banks," <u>Administrative Science Quarterly</u> 25 (1980): 252-267.

26. For a full discussion concerning the survey and its implementation see James L. Bowditch and Anthony F. Buono, <u>Quality of Work Life Assessment: A Survey-Based Approach</u> (Boston: Auburn House, 1982).

27. Anthony F. Buono, James L. Bowditch, and John W. Lewis, "When Cultures Collide: The Anatomy of a Merger," <u>Human Relations</u> 38 (1985): in press.

# 6

# THE DYNAMICS
# OF SOCIAL POLICY II:
# CONFRONTATION AND CONFLICT

Corporate social responsiveness can perhaps best be characterized as an interpretive process which involves a continuous (implicit or explicit) appeal to certain standards of behavior. To be truly "responsive," socially oriented policies must somehow be considered right or just in terms of a perceived fit between specific corporate actions and appropriate standards of judgment. Within this context, attention has most often centered on organizational policy development, and on processes of organizational learning and institutional commitment which lead to justification of plans of action within policy-making units.[1] This orientation was the focus of Chapter 5.

As pointed out in earlier chapters, however, social responsiveness may be variously defined by a number of interested parties. Research has indicated that behavior perceived as responsive by an organization's management may be viewed quite differently by industry regulators.[2] Other studies have pointed to even wider discrepancies between the perspectives of organizations and those of critical constituencies such as local civic associations and public-interest advocacy groups.[3] The practical result of such interpretive disparities has been a significant amount of conflict, complicated and reinforced by attitudes of mutual suspicion. Business organizations sometimes feel that outsiders do not appreciate the problems they face in competitive markets, while external groups that are affected by corporate policy often conclude that organizational commitments to social concerns are merely exercises in public-relations rhetoric.

The banking industry offers an appropriate context for the investigation of these issues, especially in the wake of economic deregulation, interstate banking initiatives, and the advent of electronic funds transfer operations. Existing studies have demonstrated significant variations in both interpretation and performance of social responsiveness among different banks. Some observers have contended that the industry has steadily incorporated more of the demands of its relevant publics,[4] but others have documented important differences in the policy areas of hiring and treatment of women and racial minorities, loans for low-income housing, commercial lending to minority business, and responses to the Community Reinvestment Act.[5] These discrepancies highlight the need to examine the dynamics of external legitimation, or validation, of organizational policies.

The Community Reinvestment Act (CRA) provides a wealth of material for the study of conflict over responsiveness policies. Over the past several years, dozens of formal challenges have resulted from the passage of the CRA. As indicated in Chapter 5, as part of the regulatory process underlying this act community groups may challenge bank attempts to open or close branches, merge with or acquire other banking institutions, all on the basis of insufficient CRA activity. While many of these challenges have simply led to the expression of pent-up emotion, others have resulted in improved communication between banks and their surrounding communities. The resultant dialogue has created many instances of "affirmative lending agreements" which have increased the resources available to local communities.[6] A small percentage of these challenges, however, have had significant repercussions for large financial institutions, blocking their efforts at branching, merger, or acquisition. In the process, an array of grassroots networks have been formed, such as the Missouri Coalition for Lending, the Buckeye-Woodland Community Congress, the Neighborhood Revitalization Project in Washington, D.C., and the Angry Citizens of East Twenty-Third Street Urban Renewal Area in Kansas City.[7] The disputes between these groups and surrounding large thrift institutions have made a significant mark on contemporary banking. Moreover, it has been suggested that as the recent trend toward bank mergers continues to escalate, the use of the CRA by such groups could have a major impact on the approval process.[8]


CONFLICT OVER REINVESTMENT:
THREE CASES

As the different interpretations of and policy initiatives for the CRA discussed in Chapter 5 readily suggest, there is a high potential for divergent perceptions and conflict in the evaluation of corporate policy. To further explore this issue, the present chapter focuses on cases of conflict (1979-1981) concerning the CRA-related performance of three Boston-area banks. These disputes provide a useful sequel to the analysis in Chapter 5 and contain much relevant data for the development of our conceptual approach. Information concerning these disputes was gathered through interviews with some of the participants representing the various sides and examination of documentary evidence available through the Massachusetts Banking Commission.

### Case D

The first confrontation, which extended over a period of approximately two years, was initiated by the application of the largest savings bank in Massachusetts to open a branch in an affluent suburb. Although the area in question already had several thrift institutions, the applicant argued that a new bank was justified on the basis of recent growth trends in deposits. Moreover, the institution pointed out that the new branch would not be limited to the existing market, because it planned to offer a variety of services not presently available in the area. In the wake of the CRA, which had been passed the year before, local individuals and groups could express their opinions on the application during a public comments period. Most of these inputs were negative. After evaluating the relevant materials, Carol Greenwald, the commissioner of banks, denied the institution's application.

In a public memorandum, the commissioner set out the primary considerations underlying the negative verdict. The bank, she argued, seemed to consider deposit growth much more important than affirmative lending in its community. The bank's ratio of loans to assets was quite low, compared with other area banks, while its ratio of securities was comparatively high. When the bank did make mortgages available in low- and moderate-income areas, moreover, it generally did so only within federally guaranteed programs. The institution did not participate in the state-guaranteed student loan program. Finally, members of the neighborhoods served by the bank were not represented on its board of trustees. [9]

The bank rebutted the commissioner's statement, arguing that it was inaccurate and even arbitrary in nature. To begin with, why should the institution's pursuit of deposit growth be grounds for criticism? The policy was simply good business practice, since

> Our overall objective, as molded by our charter,
> our by-laws, and the banking laws and regulations,
> both state and federal, is to provide a sound and
> secure depository for the funds which are entrusted
> to us in a fiduciary capacity and to provide a reason-
> able return to the depositors. Deposit growth can
> be just as important to our ability to meet our fidu-
> ciary responsibilities as providing loans to our
> community.[10]

In addition, the bank asserted, its mortgage lending had been
significantly on the increase. Participation in governmentally
guaranteed programs, far from being reprehensible, was deserv-
ing of praise, since these programs were very beneficial. In
sum, the institution's management remained adamant:

> We believe the Commissioner is wrong to have used
> this opportunity to express opinions which are
> slanted, full of conclusions which have no mean-
> ing when drawn from raw statistics while ignoring
> some of the reasons behind the figures, and which
> question the ability of those people designated by
> statutes and by law to maintain the safety and
> soundness of the Bank.[11]

Between the lines were hints that the bank regarded the commissioner as an extreme consumerist and a bit of a crusader.

Within the year, with the election of a new governor, a
new commissioner had been appointed who was generally considered to be much more favorable to business. The bank
reapplied for permission to open its suburban branch, and
made a serious effort to dispose of the CRA-related objections.
In materials presented to support the request, the institution
cited community outreach activities and sensitivity to community
concerns. Outreach efforts had included meetings with political
leaders in the suburban town, as well as the local chamber of
commerce, the community's land use committee, a neighborhood
association and a local church.[12]

A second phase of controversy now began, with the opposition spearheaded by a local community advocacy group, the
Massachusetts Urban Reinvestment Advisory Group (MURAG).
This group identified itself as "a non-profit public interest
organization promoting community reinvestment partnerships
between financial institutions, local government, and community-
based organizations."[13] While MURAG is characteristic of the

various community-based organizations prompted by the passage of the CRA, it has been called "far and away the most sophisticated local group working with the CRA."[14]

MURAG's brief against the application reviewed the major points of the previous commissioner's memorandum and argued that the indictments remained valid. One comment in particular captures the intensity and flavor of MURAG's challenge:

> The Board of Trustees seems to be more representa-
> tive of the Myopia Hunt Club than that of a mutual
> institution. Of the 38 trustees, 4 live in Dover, 3
> live in Hamilton, 4 in Beacon Hill, 2 in Brookline,
> 2 in Manchester, 2 in Beverly Farms, 2 in Newton
> and 2 in Lincoln.* None of the trustees live in the
> neighborhoods where the branches are located . . .
> [Emphasis added].[15]

Gerald Mulligan, the new commissioner of banks, reaffirmed the verdict of his predecessor, concluding that the proposed branch would not promote public convenience and advantage. The CRA-based challenges of the critics were pronounced valid. In addition, however, Mulligan found that the application should be denied even on narrower business grounds, for, strangely enough, there was a "pattern of disinvestment in Boston neighborhoods after the establishment of a branch office" by this bank (emphasis added).[16] The bank, it turned out, had applied for permission to open five local branches over the past few years, and four of these requests had been granted. In each instance, both commercial and mortgage lending to the bank's customers had subsequently decreased. Consequently, the commissioner, while holding out some hope of favorable action in the event of changed bank policies, felt compelled to join the nearly unanimous chorus of criticism.

### Case E

The second conflict actually refers to two related disputes which occurred over a period of approximately one year. In an effort to sharpen the issues and to develop topics that might be passed over if only one dispute were covered, selected

---

*Each of these communities represents quite well-to-do neighborhoods and suburbs in the Boston area, and a town in New Hampshire, just over the state line.

details of these confrontations are combined and compressed.
In each controversy, a large bank holding company's plans for
expansion were opposed by MURAG. The setting for the exchange was Massachusetts's three-member Board of Bank
Incorporation, which included the commissioner of revenue and
the treasurer in addition to the commissioner of banks.

In the summer of 1980, the bank holding company, the
largest banking organization in the state, applied to the Board
for permission to acquire a small bank in western Massachusetts.
This action, the company alleged, would benefit the bank to
be acquired because it had found itself in a very disadvantageous
position. All other commercial lenders in its town were affiliated
with bank holding companies, permitting them to draw on greater
resources and to provide services which it could not match. As
a result, the bank was experiencing little growth in deposits
and found itself in an uncomfortable defensive posture.[17] As
the sixteenth-largest banking organization in the United States,
which already had nine subsidiaries in the state, the holding
company argued that it was in a position to resolve these difficulties.

In response to the application, MURAG executed a legal
maneuver: it requested "permission to intervene in this action
so that we may become an original party to the proceedings."
If successful, this tactic would improve the advocacy group's
status within the context of the dispute, permitting it to
"present testimonial evidence, cross-examine witnesses, submit
rebuttal evidence, and have access to crucial data not presently
available to us, in order to present a comprehensive protest."[18]
Citing a variety of laws and cases, MURAG argued that its
interests were directly affected by the case, and that it would
be damaged if its petition were denied.

The Board of Bank Incorporation, however, turned down
the request, concluding that MURAG was not "substantially
and specifically affected," despite the fact that one of its
members did live in the relevant town. The organization would
still be allowed to participate in hearings on the acquisition,
but not in the central role that it desired.[19] Several months
later, the request for acquisition was approved.

A second application by the bank holding company closely
resembled the first. Three other commercial banks in another
small town of interest enjoyed the advantage of affiliation with
large financial institutions, while four other thrift institutions
in the area were larger in terms of amount of deposits. Acquisition by the holding company would allow the local bank in
question to offer a variety of new services, including IRA

accounts, 90 percent residential mortgages, and international transactions, and, as a result become a more stable and more competitive bank.

Once again, MURAG renewed its challenge, thereby creating a series of unprecedented difficulties for the Board of Bank Incorporation. The bank holding company operated under a federal or national charter, and this circumstance placed its CRA activity beyond the jurisdiction of the state regulators. At the same time, however, the Massachusetts Board was committed to giving CRA performance the most serious consideration, having adopted the federal CRA as a component of its own operation. Pursuant to this commitment, the Board requested permission from the appropriate federal agency, the Comptroller of the Currency, to conduct an on-site investigation of the community reinvestment performance of the organization. This request was refused, and the Board found itself in the frustrating and embarrassing position of being unable to comply with its own policy directives.

Under the pressure of its own commitment, the Board devised an indirect assessment procedure: it would focus on the four state-chartered subsidiaries of the holding company, since these were required to submit the necessary information. As a result,

> All four were found to have satisfactory records of performance. Three of the four institutions . . . have become very active in the home mortgage market over the past eighteen months, primarily due to a substantial downstreaming of funds from the affiliated [bank]. Thus, the local communities served by the state-chartered subsidiaries have benefited from funds invested by [the bank]. These institutions have also initiated outreach programs to real estate brokers and community development organizations over this same period.[20]

On this basis, the Board approved the acquisition request.

There were, however, some lingering questions and doubts, which the Board acknowledged in a reference to the "large number of individuals and groups testifying in opposition to (the bank's) acquisitions at the Board's hearings and the serious nature of their allegations."[21] It was the contention of MURAG, for example, that the bank holding company

> has been acutely negligent in meeting its obligations pursuant to the CRA and that its lack of

concern is indicative of its banking policies to ignore
the CRA community in favor of high yield, short
term investment outside of Massachusetts. MURAG
further asserts that even the small amount of local
investment has been directed at the high income
neighborhoods and that this investment policy
retards the revitalization of urban areas.[22]

The credibility of these charges was enhanced by a mandate
from the Federal Reserve Board to the bank holding company,
which called for greater efforts to meet with community groups.
Consequently, the Board of Bank Incorporation was left with
a troublesome unanswered question: Could a large financial
institution shirk its own CRA responsibilities by the device of
acquiring responsible subsidiaries? Could it meet the letter
of the law while eluding its spirit?

A further policy issue arose in this case. Unlike other
opponents of MURAG, the bank holding company refused to
submit a CRA statement, thus reducing the size of the potential
target. Because of the federal chartering provisions already
mentioned, MURAG could not obtain data on mortgage and
small-business lending. The nonsubmission rankled MURAG
and resulted in some harsh language in the community organization's challenge. In the end, however, the bank had successfully implemented its strategy of avoidance. Despite being
challenged, it had not permitted the community advocacy group
to do battle on its favorite terms and most familiar turf. In
this instance, silence had proven to be golden.

## Case F

The final controversy which will be considered arose from
a merger application that was submitted by a Boston savings
bank, the third largest thrift institution in Massachusetts. Its
prospective partner was another savings bank located in a small
city next to Boston, which operated a main office and four
branches. This latter institution had recently depleted its
capital resources through participation in a local commercial
development, and was therefore attracted to the strong capital
and management of the larger bank. If allowed to merge, the
banks argued that prospective benefits to customers would
include such expanded services as FHA and VA mortgage loans,
food stamps, commercial loans, and group insurance plans.

As part of the application, both banks produced statements
of their community reinvestment activity in which two points
were emphasized: 1) active involvement in their local communities,

and 2) sensitivity to the credit needs of low- and moderate-income persons. The larger institution also pointed to its record as the leading mortgage lender on residential properties in Boston, and the highest lender to students of all savings banks in the state. Further evidence of its commitment was to be found in its internal Community Reinvestment Act Committee, which would be expanded to include representatives of its merger partner. In sum, the responsible community-oriented activity of the past would be increased "in the resulting institution through the expansion of our real estate broker visitation program, frequent use of broker bulletins, participation and sponsorship of housing workshops and seminars, expansion of the student loan call program and other similar involvement."23

The merger application elicited a fierce response from MURAG, which regarded the larger bank as the "worst redliner in Boston" with a long history of ignoring the credit needs of low- and moderate-income persons. In a very substantial brief, the community advocacy group put forward a series of serious accusations, including "a total unwillingness to meet the legitimate credit needs of its local community"; token lending in city neighborhoods; the limitation of inner-city lending to affluent projects (gentrification); failure to work with community-based groups to develop cooperative or low cost housing; disproportionately high mortgage lending in suburban towns (79 percent); and the virtual redlining or exclusion of several specific neighborhoods in Boston.24

In rebuttal, the accused institution submitted a supplement to its CRA statement, which focused on its activities over the past year and a half. This document detailed a field representatives program to identify credit needs via meetings with realtors, a professionally compiled credit needs survey, a program of meetings between bank personnel and real estate brokers (in addition to the field representative program), and two loan centers in low-income neighborhoods. Other special CRA-related services included: distribution of booklets on purchasing a home; local financial planning sessions and home buying workshops; and participation in the Urban Edge Vacant Housing Program, the Boston Urban Mortgage Review Board, and the efforts on behalf of lower income persons of the Massachusetts Home Mortgage Finance Agency. Statistics on this last program showed a commitment of some $2.6 million including 15 loans for housing rehabilitation, and 20 for neighborhood preservation areas.25

Confronted with two masses of conflicting data and interpretations, the commissioner of banks (Mulligan) sided with the savings institutions while expressing partial agreement with the MURAG protesters.  On the basis of a detailed investigation by the Division of Banks, Mulligan concluded that the CRA record of the larger savings bank was generally satisfactory, though there was room for improvement.  In particular, the bank was vindicated on the issues of total lending, lending in Boston, lending in low- and moderate-income areas, and redlining.

The commissioner's reservations centered on the outreach activities of the institution.  While praising the bank for some of its community development activities, he expressed the opinion that much more could be done in view of opportunities existing in Boston.  The common good would be served if the institution would be more aggressive and more systematic in its outreach.  In sum, "The Division believes that [Bank F] could take a leadership role in community development and thereby improve its community reinvestment performance and image in Boston."[26]

The decision was noteworthy also for the effort by the commissioner to reduce the conflict between MURAG and the savings institution.  Consideration of the longstanding hostility between the opponents prompted Mulligan to comment that

> the Division finds troublesome the degree of animosity existing between [Bank F] and the Protestant.
> The animosity appears deeply rooted and, significantly, shared by both parties.  It is characterized by the reluctance of [Bank F] to acknowledge the potential contributions of the Protestant in identifying community credit needs, and by the reluctance of the Protestant to acknowledge the legitimate accomplishments of [Bank F].[27]

So long as this situation persisted, he concluded, everyone would suffer.

## CASE ANALYSIS AND INTERPRETATION

These cases resulted from divergent perceptions concerning responsibility and performance, the most important of which are summarized in Table 6.1.  The extreme polarity in views displayed there points to some of the difficulties confronted when socially oriented policies and practices are assessed from different perspectives.

Under the CRA, when such divergence occurs, the groups involved are provided with a framework for programmatic, as opposed to rhetorical, solutions through formal challenge and

TABLE 6.1

Divergent Views of CRA Related Performance

| Bank's Perception | Community Group's Perception | Bank Commission's Perception |
|---|---|---|
| **Bank D** | | |
| Active formulation of affirmative CRA commitment | Lack of affirmative CRA policy | Disapproval of "general operating philosophy" |
| Despite severe deposit outflow, continued mortgage lending throughout community | Lack of significant mortgage lending, especially in low- and moderate-income areas | Refusal of mortgage for 90% of property values leads to hardships in these areas |
| On-going surveys undertaken to assess community credit needs | Lack of any continuous effort to assess community credit needs | Insensitivity to credit needs of community |
| Participant in community development projects | Community development participation deceiving and token at best | Applicant's "apparent isolation from all levels of its community structure" |
| **Bank E** | | |
| Not required to submit data to state agency for subsidiaries under national charter | Failure to include CRA statement reflects bank's insensitivity | No statutory authority to investigate national charter banks |
| Record of state subsidiaries speaks for itself | Bank's overall policy retards revitalization of urban areas | State-chartered subsidiaries' CRA records satisfactory |

| | | |
|---|---|---|
| Wide-ranging investments appropriate to function as nationally chartered commercial banking institution | High-yield, short-term investments outside the state reflect indifference to CRA community | Recent activity in home mortgage lending in community |
| | | Community group raised valid concerns |
| **Bank F** | | |
| History of mortgage lending demonstrates commitment to entire CRA area | Historically worst redliner in city | "Superior mortgage lender of late" |
| Formulation of specific outreach function via marketing, credit informational programs and seminars | Current practices merely disguise continued discriminatory policies | Evidence does not support allegation of discriminatory outreach practices |
| Specific lending in low- and moderate-income neighborhoods leading to genuine rehabilitation | Lending in low- and moderate-income neighborhoods restricted to incoming upper income residents leading to gentrification and displacement of long-time residents | Most lending has occurred in area which complainant has characterized as not undergoing gentrification or displacement |
| | | Dispute reflects continuing ill-will between parties |

confrontation. Since the structure of the CRA essentially
dictates the structure of the challenge (that is, the application-
disputing process), each of the three cases presents a similarity
of charges and a similarity of defenses. Yet, in spite of the
similarity of arguments and perspectives put forth in the hearings, in each situation quite a different decision was reached.
Bank D was censured and denied its request for suburban
expansion; Bank E was criticized for its approach to the CRA
but its request for acquisition was reluctantly approved; and
finally, while the Banking Commissioner's Office shared the
concerns expressed by the community advocacy group in Bank
F's case, it vindicated the institution's performance as superior
to the industry in general and approved its merger application.

At this point, a basic analytic question emerges as to why
such different decisions were reached in spite of the similarities
in challenges and defenses. What is particularly intriguing
about these three cases, therefore, is the process by which
these major banking institutions received these different outcomes.

## Dispute Origins

An understanding of the dynamics of the conflicts begins
with the sociolegal principle that every law creates interpretive
problems. The function of the law is to set down broad and
general guidelines, rather than to provide for all the complications that might arise in practice. The ambiguity of the law
at all levels is perhaps most dramatically shown by the vast
social apparatus that exists to interpret, apply and modify it—
namely, the legal profession and the labyrinthine court system.
Difficulties of interpretation, however, do not, by themselves,
show that a law is poorly written, for they may reflect simply
the problems of formulating adequate principles and the unfore-
seen consequences of changing conditions.

The Community Reinvestment Act (CRA) provides an
excellent illustration of such issues. As suggested by the
discussion in Chapter 5, the CRA underscores the importance
of and the need to consider community interests in bank policy
making. The Act is designed to ensure that the flow of funds
through banks meets the specific needs of low- and moderate-
income neighborhoods for mortgages. Moreover, since it was
felt that stable, livable neighborhoods require credit for activities other than housing purchase, the CRA is intended to
prompt financial institutions to assist in meeting other credit
needs of their surrounding communities as well.[28]

Essentially, the CRA states that a bank has an "affirmative obligation" to meet the "legitimate credit needs" of its "community" as defined by local "convenience and needs." Although the Act emphasizes that these considerations should be met in ways which are consistent with "prudent lending practices," its norms are far from clear. In fact, the key terms—community, legitimate credit needs, and convenience and needs—and the basis for their assessment are not defined with any precision. Instead of embodying a series of standards that regulators and community groups could use to assess and, if warranted, challenge the applications of financial institutions (as well as the subsequent decisions by the regulatory bodies), the CRA contains the far less specific requirements that bank regulators "assess the institution's record" and "take such record into account" when evaluating branching, merger, or acquisition applications. Carol Greenwald, former commissioner of banks in Massachusetts, argues that although more precise standards were initially specified, due to the bill's controversial nature the CRA was "watered down in committee as the price of passage."[29] As a result, the law does not require banks to make specific types of loans nor to allocate credit in fixed ratio to deposits in a given area. Furthermore, it leaves the final evaluation of such performance, which also remains undefined, to the regulators. Thus, even MURAG, the community advocacy group in the above set of cases, has complained that the law is "vague legislation."[30]

Further complicating the situation is the fact that the law was formulated during a period when the banking industry was relatively stable. Due to subsequent deregulatory interventions and the volatile economic climate of the late 1970s and early 1980s, however, the Act was implemented during a time of intense pressure and change for the industry. During 1981, David Elliott, vice president of the Federal Home Loan Bank of Boston, argued that "the central issue to thrifts today is not community investment. It is survivability."[31] Many savings banks, for example, found themselves in a situation where they had to pay 14 to 15 percent in interest for their six-month money market certificates, while approximately 70 percent of their mortgage portfolio was earning less than 10 percent—and would not be entirely off the books for another 15 to 20 years.[32]

Observers of the industry even questioned the impact the law would have on meeting the "convenience" of community members through branching extensions:

The impact of the CRA on the provision of convenient banking services in low- and moderate-income neigh-

borhoods is questionable. On the one hand, the
Act may encourage banks to establish branches in
these areas; on the other hand, the law does not
require banks to maintain unprofitable office locations. Naturally, the CRA does not change the
branching prohibitions which may limit the ability
of banks to provide convenient offices in those
areas which could generate enough business for
a profitable branch but not enough business to
justify the establishment of a de novo bank.[33]

As a result of these pressures and changes, critics argued that
those individuals without sufficient income to repay loans at
higher interest rates—the low- and moderate-income groups
to whom the law was initially addressed—would not benefit
directly from its passage. At the same time, however, the law
made it clear that reinvestment in a bank's community and a
demonstration of commitment to that community was going to
be part of the regulatory decisions concerning branching,
merger, and acquisition activities. The statute, thus, forced
the parties involved to come to terms with rather ambitious and
ambiguous goals and vaguely defined performance standards.
Subsequently, the actual interpretations of a bank's "affirmative
obligation" have ranged from an absence of overt discrimination
to aggressive policies for "greenlining" and active retirement.[34]
    Whatever the shortcomings of its language, and despite
the pressures brought about by changing economic and industry
conditions, the CRA affected all banks and therefore forced
them to act. In effect, it handed down an interpretive mandate
which required that financial institutions make specific interpretive commitments regarding goals and standards of performance. Due to the ambiguities surrounding the law, however,
the accuracy and adequacy of such interpretation would have
to be assessed gradually, through regulatory decisions and
grassroots challenges.
    A critical interpretive commitment in the three cases
summarized above focused on the meaning of the term community.
This concept, though commonly used, has always defied precise
and final definition, as demonstrated in a study which detailed
96 variants of the term.[35] In the three Boston controversies,
the opposing sides disagreed on whether community should be
thought of as "neighborhood" or as "marketing area." The
banks favored the more general and impersonal usage of community as Standard Metropolitan Statistical Area (SMSA), while

MURAG selected the specific neighborhood meaning and discussed the city in terms of 15 identifiable communities specified by the U.S. Bureau of Census. These choices seem to be consistent with the perceived self-interest of the parties, since large banks must think in terms of aggregates and markets, while MURAG is devoted to the cause of bringing banking down to human scale.

The point may be clarified further by a brief sociological comment. Human groups can be ranked according to their degree of organization, from those that are minimal unities to others that are fully organized systems. At the threshold are purely nominal groups, such as all left-handed or red-headed persons. Members of such conceptual units do not know one another, and do not interact on the basis of their shared criteria (with the exception of rare cases like the "red-headed league" solved by Sherlock Holmes). Slightly higher on the scale of organization are temporary groups such as crowds or audiences that have a short-lived sense of shared identity, and interact in limited ways. They have some characteristics of social systems, and constitute part of a semi-organized range. The end point of the continuum is reached with fully organized systems such as families, which are often intimately bound together over many generations, and think, feel, and act as self-conscious units.[36] In our cases, the financial institutions looked at community as a semi-organized group, while MURAG chose to regard it more as an actual or potential family, that is, as a social system with a self-consciousness and history. This distinction, thus, becomes especially significant for validating specific policies since the aggregate interpretation of the banks focuses on several million people, while MURAG focuses on units of several thousand people. As a result, the advocacy group charged that bank practices essentially disguise discriminatory lending through an appearance of widespread mortgage and small business lending, while banks argued that their policies serve their "true" community. Thus, each group made an interpretive commitment to this aspect of the CRA which then became the critical point underlying its evaluation of the legitimacy of specific policies and practices.

Once such contrasting interpretive commitments have been made, the potential for confrontation exists but conflict is not yet inevitable. A further strategic decision must be faced: Are the divergences of perception and interest significant enough to justify disputing? Each of the cases under discussion resulted from an affirmative answer to this question. Other basic options

might also have been exercised, either to tolerate some discrepancies or else to postpone conflict because of practical
difficulties such as limitations of resources available for disputing.

It is important to emphasize here that at present CRA
conflicts arise almost entirely as a result of grassroots initiatives.
In theory, this is not the case, since four major federal regulatory bodies are bound by law to monitor the community reinvestment performance of the institutions. Very rarely, however,
do bank examiners instigate conflict with those they regulate
on CRA grounds. The practical consequence of this situation
has been a clustering of confrontations in urban areas with
particularly skillful activists. Or, putting it in slightly different
form, "Outside cities like Chicago and Cleveland and Philly,
where national coalitions of community groups are very powerful,
you're unlikely to get a lot of complaints that are very sophisticated."[37] Boston, with a skilled and committed community
group, has thus emerged as a center of CRA activity.


Dispute Outcomes

Resolution of disputes can be achieved through three basic
processes: avoidance, informal disputing, and formal disputing.[38]
Avoidance appears to have been the primary mechanism by which
potential confrontations over corporate policy were dealt with
before about 1965. Since that time, social controversies have
often been handled through an informal disputing process which
is highly dependent on the relative power of the groups involved
(for example, the farm-worker-sponsored consumer boycott of
California lettuce and grapes in the early 1970s, the recent
consumer boycott of Nestle's products). In recent years, more
formal disputes have become widespread as a result of the expansion of legal rights (such as "standing to sue" in court,
which many environmental groups have successfully employed),
and the provision of numerous specific formal mechanisms of
redress such as the Board of Bank Incorporation in the above
conflicts.

Because of the availability of the formal disputing mechanism and its selection by the challenging group, the interpretive
commitments made by the Banking Commissioner's Office and the
Board became critical in the resolution of these confrontations.
In the cases outlined, the most important of these interpretive
commitments was the decision to employ professional peer norms
as the central criterion for evaluating the merits of the CRA
challenges and defenses. This decision was reflected in each
of the three cases as the following statements explicitly show.

(1) In its denial of Bank D's request for a suburban branch, the Board of Bank Incorporation argued:

> In any mortgage lending comparison using publicly available mortgage disclosure data for the four largest Boston based savings banks, Applicant is found wanting.  In a peer group comparison [emphasis added] of one to four family conventional mortgage loans in the BSMSA as a percentage of total assets, Applicant ranks last of its three peers.[39]

(2) In validating Bank F's policy, the Board again emphasized performance relative to the institution's peers:

> . . . if standards applied by the [community group] to [Bank F] are applied to other large savings banks in Boston including those never challenged by [community group], [Bank F] appears to be a superior lender of late.[40]

For purposes of these evaluations, the Banking Commission thus operationalized its notion of peer norm as "the four largest savings banks in the Boston area."
(3) This norm was also employed in the case of Bank E, even though federal and state subsidiaries were involved.  Although the Board had no jurisdiction over the federally chartered subsidiaries, it argued that with respect to Bank E's state subsidiaries,

> . . . in a relatively short period of time [Bank E] achieved a level of mortgage lending commensurate with that of the three major thrift institutions in the city. . . . In light of the above, the Board finds that the state-chartered subsidiaries are performing satisfactorily with respect to the Board's standards for active community reinvestment.[41]

Although the Board felt that due to the size of both Bank E and Bank F they could take on a greater "leadership role" in community development and be more "aggressive and systematic" in their outreach efforts, their records were "satisfactory and consistent with the approval" of merger and acquisition applications.  Thus, as part of its formal interpretation of the meaning of responsiveness, the Board relied quite heavily on relative responsiveness as compared to similar banking institutions.

Structured Ambivalence

While the peer norm was, thus, the Board's key interpretive
commitment and does help us understand the varying outcomes
of the cases, other interpretive decisions exhibited an inconsistency which complicates our analysis. Most importantly, in
its written decisions the Board adopted at different times the
two opposed definitions of community discussed earlier. In
the cases of Banks E and F it agreed with the institutions and
accepted SMSA; in the case of Bank D, however, the Board
accepted the definition of "community as neighborhood" put
forth by the challenging advocacy group. Such apparent
inconsistency raises the question of what other factors influenced these critical choices.

We believe that the apparent inconsistency in the interpretations of the Board of Bank Incorporation is best understood
in terms of a basic dualism in the role or function of the Board.
It appears that the Board operates under a double mandate:
to preserve a healthy financial climate in the banking industry,
and to act as advocate for the general public. To put it another
way, the Board is required to serve the interests of two groups
whose interests may not coincide in particular cases. In sociological terms, there is an ambivalence of function which is built
into the everyday workings of the Board.[42] This dualism has
been reflected in discussions about alternative types of behavior
regulatory agencies engage in when interpreting public policy:
a buffer role (in which the regulator defends organizations
against direct and immediate public pressure for change) and
a change agent role (in which the leadership of the regulatory
agency is committed to forcing changes in industry practices).[43]

To understand how this is manifested in practice, it is
necessary to take the analysis one step further. Thus far,
the discussion has focused primarily on the cultural (public
policy) and social (organizational policy) levels of analysis.
Decisions made at these levels, however, create important
correlates at the psychological/attitudinal level. Historically,
private-interest-generated legislation developed strong social-
emotional bonds between regulatory commissions and the industries they governed. With the advent of public-interest-generated
legislation, however, regulators were forced to broaden their
perspectives and to extend their loyalties to outside interest
groups.[44] The double mandate of such laws thus creates
attitudinal difficulties for groups like the Massachusetts Board
of Bank Incorporation which are not experienced by other
parties to the disputes we have been considering. The community

advocacy group (MURAG), with its distinctive culture of an ethical idealist, redistribution ideology, has developed a critical and sometimes adversarial posture toward the banking industry. The banks, committed as they are to a free-enterprise type of ideology, understandably view their social policies in much more favorable terms.

It is important, however, not to overstate MURAG's tendency to take an adversarial posture toward the banking industry. Although there has generally been a divergence of perceptions concerning responsive performance between banking institutions and the community advocacy group, perceptual convergence has also occurred. When Bank C (discussed in Chapter 5) applied for a merger with another savings institution, MURAG supported the application, primarily due to the bank's progressivist policies and performance. Analytically, MURAG has elements of both ethical idealism and progressivism in its interpretation of the CRA. Its main desire is oriented to redistribute capital allocations and to rekindle a spirit of community. MURAG's executive director, for example, has argued that "It is important to steer [bank] reinvestment to make sure that it doesn't all go to gentrified neighborhoods. The challenge is, how much of it can we control and retain for the people already living in a [low- and moderate-income] neighborhood."[45] In interviews, however, MURAG personnel admitted that they are ultimately guided by "what is possible," which reflects a realization of some of the limitations of such idealist sentiments and, at least, an implicit acceptance of progressivism on the part of banks. Thus, despite the community advocacy group's ethical idealist interpretation of the meaning of responsiveness, in practice it appears willing to accept (at least for the present time) progressivist policies. It is quite ready to challenge those policies, however, that remain productivist or minimally philanthropic in nature.

With respect to the cases outlined in this chapter, it appears that in formulating its attitude toward the specific challenges and defenses, the Commissioner's Office and the Board of Bank Incorporation sought a pragmatic blending of the elements of the competing orientations—attempting to serve the public interest (change agent role) while tending to give the benefit of the doubt to the banking industry (buffer role). The effort to create such a pragmatic blend is reflected in the Board's interpretive commitments. In the case of Bank D, the Board's loyalty to the general public apparently prevailed, though its loyalty to the industry (peer norm) was also evident in its censure of Bank D's performance. In the cases of Banks E and F, by contrast, the Board's loyalty to the industry appears to be paramount. Faced with situations where smaller banks were in some financial danger, the Board approved two "rescue operations" despite some reservations about the CRA-related policies and performance of the two larger (E and F) banks.

We gain perhaps some further insight by noting a correlation between interpretive commitments and type of application: Loyalty to the public seems to have been decisive in a branching decision which would have affected a well defined neighborhood, while loyalty to the industry seems to have won out in merger and acquisition decisions affecting larger, and in a sense, more impersonal, markets. While this relationship may oversimplify matters, it does help us to understand how structured ambivalence forces the Board into a constant problem of weighting its competing duties and loyalties while shifting between buffer and change agent roles.

## TOWARD A MODEL OF POLICY DISPUTES

The above discussion provides us with some basic features of a rough model of policy disputing, which is illustrated in Figure 6.1 and will be briefly elaborated in this section. The starting point, as illustrated by the preceding cases, was located in certain problematic choices that were dictated by the passage of the Community Reinvestment Act. Such precipitating factors in policy formulation may be usefully summarized under the heading of a dynamic normative environment. This concept refers to change at the cultural level, that is, the changes in the ideas or beliefs, values, and norms or standards of a group, as well as in the specific behaviors and materials which embody them.[46] In the context of the present research, this would specifically denote the concept of banks as quasi-public institutions; the notion of community; the belief in the ability of the private sector to address large social problems; the norm of affirmative obligation; and the norm of the convenience and needs of local communities as codified by the CRA. Other examples might be found in the environmental legislation or affirmative action laws of the past decade.

The dynamic normative environment leads, in cases such as those we have followed, to a series of related actions and reactions which occur in the dynamic institutional environment. This concept refers to changes that take place at the specifically social level, such as the array of changes in contemporary banking from the expansion of financial services and the growing

FIGURE 6.1

Assessment and Validation of Corporate Social Policy: A Process Model

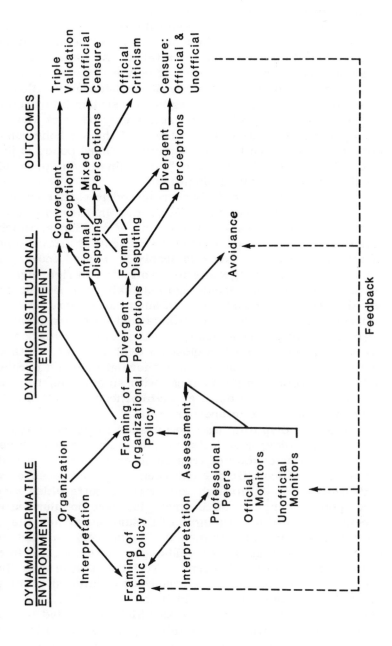

popularity of mergers and acquisitions, to the effect of regulations like the CRA and the emergence of community advocacy groups specializing in banking issues. As indicated by the preceding cases, business organizations interpret the emergent guidelines as they affect their activity, and begin to frame policies based on such understandings. As illustrated in the preceding chapter, the courses of action that may arise from such understandings can vary quite considerably. Meanwhile, other affected groups are engaged in a similar interpretive process. When a specific corporate policy becomes known to such groups, they assess it in terms of the symbolic constructions that they have been developing. Where policy is judged to be "incorrect," "inadequate," or "unjust," the preconditions for disputing have taken shape.

At this point, the decision referred to earlier arises, namely, whether or not to dispute, and whether to pursue formal or informal means. The option of avoidance, which is often overlooked, raises particular difficulties from the point of view of research. There is simply no way of knowing how often individuals and groups feel motivated to fight against corporate policy, but decide against taking the risk or expending the necessary resources. In such cases there are several courses of action. The perceptions that create frustration may be blocked out psychologically, or the conflict situation itself avoided, as when a person closes a bank account, quits a job, or moves. On the corporate side there are certain parallels: A firm may refuse to do business with an antagonist or relocate, as when a bank shuts down a neighborhood branch or a business moves its operations to another state.

Informal disputing may be pursued in myriad ways. One can write an anonymous letter, make an anonymous phone call, or mobilize a delegation of frustrated consumers for a visit to a manager's office. Or one can seek to apply pressure in more organized ways, as through consumer boycotts which seek to force policy changes. Such strategies were popularized in recent years by the campaigns of Cesar Chavez and the United Farm Workers against supermarket chains carrying certain products, as well as by the challenges to Nestle, and to corporations investing in South Africa. To label such efforts "informal" means that they occur without clearcut ground rules for the resolution of the conflicts, and that they tend to be both fluid and short-lived. CRA challenges which are settled by negotiations leading to affirmative lending agreements fall into this category. An appropriate comparison can be drawn with out-of-court agreements arranged by lawyers, with details typically kept confidential.

Formal disputing occurs within public contexts under relatively clearcut rules of procedure. The best known example is undoubtedly that of trials in the courts, where complex procedural codes define the offenses, rules of evidence, and criteria underlying verdicts (such as guilt beyond a reasonable doubt). The cases considered in this chapter belong in this class. As we have noted, the structure of the CRA dictated the structure of the challenge: There were requirements for notification of proposed mergers, acquisitions, or branches; a period was set aside for public comment; and, finally, a written decision had to be published, setting out the specific reasons for approval or disapproval of the requests from the financial institutions. The sequence of proceedings was thus regular and somewhat ritualized.

Upon the completion of some phase of formal or informal disputing, the perceptions of the participants may converge or diverge or be mixed. Citizen groups may realize that they have been mistaken about a bank's policies and performance, or a bank may realize that it needs to change its policies, extend extra credit to a particular area, and so forth. If the relevant regulatory bodies also concur, we may speak of a "triple validation" of some course of action. Where regulators and one of the disputants only agree, the result is mixed. This occurs also when a regulatory agency accepts portions of both competing views, as in Case D. These various outcomes may be followed by further phases of policy development and assessment, and new cycles of disputing, as part of an open-ended dynamic process.

## CONCLUSION

While Chapter 5 illustrated how definitions of responsive performance are established in different organizational settings, this chapter analyzed how such definitions are subsequently interpreted and redefined by the different groups involved. As the analysis in both chapters suggests, for a complete understanding of corporate responsiveness, questions must be posed with respect to corporate behaviors themselves and to the framework of public policy that provides the initial criteria for assessing social performance.[47] Thus, it is necessary to conduct analyses of both the dynamic normative (cultural) and dynamic institutional (social) environments. These two levels of analysis are respectively reflected by the sociological concepts of <u>role making</u> (that is, the establishment of the "initial rules of the game" which sets the foundation for organizational decision making) and role taking (or assessing what the new rules will actually mean in practice). In the present discussion, this refers to the development and passage of the CRA in 1977 (role making), and the specific policies formulated by the individual banks, by community groups in the emergent role of "bank examiner," and by the Banking Commissioner's Office and the Board of Bank Incorporation (role taking).

It is important to emphasize that these two environments— the dynamic normative and the dynamic institutional—continually interact with each other, leading to a reinterpretation of the situation of responsiveness and eventual clarification of what actually constitutes acceptable performance. Since this is an ongoing process however, the outcomes are necessarily tentative. In the case of Bank D, for example, having been denied its application for a suburban branch extension under one commissioner (the Greenwald administration), it reapplied under a new administration. While the denial prompted the bank to make some changes in its CRA statement and branch proposal, the second commissioner (the Mulligan administration) upheld the initial decision arguing that the bank had still not translated its intentions into concrete policies and performance.

The open-endedness of this process is even more strikingly manifested by the response of the community advocacy group in the decision in case F. As noted earlier, there was long-standing animosity between the disputing parties which led to MURAG's unwillingness to accept the commissioner's decision (merger approval), especially its criterion of performance based on peer norms. MURAG appeared to feel that since the CRA, in effect, imposed new norms on the industry the continued use of peer norms and relative responsiveness as a way of legitimatizing bank policy would tend to justify the status quo rather than bring about the type of change advocated by the legislation. Thus, despite the decision made by the Board, MURAG's divergent perception concerning the use of peer norms led to its decision to enter a new phase of disputing. The community group, again selecting a formal adjudicatory mechanism, subsequently took its challenge to the Federal Deposit Insurance Corporation.[48]

Such open-endedness in the assessment of corporate social performance thus reflects the inevitability of some conflict and confrontation in the external legitimation or validation of organizational policy. This chapter has attempted to show how such disputes emerge and the processes they undergo toward accommodation. Since resolution or consensus is highly problematic at best in a pluralistic society such as ours, the type of dynamic framework presented in this chapter is necessary to appreciate the complexity of corporate social performance.

NOTES

1. See, for example, Robert Ackerman, "How Companies Respond to Social Demands," Harvard Business Review 51 (July-August 1973):88-98; Robert Ackerman, The Social Challenge to Business (Cambridge: Harvard University Press, 1975); and Michael J. Merenda, "The Process of Corporate Social Involvement: Five Case Studies," in Research in Corporate Social Performance and Policy, Vol. 3, ed. Lee E. Preston (Greenwich, Conn.: JAI Press, 1981), pp. 17-42.

2. P. Posey and A. Bhambri, "Corporate Social Performance: Assessments in a Regulated Industry," paper presented at the 42nd Annual Meeting of the Academy of Management, New York City, August 16, 1982; and James E. Post and John Mahon, "Articulated Turbulence: The Effect of Regulatory Agencies on Corporate Response to Social Change," Academy of Management Review 5 (July 1980):399-407.

3. Jeffrey Sonnenfeld, Corporate Views of the Public Interest (Boston: Auburn House, 1981). See also Robert Ford and Frank McLaughlin, "Perceptions of Socially Responsible Activities and Attitudes: A Comparison of Business School Deans and Corporate Chief Executives," Academy of Management Journal 27 (September 1984):666-674.

4. G. Haugue, "Some Comments on the Social Responsibility of Banking," in The Changing World of Banking, ed. H. V. Prochnow and H. V. Prochnow, Jr. (New York: Harper & Row, 1974).

5. See Council on Economic Priorities, Short-Changed: Minorities and Women in Banking (New York: Council on Economic Priorities, 1972); A. J. Thiebolt, The Negro in the Banking Industry (Philadelphia: University of Pennsylvania Press, 1970); E. Murray, "The Social Response Process in Commercial Banks: An Empirical Investigation," Academy of Management Review 1 (January 1976):5-15; and Banwari L. Kedia and Edwin C. Kuntz, "The Context of Social Performance: An Empirical Study of Texas Banks," in Research in Corporate Social Performance and Policy, Vol. 3, ed. Lee E. Preston (Greenwich, Conn.: JAI Press, 1981), pp. 133-154. For a comparison of CRA-related performance critiques see ABA Banking Journal, "BHC Steps Up Its Role in Inner-City Renewal,"

ABA Banking Journal 71 (April 1979):22; ABA Banking Journal, "Focus on Community Banks," ABA Banking Journal 71 (October 1979):126; ABA Banking Journal, "Action Under the Community Reinvestment Act," ABA Banking Journal 71 (August 1979): 39-42; and N. Weber, Banks, Neighborhoods, and the Community Reinvestment Act (New York: The Conference Board, 1981).

6. See Neal R. Peirce, "Mergers Activate Banks' Social Consciences," The Hartford Courant, July 8, 1984, p. B4.

7. Kirk Scharfenberger, "The Community as Bank Examiner," Working Papers for a New Society 7 (September/October 1980):30-35; and Harold E. Mortimer, "Current Developments in CRA Enforcement," Banking Law Journal 98 (August 1981):604-615. See also Special Report No. 36, Washington Federal Reporter.

8. Peirce, "Mergers Activate Banks' Social Conscience."

9. Carol S. Greenwald, "Memorandum to the Provident Institution for Savings," Public Comment File (Community Reinvestment Act), Commonwealth of Massachusetts, 1979.

10. The Provident Institution for Savings, "Response to the Commissioner of Banks Memorandum," January 30, 1979, pp. 1-2.

11. Provident, "Response to the Commissioner," p. 11.

12. The Provident Institution for Savings, "Materials submitted to the Commissioner of Banks in Support of its applications for a Branch office in Newton, Massachusetts," 1980.

13. Massachusetts Urban Reinvestment Advisory Group, "Petition in Opposition to Application, in the Matter of the Application of the Provident Institution for Savings to Open a Branch Office in Newton Center, Massachusetts," 1979, p. 1.

14. Scharfenberger, "Community as Bank Examiner," p. 30.

15. Provident, "Response to the Commissioner," p. 6.

16. Gerald T. Mulligan, commissioner of Banks, "In the Matter of the Provident Institution for Savings, Boston, Massachusetts, Application to Establish a Branch Office at 1255 Centre Street, Newton Center, Massachusetts," 1980, p. 7.

17. Board of Bank Incorporation, Commonwealth of Massachusetts, "In the Matter of the First National Boston Corporation, Application to Acquire the Haverhill National Bank, Haverhill, Massachusetts," May 28, 1981.

18. Massachusetts Urban Reinvestment Advisory Group, "Petition to Intervene," August 12, 1980.

19. Board of Bank Incorporation, Commonwealth of Massachusetts, "Decision, First National Boston Corporation," September 2, 1980.

20.  Board of Bank Incorporation, Commonwealth of Massachusetts, "In the Matter of the First National Boston Corporation, Application to Acquire County Bank, N.A., Shelburne Falls, Massachusetts," January 20, 1981, p. 5.

21.  Commonwealth of Massachusetts, "First National Bank," p. 4.

22.  MURAG, "Petition to Intervene," p. 7.

23.  The Boston Five Cents Savings Bank and The Atlantic Savings Bank, "Community Reinvestment Act," February 1980, p. 2.

24.  MURAG, "Brief of the Massachusetts Urban Reinvestment Advisory Group in Opposition to the Application for the Merger of the Boston Five Cents Savings Bank and the Atlantic Savings Bank," June 16, 1981.

25.  Boston Five Cents Savings Bank, "Supplemental CRA Statement," undated, circa June 1981.

26.  Office of the Commissioner of Banks, Commonwealth of Massachusetts, "In the Matter of the Boston Five Cents Savings Bank, and Atlantic Savings Bank, Application for Merger," July 15, 1981, pp. 2-5.

27.  Commissioner of Banks, "In the Matter of the Boston Five Cents Savings Bank," pp. 5-6.

28.  Carol Greenwald, Banks Are Dangerous to Your Wealth (Englewood Cliffs: Prentice-Hall, 1980), pp. 171-173.

29.  Ibid., pp. 171-172.

30.  Massachusetts Urban Reinvestment Advisory Group, Bank Change and the Community Reinvestment Act (Boston: Metropolitan Area Planning Council, undated research report, circa 1981), p. iii.

31.  Bruce A. Mohl, "Bankers Told Survivability Is the Issue," Boston Globe, September 12, 1981, p. 16.

32.  Beatson Wallace, "A Problem for Banks," Boston Globe, April 16, 1981, p. 27. See also, Newsweek, "How Safe Are Your Savings?" Newsweek, March 15, 1982, pp. 50-55.

33.  D. T. Savage, "CRA and Community Credit Needs," in Bank Management: Concepts and Cases, ed. J. R. Brick (Richmond, Va.: Robert F. Dame, 1980), p. 503.

34.  See ABA Banking Journal, "BHC Steps Up Its Role in Inner-City Renewal," p. 22; ABA Banking Journal, "Focus on Community Banks," p. 20; Savage, "CRA and Community," pp. 497-504; and Savings Bank Journal, "CRA Upfront Issue in Massachusetts," Savings Bank Journal 60 (November 1980): 64-65.

35.  C. Bell and H. Newby, Community Studies (New York: Praeger, 1972).

36. See P. A. Sorokin, Society, Culture, and Personality (New York: Harper & Row, 1947).

37. Scharfenberg, "Community as Bank Examiner," p. 33.

38. See B. S. Alper and L. Nichols, Beyond The Courtroom (Lexington, Mass.: D. C. Heath, 1981).

39. Mulligan, "In the Matter of the Provident Institution for Savings."

40. Commissioner of Banks, "In the Matter of the Boston Five Cents Savings Bank."

41. Board of Bank Incorporation, "In the Matter of the First National Boston Corporation."

42. See Robert K. Merton and E. Barber, "Sociological Ambivalence," in Sociological Theory, Values, and Sociocultural Change, ed. E. A. Tiryakian (London: Free Press, 1963).

43. Post and Mahon, "Articulated Turbulence."

44. P. Weaver, "Regulation, Social Policy, and Class Conflict," Public Interest 50 (Winter 1978):45-63. See also Murray Weidenbaum, "The Changing Nature of Government Regulation of Business," in Business Environment/Public Policy: 1979 Conference Papers, ed. Lee E. Preston (St. Louis: AACSB, 1980).

45. Scharfenberg, "Community as Bank Examiner," p. 33.

46. See Sorokin, Society, Culture, and Personality.

47. James E. Post and Edward Baer, "Analyzing Complex Policy Problems: The Social Performance of the International Infant Formula Industry," in Research in Corporate Social Performance and Policy, Vol. 2, ed. Lee E. Preston (Greenwich, Conn.: JAI Press, 1980), pp. 157-196.

48. D. Lowery, "Watchdog on Boston Five: MURAG Renews Fight Against Chelsea Acquisition," Boston Globe, August 22, 1981, p. 9.

# 7

# CORPORATE RESPONSIBILITY
# AND SOCIAL CHANGE

Discussions of corporate social responsibility have long been linked with the issue of social change. Business writers have generally referred to a "movement" among corporations which has sprung from important changes in the larger society. As we have seen in earlier chapters, however, there are significant differences both in perception and evaluation of such trends. In general, the business and society literature reflects considerable agreement with the premise that we are entering an era of "responsive capitalism" which is characterized by the increasingly cooperative interaction of business, government, and the larger society.[1] Some observers, however, are much more reluctant to accept the emergence of a "new corporate personality," while others even dismiss corporate efforts as the merest "shell game."[2] Since there has been a strong tendency among writers in the field to express such overall positive or negative judgments about the responsiveness process, these global categorizations may be usefully summarized under three headings: optimists, pessimists, and critics.

Those whom we refer to as optimists believe that a process of substantial change is under way, and, as a result, expect tangible benefits for the quality of our lives in the near future. At the opposite pole, pessimists hold to a negative verdict: Either there has been no significant change or else the modifications that have occurred must be seen as damaging to business or society. A middle group, called critics, focus on perceived problems in recent developments, in terms of either the quantitative extent of change, or qualitative omissions. Illustrations of these respective positions are summarized in Table 7.1. Similar

TABLE 7.1

Alternative Conceptualizations of Transformations in Management Orientations

| Reference | Phase 1 | Phase 2 | Phase 3 |
|---|---|---|---|
| **Optimists** | | | |
| Bruyn (1977) | Corporate economy: Emphasis on traditional market and legal structures | Federal/international economy: Emphasis on "macrosystem" issues with self-monitoring and self-governance of alternatives | Social economy: Emphasis on the social and personal dimensions of economic life |
| Harrington (1976) | Laissez-faire capitalism: Exploitation of working classes | Welfare capitalism: Modified exploitation, with some social rights | Socialism: Eventual resolution of internal conflict of capitalism |
| Hay and Gray (1974) | Profit maximizing management: only objective is to maximize profits | Trusteeship management: management as trustee for various contributor groups as well as agent of owner | Quality of life management: management and company deeply involved in solution of social problems |
| Holmes (1976) | Classical view: economic criteria primary measure of performance; growth in production of goods and services | Managerial view: management responsible for balancing claims and rights of many diverse groups | Public view: management must insure that business operates in harmony with the public interest |
| Parket and Eilbert (1975) | Self-defense/payoff reaction: responsible actions taken | Fashionable reaction: business swept by fads; re- | Reflection of corporate personality: company policy reflects |

184

| | | | |
|---|---|---|---|
| Preston and Post (1974) | Hierarchical structures: initial specialized functions of management: internal coordination and decision making | Professionalization: separation of ownership and control in large organizations; growth in scale and complexity of managerial roles and widening of concerns | Participation: participative management within organizations and external social participation in management process |
| Zenisek (1979) | Owner-manager/organization participant: profit and resource use main goals | Task environment: emphasis on market sphere | Societal: focus extended to societal welfare |
| Critics | | | |
| Henning (1976) | Traditional capitalism: focus on traditional market forces: competition, optimum economic efficiency and survival | Protective self-interest: responsibility hype; corporate social activity more myth than reality; massive PR effort | |
| Krishnan (1973) | Profit maximization: only objective: maximize profits for stockholders | Profit maximization with responsibility to claimant groups: consumer groups, minorities etc. as well as stockholders that demand attention | |
| Nader-Green (1976) | Competitive capitalism: Economic domination by the wealthy within relatively small corporate structures | Corporate socialism: Emergence of giant firms which own most national resources | |

(continued)

Table 7.1 (continued)

| Reference | Phase 1 | Phase 2 | Phase 3 |
|---|---|---|---|
| Pessimists | | | |
| Browne (1972) | Monopoly capitalism: focus on profit and self-interest; social response as myth | | |
| Friedman (1962; 1976) | Free enterprise: market economy with internal checks and balances | Excessive regulation: counterproductive efforts to legislate social responsibility | |
| Hayek (1967) | Liberal capitalism: healthy free-enterprise economy | | |
| Herman (1981) | Irresponsibility bias: profit motive and competition override environmental and community concerns; business interfering with the process of government | Totalitarian drift: private control lost to state planning | |

to our earlier discussions of the need to use an integral approach to examine perceptions of corporate responsibility, each of these perspectives should be considered in assessing the extent to which social change in this area has indeed occurred.

## A THEORETICAL APPROACH TO CHANGE

In order to move beyond the basic situation depicted in Table 7.1, we must come to terms with the difficult general issue of the meaning of change. Within the social sciences, however, there has been no real consensus on this question. For purposes of this discussion, therefore, we shall suggest our own model of change, and then relate it to the four types of responsiveness presented in earlier chapters.

### Major Processes of Change

It seems to us that the best starting point for considering change is in the concept of process. As discussed by sociologist Pitirim Sorokin, process refers to "any kind of movement, or modification, or transformation, or 'evolution,' in brief any change, of a given local subject in the course of time, whether it be a change in its place in space or a modification of its quantitative or qualitative aspects."[3] This statement, as Sorokin admits, is rather tautological or self-evident, but this outcome is unavoidable, since "the concept of change or process in the above sense is an irreducible ultimate category of human thought and therefore indefinable in terms of another more ultimate category."[4] Thus, using the notion of process, we might replace global statements about the presence or absence of change with more specific generalizations about the operation of particular dynamics.

While the concept of process makes the notion of change more comprehensible, it does not by itself make the analysis of change manageable. Many hundreds, if not thousands, of processes have been identified in social science and business literatures. Some of the best known would include interaction, growth, cooperation, competition, exchange, conflict, adaptation, influence, social and cultural mobility, accommodation, invention and diffusion, socialization, alienation, and revolution. The lengths to which such a list might be taken have been indicated by sociologists Becker and von Wiese, who produced a catalogue of several hundred major and minor processes.[5] If all of these dynamics had to be considered in studies of corporate social responsibility, such research, especially in its exploratory phases, would clearly become impossible. Some strategic simplification is therefore necessary. Based on our analysis of sociological works on change, we suggest four processes which merit special attention: differentiation, restratification, cultural innovation, and attitudinal variation.

Differentiation refers to the emergence of new social structures within some particular context. These may be roles or portions of roles, statuses, networks, social systems or subsystems, collectivities (such as crowds or social movements), or institutions. Within the business sector, this may mean the emergence of a new position, program, or department, as well as a corporation or an industry (such as computers or genetic engineering). Applied to the specific question of corporate social responsibility, differentiation refers to such things as the appearance of positions like social issues specialists, committees on corporate responsiveness, task forces investigating particular concerns like pollution and product safety, or informational clearing houses on responsibility such as that of U.S. life and health insurance companies. Other things being equal, the more such specialized structures appear, the greater the degree of social change.

The emergence of new social structures is often accompanied by the disappearance of older forms. As the airline industry grew and prospered, for example, many railroads gradually went out of business. In the same way, thousands of small family farms have vanished as residential subdivisions and industrial parks have sprung up on the borders of metropolitan areas. Therefore, it seems best to regard differentiation as a two-sided process.

A second major model of change is the process of restratification, whose defining characteristic is a shift in the social position of one or more groups. Like differentiation, the process should be thought of as a reciprocal movement, for as the position of one group improves, that of another in some sense declines. This is true whether the relative positions are measured in terms of power, wealth, prestige, or other qualities. The spread of unions, for example, indicated an increase in the power of labor and a decline in that of management. As foreign auto makers have entered the American market, domestic firms have lost business. Corporate conglomerates have grown by assuming control over matters formerly decided by acquired firms. Increases and decreases in governmental regulation of business further illustrate the meaning of change in terms of restratification. Within the context of corporate social responsibility, change in terms of restratification may mean that minorities can demand access to jobs and promotions via affirmative action, or that local communities can exert greater control over business operations, exercised through public directors on corporate boards.

Cultural innovation, our third model of change, refers to a shift in our way of thinking, which is expressed in new ideas, values or priorities, and norms or standards. We can get a sense of what is meant here by briefly recalling some fundamentals of American history. When the nation was established, the idea of monarchy was rejected in favor of the concept of a republic; the value of freedom was elevated above that of the security offered by the British Empire; and the norm of government "of the people, by the people, and for the people" became the standard which has been pursued to this day. Focusing on the issue of corporate responsiveness, we might see cultural innovation in the "stake-holder" concept of the business organization, as well as in the value of "corporate citizenship," and the norm of "budgeted nonfinancial objectives." Other examples may be found in the notion of "economic democracy," the norm of employee-owned and employee-controlled firms, or in Schumacher's value, "small is beautiful." Important change, in terms of this paradigm, would therefore be marked by the appearance of new ideas, values, and norms within a relatively short period of time.

The fourth proposed model of change, attitudinal variation, refers to alterations in the way people perceive and feel toward particular objects, and secondarily to the behavioral tendencies which result from such modifications. Suppose, for example, that a firm has "racist" or "sexist" attitudes. This would mean that it tends to perceive members of specific groups (for example, blacks and women) in certain limited ways (perhaps as unambitious or not fully competent), to feel negatively toward them (disrespect, hostility, and so on), and to engage in certain behaviors (for example, not hiring them or not promoting them beyond certain levels). As more tolerant, nonracist and nonsexist attitudes begin to form, the firm changes its perceptions (perhaps recognizing potential managerial talent), its feelings (to respect and even enthusiastic support), and its behavior (to recruiting and promoting). Changes in the area of corporate responsiveness have included such attitudinal shifts as support for charitable donations, tolerance of increasing governmental regulation, dissatisfaction with an exclusive emphasis on profits, and increased concern for employee rights. The degree of change will be reflected in the frequency of such perceptual, emotional, and behavioral shifts.

One may well wonder at this point about the relations between the four processes we have been describing. Is one more important than another? Do they occur in any predictable order? Can one process be reduced to another? Our response is summarized by the concept of an integral model of change: 1) the study of change necessarily involves the study of all four processes, because they are generic to change; 2) though the processes are all closely interrelated, each has a certain margin of autonomy from the others; 3) in any particular case of change, one process might be more significant than another; and 4) it is therefore not possible to specify in advance the relative importance of the processes, nor to determine their sequence in time. An investigator who studies change in terms of these four processes, we believe, will not miss anything of fundamental importance. At the same time, this integral, four-process model of change is manageable in exploratory research, such as that which might be undertaken into corporate responsiveness to social issues.

## Change and The Community Reinvestment Act

The model of change developed above can be readily applied to the material on the CRA presented earlier. Differentiation of new social structures would refer to groups such as the Massachusetts Urban Reinvestment Advisory Group (MURAG), and to positions within banks specifically created to deal with new duties imposed by the legislation (social issue specialists), as well as to new roles on such bodies as the Massachusetts Banking Commission which have a regulatory function. Change in terms of restratification can be seen in the empowerment of citizen groups like MURAG, which are now consulted by banks, especially in the wake of successful challenges which have prevented financial institutions from branching or merging.[6] They thus exercise a tangible influence on the internal policy making of the largest banks in urban areas like Boston. Cultural innovation, of course, appears in the new legislation itself, especially in its central concepts of banks as "quasi-public" institutions, which have "affirmative obligations" to preserve the quality of life in urban areas. These ideas are supported by the critical normative concept of the "convenience and needs" of a community, the standard which the CRA imposes on regulators in their evaluations of bank actions. Attitudinal variation, finally, is clearly implied in the legislation, which requires increased concern for local needs, plus a new willingness to communicate and lend practical aid, and a decrease in the tendency to perceive issues solely in terms of self-interest and profit.

One might ask whether anything can be said in this case about the relative importance of the individual change processes, or about their sequence. The most crucial fact certainly seems to be the passing, in 1977, of the CRA legislation. A question that arises, however, concerns the factors that cleared the way for this decision, and the process of attitudinal variation immediately comes to mind. That is to say, the formulation of new laws seems logically to require a prior change in perceptions and feelings. One could therefore conclude that the sequence occurs as follows:

1) Attitudinal Variation ⟶ 2) Cultural Innovation ⟶
3) Differentiation ⟶ 4) Restratification.

Such a formula would be both intuitively and conceptually appealing. However, it would still not take adequate account of the dynamics of change (that is, how were the attitude changes themselves produced?). One answer would be through the influence of well-organized advocacy groups, such as those lobbying on behalf of consumer rights, cities, and minorities. But this brings us back to an earlier phase of differentiation, in which these groups were created. At the same time, we would have to consider that the success of such lobbying indicates that some power relations were shifting, and thus the process of restratification was operative prior to the passage of the CRA. Therefore it is clear that all four processes are continually encountered each step of the way. Determination of their relative importance or causal influence would require a significant amount of theoretical and empirical analysis.


The Degree of Change and Corporate
Social Responsibility

The study of change includes the difficult issue of the degree of change, that is, of its comparative extent and importance. We know, in a common-sense way, that all changes are not equal, that some are much more significant, with longer lasting effects. We therefore speak of "minor," "moderate," and "major" changes. Which of these labels best applies to any case of change, however, can be and has often been a very

controversial question. In our earlier consideration of "optimists," "pessimists," and "critics," for example, we saw how
different observers disagreed about the extent of change which
has occurred as a result of the corporate social responsibility
movement. Accordingly, we would like to indicate how this
issue may be approached within the model of change developed
above. Our point of departure, as one might expect, will be
the four types of responsiveness developed in Chapters 3 and 4.
How much change is implied by the move from a policy of productivism to one of philanthropy, or from a stance of progressivism
to ethical idealism, or from any one type to any other?

Despite the difficulty of an adequate response, it appears
that some rough generalizations can be made. The first point
would relate to fluctuations <u>within</u> the individual groups. Though
we have sometimes described these orientations as four points
along a continuum, they are really best understood as <u>four</u>
<u>ranges</u>. Within productivism, for example, Friedman's model
might actually be a bit closer to philanthropy than that of Hayek,
while within the ethical idealist range Bruyn's approach stands
nearer to progressivism than does that of Kavanaugh (see Chapter
3). It seems best to refer to fluctuations within the four
individual types as "minor" changes. This does not imply that
shifts on this level are not important: They might be extremely
important to the people involved, and may serve also as indicators
of emergent trends. For example, if we consider the approach
of the federal government, it should be apparent that it did not
suddenly move from the productivism of the 1790s to the progressivism of the New Deal in the 1930s. Along the way were a
series of measures which might fall under the heading of
philanthropy—especially in terms of limited welfare programs
for the most extreme cases of need.

Changes across one category, that is, from one type to a
neighboring type on our continuum, will be understood as
"minor to moderate." Again, the issue of internal ranges within
each type is important (see Chapter 5). A shift from the
most philanthropic version of productivism, for example, to
the most productivist variant of philanthropy—a "short trip
across the border," in effect—should be thought of as minor,
while a move from the most extreme productivism to the most
progressive philanthropy may be considered a "moderate"
degree to change. Shifts across two or three categories will
be considered major, such as going from productivism to progressivism; productivism to ethical idealism; philanthropy to
ethical idealism; progressivism to productivism; ethical idealism
to philanthropy; and ethical idealism to productivism. These
concepts are depicted in Figure 7.1.

FIGURE 7.1

Illustrations of Minor, Moderate, and Major Change

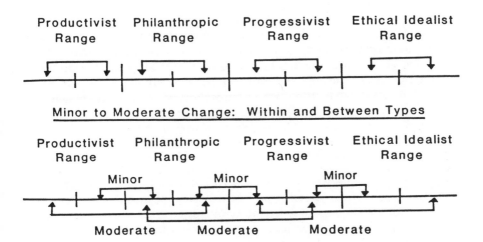

### Minor Change: Within Types

Productivist Range  Philanthropic Range  Progressivist Range  Ethical Idealist Range

### Minor to Moderate Change: Within and Between Types

Productivist Range  Philanthropic Range  Progressivist Range  Ethical Idealist Range

Minor  Minor  Minor

Moderate  Moderate  Moderate

### Major Change: Between Types

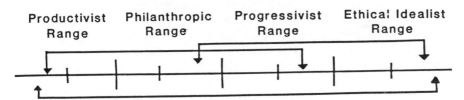

Productivist Range  Philanthropic Range  Progressivist Range  Ethical Idealist Range

In sum, this approach recognizes 14 distinct types of minor change, six types of moderate change, and six types of major change. Others could be added by breaking each range into thirds or fourths instead of halves, but these seem sufficient for present purposes. We leave aside for the time being other interesting questions which might be pursued in this context. One might argue, for instance, that some movements across an equal number of categories are more important than others, specifically, that a shift from productivism to philanthropy, or from progressivism to ethical idealism, is really more of a departure than a change from philanthropy to progressivism, or from progressivism to philanthropy. Since such assessments appear to be more value oriented than analytic, however, the remainder of our discussion proceeds as though all of these changes were equal in degree.

## Sources of Change

An important consideration in assessments of patterns of organizational responsiveness focuses on questions concerning the impetus for change. Is change precipitated by forces outside the organization? Or does change occur more readily from sources internal to the firm in question? These concerns have led to different interpretations of the extent to which such change is initiated on an external or internal basis.[7]

### External

Social change, as it relates to corporations and their policies, has often been interpreted and explained in terms of alterations in some relevant environment. Numerous texts in the field of business and society have explicitly linked corporate behavior to fluctuations in politics (increased governmental regulation), economies (availability of energy resources), technology or social demands in general (as in demands for day care facilities or for more meaningful work experiences). Indeed, university courses in management and social issues have often been given under titles like "The Changing Environment of Business." The unstated assumption within this approach is that of stability: Left to itself, business would pursue a relatively constant course of action, and in fact seeks to do so, while adjusting to significant environmental changes.

The environmental perspective described here closely resembles a well-known school of thought in sociology called functionalism (or structural-functionalism). The most important theoretical source for this viewpoint is the work of American sociologist Talcott Parsons. In his major writings, especially The Social System, Parsons develops the thesis that all social systems have a tendency to seek stability or steady states, and refers to this process of structural maintenance as "homeostasis." Groups or systems which successfully preserve stability are said to be "in equilibrium." Change occurs as the result of some external disturbance which alters the relationship between system and environment, and produces "strain." Systems adapt to such strains and eventually reach some new state of equilibrium. The most typical adaptive strategy is said to be specialization, most commonly seen in the creation of new roles or role components.[8]

Case studies following this model of change are plentiful. Reynolds Metals, faced with economic and political obstacles to its supply of minerals, achieved stability by developing an ambitious recycling program. Weyerhauser, responding to ethical challenges to the legitimacy of business in general and to foreign payments practices in particular, set up a task force to draft an ethical code for the company. Confronted with sharply rising energy costs, 3M introduced energy conservation measures and strict monitoring procedures, as well as a transportation pool for employees to cut down on gas consumption. Abbott Laboratories created positions whose purpose was a dialogue with proxy critics of its international infant-formula marketing.[9]

## Internal

Critics of the functionalist view argue that it suggests a kind of paralysis: If all systems tend toward equilibrium and do not change until their environments change, then how does the process of change ever get started? The analysis of change, they conclude, must rest on some assumption of an internal dynamism in all systems. Marx, for instance, contended that "motion is the mode of being of matter"—that is, everything is moving all the time. Other theorists have made similar responses, while pointing to various sources of movement.

The most fully developed statement of this approach is reflected in Pitirim Sorokin's major works, especially Social and Cultural Dynamics and Society, Culture, and Personality. There are two major principles within this treatment: 1) that systems change continually, simply as the result of their own activity, even in a static environment; and 2) that such internal dynamics are far more important in understanding the life-course of systems than environmental factors. This can be seen more clearly by considering the three main components of sociocultural systems, their human members, the cultural meanings they share, and the physical vehicles which carry out their purposes. Sorokin explains the issue as follows:

> Since any sociocultural system is composed of human beings as one of its components, and since any organism, so long as it exists, cannot help changing, the sociocultural system is a "going concern" and cannot help changing so long as it exists, regardless of its external conditions, even when

they are absolutely constant. The very performance of any activity, any reaction or response, to
a given environment A, changes the system and
makes it react differently a second time, and then
a third time, and subsequent times. Other components of any sociocultural system are meanings
and vehicles. These also bear in themselves the
seeds of their, and of the system's change.[10]

Applied to cases of corporate change, the internal and
immanent approach leads us to view later choices as consequences
of earlier choices that unfold the logical possibilities of those
previous decisions. Thus, returning to the Weyerhauser case
mentioned above, we note that Weyerhauser had always regarded
itself as a very ethical company, and had enjoyed a widespread
reputation as such. Its development of an ethical code was
therefore a change which flowed out of its particular identity,
and is much better explained in terms of that identity than in
terms of external factors. Other corporations, confronted with
the same external changes faced by Weyerhauser, did not
respond in the same way.

## An Integral Conception

As Sorokin notes, the two views of the origin of change
are both useful and true. One is, however, forced to make a
kind of philosophical choice in this matter, since it is difficult
to consider each as equally important. While utilizing both
models, we shall therefore give priority to the second, and
base our analysis on the premise that human social groups
create and modify their own worlds of meaning. This is their
most fundamental and characteristic activity, and the most
important determinant of changes in their social, cultural, and
psychological aspects. Change, of course, always occurs in
environmental contexts, but these will not be treated as the
ultimate or primary causes of change.

Applied to the specific issue of corporate social responsibility, the notion of sources of change raises some provocative
questions. If environmental factors are really the causes of
the contemporary movement, for example, then perhaps its
roots are not very deep after all. It might pass away as quickly
as it started, should conditions in the environment reverse
themselves. Such an outcome would make the trend look, in
retrospect, like the "shell game for the seventies" which some
critics have seen in it. On the other hand, if the movement
flows from the character of U.S. business itself, as an internal

development, then it may persist irrespective of fluctuation
in environmental factors. Its institutionalization will be more
likely, and its future more secure, despite differences among
schools of thought on the proper content of corporate responsibility.[11]


The Direction of Change

Whenever we speak of social change, we require some
notion of direction with respect to particular processes. That
is, we need some sense of a starting point and a possible or
actual end point, a notion of "from" somewhere "to" or "toward"
somewhere else.[12] In some discussions of change, explicit
reference is made to the direction of social processes, but in
many cases it is assumed or implicit. Thus, when we speak of
a society undergoing "modernization," we mean that it is moving
from a traditional, or nonmodern situation toward a situation
characterized by certain features of contemporary life such as
industry, mass education, and high mobility. References to
"evolution" usually indicate a movement from a less complex to
a more complex form of organization. And processes of "alienation" imply movement from an attitude of greater satisfaction
toward one of lesser satisfaction. Application of the idea of
direction to our four-process model of change means that we
should try to specify as clearly as possible the starting points
and end points of differentiation, restratification, cultural
innovation, and attitudinal variation.

Among the most important aspects of direction is what may
be referred to as its path. In particular, we may inquire
whether a process is better described as "linear" or "nonlinear,"
and within the latter type, as "cyclical" or "noncyclical." The
general meaning of linearity is that of a steady trend, or of
consistent movement toward a fixed goal, so that a process may
be thought of as taking the form of a straight line. Urbanization
as a social process has often been linear in this sense, as more
and more people have become residents of cities, and more and
more land that was previously rural or agricultural has been
converted into urban uses. Nonlinear processes are characterized by reversals, or changes of direction. Thus, the process
of governmental regulation of business has seen many fluctuations
between increasing control and the lessening of control reflected
in recent policies of partial deregulation, as in the airline and
trucking industries. In some cases, social processes may move
through a fixed series of phases in a cyclical or circular manner.

The well known stages of the business cycle provide a good illustration (boom, decline, recession, recovery).

Application of these ideas to the case of corporate social responsibility leads to the following question: Do we observe any steady trends in the four major processes of change, or are events in the area of social responsibility characterized by fluctuations or fixed cycles? The existing literature, not surprisingly, offers contradictory answers. Perhaps the best illustration is provided by the main progressivist texts in the field of business and society, which argue that responsiveness has been a linear trend.[13] The social awareness of business, it is said, has been steadily increasing in recent decades, and will continue to do so for the foreseeable future. We have noted this view at the start of the chapter, in our brief summarization of optimists. Productivist writers such as Friedman and Hayek have also put forward a linear interpretation of recent trends, expressing this primarily in terms of the process of restratification. In their opinion, increasing governmental regulation under the banner of responsiveness has steadily reduced the freedom of action as well as the power of private business.[14] Other critical observers have explained both corporate and governmental actions in terms of nonlinear fluctuations, contending that responsiveness policies vary with the public mood or the condition of the economy.[15]

Our view of the issue is open-ended. We believe that researchers in the field should be aware of both linear and nonlinear patterns of movement, and should be prepared to interpret particular cases in terms of either. That is, they should not allow their own philosophies or personal preferences to dictate a rigidly linear or nonlinear view of particular events in the world. It may be that a certain policy-making unit, such as a corporation, does show steady change of a certain kind during a particular period of time, such as attitudinal variation in the direction of increasing awareness of social responsibility. But it may also happen that a group's policy fluctuates from one type to another, possibly as the result of changes in managerial personnel (differentiation), as we saw in one of our cases in Chapter 5. External factors such as the general economic climate and fluctuations in market shares are also of obvious relevance for changes in social responsibility orientations. It is considerably easier, for example, to adopt a progressivist stance when high earnings permit expansion of special programs such as hiring the hard-core unemployed. A sharp and sudden recession, however, can result in new policies of fiscal restraint in which productivist principles will come to the fore.[16]

Starting Points for Change

Before proceeding, it is important to reiterate and clarify the principle set out earlier in this chapter that change represents a movement from some starting point toward some destination. Students of corporate social responsibility must therefore pay particular attention to the situation preceding change, that is, to the social, psychological, and cultural structures which exist at a given point in time. We have often spoken of the "traditional mission of American business," as though the starting point for change was a situation in which productivism was dominant. While this may be roughly accurate as an overall sketch of trends in this century, it represents only one of the four basic possibilities. Let us briefly review some other alternatives.

Within communist nations, the official doctrine on corporate social responsibility has always been ethical idealism: wealth-producing organizations, according to the dogmas of Marx, Engels, Lenin, Stalin, Mao, Castro, and others, must function as part of a larger effort to create a more just society in which social ownership will abolish the exploitation of labor. As such, they are training grounds for a new type of human personality, one that will be motivated by social rather than merely egotistical purposes. Traditional incentives, such as bonuses, should therefore not be necessary, and distinctions of rank could be largely done away with. Competition, too, would naturally tend to give way to cooperation within the framework of economic planning by the central government. In recent years, however, such ethical idealist assumptions have been implicitly and explicitly abandoned in several prominent communist nations, to be replaced by elements of the progressivist and even the productivist views. Eastern Europe has witnessed the reintroduction of bonuses for managerial performance, as well as open competition for top executive talent. China has begun to emphasize modernization, productivity, and efficiency, while accepting as inevitable certain differences in rank and reward—changes that might vindicate the faith of the staunchest productivist. Many similar examples could be provided from current Soviet practice, as revolutionary zeal has cooled and less idealistic considerations have stamped the everyday world of work.[17]

Countercultural groups within the United States have sometimes undergone comparable experiences. In the early days of such experiments, the overriding objective may have been to satisfy economic needs according to the principles of some higher morality. As a result, no effort may have been

spared in implementing the policy of economic democracy on all
major decisions, or perhaps the groups went to great lengths
to avoid any business dealings with morally objectionable firms
such as polluters or multinationals doing business in South
Africa. With the passage of time, however, certain compromises
have eventually been made by many alternative businesses.
Some, for instance, have found that pure economic democracy
is unworkable, or else cannot be achieved once the number of
workers has risen above a few hundred.[18] Others have found
it necessary to borrow from major banks, and have decided to
make allowances for bank policies of which they do not approve.

While the overall position of such groups may still be
characterized as ethical idealism, it may be a modified version
of the doctrine, one that in practice is significantly closer to
progressivism. In our earlier analysis of the conflict between
Boston banks and MURAG (Chapter 6), for example, it was
clear that the community advocacy group held an ethical idealist
interpretation of the meanings of corporate responsibility in
general and the Community Reinvestment Act in particular.
Yet, as the case discussion indicated, MURAG supported the
progressivist policies of one of these banks. It seems that the
type of pragmatic blending attempted by the Board of Bank
Incorporation was also practiced by the community advocacy
group. Although groups like MURAG might hold ethical idealist
orientations, in practice they appear willing to accept progressivist policies, while focusing their challenges on those that
remain productivist or minimally philanthropic in nature.

These considerations should reinforce the point made in
earlier chapters that the four types of responsiveness are
broad, generic categories, rather than phases in a linear process
of change. Any policy-making unit can operate within any of
the four types at any point in time, and can shift its special
policies in various directions over some period of time.


The Problem of Persistence

A final issue which should be considered in the investigation
of change is the survival of earlier elements, whether these be
specific patterns of behavior, programs, hierarchies, values or
attitudes. The process of enduring through a period of change
has been referred to as persistence.[19] For example, we may
say that despite government regulation and criticism from
various citizen groups, the American system of free enterprise
via privately owned corporations has persisted. Thus, the

careful study of "survivals" provides another method of assessing the degree of change.  One may say, other things being equal, that the larger the number of survivals, the smaller the degree of change.

The Russian Revolution of 1917 provides an interesting illustration.  Although a revolution, by definition, involves significant change, some very provocative questions may be raised about the degree of change by focusing on the surviving elements from prerevolutionary days.  Among the major explicit goals of the Revolution, following its takeover by Lenin's Bolshevik faction, were the transformation of all private businesses into state-owned enterprises; the elimination of religion, and its replacement by militant atheism; and the equalization of status and opportunity among the population, especially with respect to such basic commodities as housing, education, and health care.  Therefore it is interesting to note, nearly seven decades later, that none of these goals has been completely achieved.  The state has become the major employer, but private enterprise has reappeared in a variety of guises, from small private gardens on collective farms, to underground construction firms that compensate for the inefficiency of their state counterparts.  Religion survives in many forms, from the traditional Russian Orthodox church to evangelical Protestant groups which have recently gained in popularity.  Moreover, equality appears no closer to realization than it was under the Tsars.  Recent accounts unanimously document the superiority of housing, health care, education, consumer goods and the general amenities available to government and Communist Party officials over those accessible to common folk.

As applied to the topic of corporate social responsibility, persistence means systematically posing a series of questions that parallel those just discussed in connection with our four models of change.  Specifically, we shall want to consider: 1) What social structures have survived from earlier periods? 2) What control relations remain intact?  3) Which ideas, values, and norms remain in the minds of corporate personnel?  4) Do any attitudes from other times continue to condition perceptions and emotional responses?  In a sense, of course, this is merely to repeat our earlier inquiries from another direction.  Yet, as any experienced teacher, researcher, or interviewer knows, such reformulation of questions can and often does yield dramatically different findings.  When we ask only about the presence and operation of the four change processes, we tend to collect data describing only change.  But when we also focus on what does not change, we create a broader perspective in which both sets of data can be properly interpreted.

An example of persistence in this area is reflected in concerns about the process of corporate governance. While much of the present debate focuses on the implications of stockholder and stakeholder models of corporate performance (see Chapter 1), and the extent to which these different viewpoints should be included on corporate boards,[20] there is still a persisting debate concerning stockholder rights and the rights of management.[21] While stockholders "own" a corporation, they do not determine its day-to-day activities. Nevertheless, both our laws and business literature pay homage to the concept of "stockholder" or "shareholder democracy," the notion that a residual power rests with stockholders so that they choose the persons to whom operational powers are delegated and participate in certain, longer-term judgmental decisions. In short, the concept of shareholder democracy essentially limits the extent of managerial power.

Managers, by contrast, typically argue that their power is based on the democratic process, and claims that such power has become unhinged from ownership are misconstrued. It is pointed out that stockholders elect the directors, who often happen to be executives and managers of the firm. Yet, although this is the law in every state, research has indicated that most stockholder voting in large corporations is achieved through the proxy process, which is controlled by the organization's management. As a result, this practice actually deters real corporate elections. Moreover, control over such elections is determined in the nomination process rather than the actual election process—and this process is controlled entirely by the corporation's management. Thus, while there is current debate over representation of "outsiders" and stakeholders on corporate boards, there is persistence in the conflict over the extent of management and stockholder rights on such boards. Other illustrations of potential or actual persistence in the business and society field are presented in Table 7.2.

## AN EMERGENT MOVEMENT:
## COOPERATIVE CORPORATIONS

As an example of social change and the way in which the model developed in this chapter can be used to assess such change, our discussion concludes with an analysis of the emergence of cooperative types of corporate bodies. Although these brief illustrations are drawn from only one of our four orientations—ethical idealism—they appear to capture some of

TABLE 7.2

Persistence and Social Responsibility

| Process | Example |
| --- | --- |
| Persistence: social structure (horizontal) | Male-dominated management<br>Private stockholders<br>For-profit corporations |
| Persistence: social structure (vertical) | Economic control by a few hundred corporate giants<br>Top-down policy making on social responsibility<br>Voting power of private directors, over public directors |
| Persistence: culture | Value: profit as a major goal<br>Priority: production over distribution<br>Belief: self-regulation of the market<br>Norm: safe and sound business practices |
| Persistence: attitudes | Opposition to increased government regulation<br>Skepticism toward economic democracy<br>Distrust of intellectuals and critics of business |

the current tension in the business and society debate as well as provide a sound basis for the evaluation of the potential significance of such changes as they unfold in our society.

In June 1984, numerous publications featured the story of Boston's new Archbishop, Bernard Law, blessing the lobster fleet in the city's harbor.[22] The occasion being celebrated was the formation of a cooperative association which brought together a number of the fiercely independent lobster fishers and set them on a common course. The combination involved in the undertaking—the Archdiocese, lobster fishers, the Industrial Cooperative Association, and local business leaders— provoked puzzlement in some, and skepticism in others. How had this come to be?

Prominent among the causes of the coalition were familiar economic factors related to the operation of markets including very large and very small producers, and other factors bound up with urban redevelopment. For some time, independent lobster fishers had found it increasingly difficult to make a living at their trade. Prices for their catch were set by the largest fishers in the industry, and their profit margins were shrinking. At the same time, locations for docking their boats became scarce, as Boston underwent a downtown building boom, and large commercial projects acquired more and more waterfront space. A crisis point was eventually reached, and a sense of desperation spread among the small operators.

This situation came to the attention of the late prelate of Boston, Humberto Cardinal Madeiros, who, having come from the fishing town of New Bedford, Massachusetts, naturally sympathized with the struggling independents. Shortly before his death in 1983, he requested that the Planning Office of the Archdiocese do what it could to help the fishers. Since the Planning Office had begun to involve itself in the formation of employee cooperatives in the wake of the 1981 pastoral letter by Pope John Paul II, On Human Labor (see Chapter 3), it was in a position to offer realistic assistance. Representatives of the Planning Office negotiated with individual fishers, and simultaneously sought funds from the national Campaign for Human Development of the Catholic church. Within a relatively short period of time, some 20 lobster boat operators were ready to participate in the experiment, and substantial monies were allocated by the Campaign for Human Development, on a matching basis with private funds. A one-year lease was secured for docking space, and negotiations were initiated with one of the city's largest businesses for a permanent site.

The lobster cooperative is illustrative of a growing trend in recent years toward the formation of worker-owned and worker-managed businesses. As in the Boston case, such groups have often come into being as last-ditch efforts to keep plants open or industries viable, and thereby to preserve jobs. Faced with an impending shut-down in Windsor, North Carolina, for instance, employees purchased a plant and converted it into the Workers' Owned Sewing Company. Workers in Philadelphia, about to lose their jobs due to the closing of numerous A & P food stores, bought some of the stores and began to run them as Employee Owned and Operated Supermarkets (O and Os).[23] In other places, cooperatives were formed at the time of incorporation. At present, there are perhaps 200 such businesses in the United States employing between 5,000 and 10,000 workers. They have been assisted in their efforts by a growing number of technical consulting groups, such as the Industrial Cooperative Association of Somerville, Massachusetts, the Center for Com-

munity Self-Help in Durham, North Carolina, the Association
for Workplace Democracy, and the National Center for Employee
Ownership in Washington, D.C. The federal government has
also contributed funds through the National Consumer Cooperative Bank (formed in 1978), and some states (like Massachusetts
and Maine) have passed legislation facilitating such organizations.

In order to place this trend in perspective, it is necessary
to explain briefly the differences between cooperative corporations and more conventional structures. Business organizations
in the modern period have generally been joint-stock corporations,
in which social rights and duties have been determined by the
ownership of property. Those who owned large percentages
of stock have had significantly greater control than others,
because voting power has been based on this criterion. Other
rewards, such as dividends and increasing equity, have been
distributed in the same way, so that the control of owners has
been continually reinforced. The dominance of the property
conception of the corporation has been formalized in law, where
a corporation is defined as a kind of property which can be
bought and sold. In theory, management and rank-and-file
workers may exercise significant control over everyday operations, but ultimately their status has been that of those who
rent out their services to owners, who are the employers.[24]*

Contemporary cooperatives are a fundamental departure
from this view, in which membership rights replace property
rights and give the corporation a predominantly social character.
All those who contribute their work to the organization, from
the highest-paid specialists to the least-skilled laborers, have
the right to cast one and only one vote on policy issues. The
result is a democratically controlled political unit. In both
cases, voting rights flow simply and directly from participation
in some functional capacity, whether it be residence in a particular territory or performance of a particular job. The right to
vote is a personal or membership right which cannot be bought
or sold.[25]

It is worth noting here that advocates of cooperatives
generally do not regard such arrangements as "socialism," but
rather as the extension of widely shared values and well established roles to all persons in particular organizations. If

---

*As discussed earlier, there is a controversy over the extent
to which this arrangement actually works in practice; see page
202.

ownership of private business is the American way, then why not include all who are involved with a firm's operation? The government is not a party to such transactions, and so the business is not "socialized" in the usual sense. In the same way, cooperatives do not lead to socialistic "equality," so far as material benefits are concerned. Some workers are more highly paid than others, though some formula may be voluntarily adopted to limit the economic gaps (such as a ceiling on salaries of three times the lowest wages). Workers with more seniority will also have acquired more than new workers in comparable job categories, through systems of internal accounts which distribute profit shares and the benefits of increasing corporate equity.

The most important model for such corporations has been the network of cooperatives at Mondragon, in the Basque region of Spain. From a single business formed in 1956, a movement has emerged which now embraces over 85 industrial cooperatives, six agricultural cooperatives, two service cooperatives, 43 cooperative schools, 14 housing cooperatives, and one consumer-worker cooperative. There is also a central cooperative bank, a polytechnical university, a technological research institute, and a social security system. In all these various organizations, members participate on the basis of voting equality, with a single vote for each. Profits are distributed by means of individual worker accounts; a fixed percentage of retained earnings is allocated for charitable purposes in the local community; and a portion is set aside in a reserve fund. The network is thus able to finance new enterprises from internal capital, which does much to account for its remarkable success.[26]

The cooperative movement furnishes an interesting case for the application of our general framework for the study of change. Table 7.3 summarizes important features of this change in terms of the four generic processes outlined in this chapter. As should be apparent from this summarization, change seems to be occurring in terms of both the conceptualization and acceptance of cooperative forms of organization. Considering the underlying rationale of such organizations, one might point to the emergence of greater consideration of social responsibilities and the development of policies which are truly responsive to the needs of various stakeholders. As argued in this chapter, however, there are a number of basic points to consider before forming such global views of the change. Observers should give ample attention to the change, its starting point and direction, and finally the persistence of older forms, such as the traditional, stockholder-oriented profit-making institution. In

TABLE 7.3

Processes of Change in the Cooperative Movement

| Process | Example |
|---|---|
| Differentiation | Formation of cooperative corporations, such as the Workers' Owned Sewing Company. |
| | Establishment of technical-assistance organizations, like the Industrial Cooperatives Association. |
| | Organization of programs of study and research, such as the Program in Social Economy and Social Policy at Boston College, or that at the School of Industrial and Labor Relations at Cornell University. |
| | Establishment of social structures to promote the movement, like the National Center for Employee Ownership. |
| Restratification | Loss of discretion by managerial strata, and acquisition of discretion by workers. |
| | Increased access of cooperatives to venture capital, through internal capital accounts. |
| | Nationwide increase in the number of businesses that have formed as cooperatives. |
| Cultural innovation | Labor theory of property. |
| | New norm: Equal voting power for all employees. |
| | New norm: Right to the fruits of one's labor. |
| | Specific legislation facilitating the establishment of cooperatives, such as the Employee Cooperative Corporations Act in Massachusetts. |
| Attitudinal variation | From fear of cooperatives as socialistic to acceptance of them as a legitimate American form of business. |
| | New proprietary attitude among rank and file (e.g., "It's my store"). |
| | Increased enjoyment of work. |
| | Strong sense of belonging (e.g., "We're all working together like a strong family"). |

this way, we will be able to assess more fully the dynamics and potential significance of changes in the relationship between business organizations and the larger society.

## NOTES

1. See Fred Fry, "A New Stage of Capitalism," Business Horizons 21 (1978):23-25; Earl A. Molander, Responsive Capitalism: Case Studies in Corporate Social Conduct (New York: McGraw-Hill, 1980); and Francis W. Steckmest, Corporate Performance: The Key to Public Trust (New York: McGraw-Hill, 1982), chap. 1.

2. Rama Krishnan, "Business Philosophy and Executive Responsibility," Academy of Management Journal 16 (1973): 658-669; and J. Henning, "Corporate Responsibility: Shell Game for the Seventies," in Taming the Giant Corporation, eds. Ralph Nader, Mark Green, and Joel Seligman (New York: W. W. Norton, 1976).

3. Pitirim A. Sorokin, Social and Cultural Dynamics (New York: American Book Co., 1937), Vol. I, p. 53.

4. Ibid., p. 55.

5. L. von Wiese and H. Becker, Systematic Sociology (New York: John Wiley, 1932).

6. For an indication of the extent to which this is occurring see Neal R. Peirce, "Mergers Activate Banks' Social Consciences," The Hartford Courant, July 8, 1984, p. B4; and Kirk Scharfenberg, "The Community as Bank Examiner," Working Papers for a New Society 7 (September-October 1980): 30-35.

7. See James E. Post, "Research on Patterns of Corporate Response to Social Change," in Research in Corporate Social Performance and Policy, Vol. 1, ed. Lee E. Preston (Greenwich, Conn.: JAI Press, 1978), pp. 55-77; James E. Post, Risk and Response: Management and Social Change in the American Insurance Industry (Lexington, Mass.: D. C. Heath, 1976); and Lee E. Preston and James E. Post, Private Management and Public Policy (Englewood Cliffs: Prentice-Hall, 1975).

8. Talcott Parsons, The Social System (New York: Free Press, 1951), ch. 11.

9. See Molander, Responsive Capitalism, cases 13, 14, 15 and 19; and James E. Post, Corporate Behavior and Social Change (Reston, Va.: Reston Publishing, 1978), chaps. 3-6.

10. Sorokin, Social and Cultural Dynamics, p. 635; see also Pitirim A. Sorokin, Society, Culture, and Personality (New York: Harper & Row, 1947), ch. 46.

11. For a good contrast between these two schools of thought, see Henning, "Corporate Responsibility: Shell Game"; and Meinholf Dierkes and Robert Coppock, "Corporate Responsibility Does Not Depend on Public Pressure," Business and Society Review (Summer 1973):82-89.

12. Sorokhin, Social and Cultural Dynamics, Vol. I, pp. 61-63.

13. See, for example, Archie B. Carroll, Business and Society: Managing Corporate Social Performance (Boston: Little, Brown, 1982); Steckmest, Corporate Performance; and George C. Sawyer, Business and Society: Managing Corporate Social Impact (Boston: Houghton Mifflin, 1979).

14. Frederick Hayek, Individualism and Economic Order (Chicago: University of Chicago Press, 1948); and Milton Friedman, Capitalism and Freedom (Chicago: University of Chicago Press, 1962).

15. For recent analyses of the role of corporate public affairs departments in this process see Edward A. Grefe, Fighting to Win (New York: Harcourt Brace Jovanovich, 1981); and Joseph S. Nagelschmidt (ed.), The Public Affairs Handbook (New York: American Management Association, 1982).

16. See William L. Kandel, "The Social Conscience in Hard Times," Business and Society Review (Winter 1974):17-20; and Grover Starling, The Changing Environment of Business (Boston: Kent, 1980), pp. 487-489.

17. See, for example, H. Smith, The Russians (New York: Ballantine Books, 1976).

18. See the Industrial Cooperative Association Bulletin, March 1984, p. 3. The classic statement of the issue of size and democratic control remains R. Michels, Political Parties, trans. by Eden and Cedar Paul (New York: Free Press, 1962).

19. For a good statement of the importance of the study of persistence, see R. DuWors, Sorokin, Sociology, and the Obdurate Facts of Social Persistence (Saskatoon, Canada: University of Saskatchewan, 1977).

20. See R. Edward Freeman and David L. Reed, "Stockholders and Stakeholders: A New Perspective on Corporate Governance," California Management Review 25 (Spring 1983): 88-106; and Anne Spencer, On the Edge of the Organization: The Role of the Outside Director (New York: John Wiley, 1983).

21. This example is drawn from Donald E. Schwartz, "Shareholder Democracy: A Reality or Chimera?" California Management Review 25 (Spring 1983):53-67.

22. Stephanie Chavez, "Archbishop Dedicates Lobster Dock," Boston Globe, June 18, 1984, pp. 19, 20. See also Peace

and Justice Commission, Archdiocese of Boston, <u>Annual Report</u>
<u>1983-1984</u>.

23.  John Egerton, "Workers Take Over the Store,"
<u>New York Times Magazine</u>, September 11, 1983.

24.  David Ellerman, "The Employment Relation, Property
Rights and Organizational Democracy," in <u>Organizational Democ-</u>
<u>racy and Political Processes</u>, ed. C. Crouch and F. Heller
(New York: Wiley, 1983), pp. 265-278.

25.  David Ellerman and Peter Pitegoff, "The Democratic
Corporation: The New Worker Cooperative Statute in Massachusetts," <u>New York University Review of Law and Social Change</u>
11 (1982-1983):441-472.

26.  John C. Cert, "The Marvels of Mondragon," <u>Common-</u>
<u>wealth</u>, June 18, 1982, pp. 369-371.

# 8

# INVESTIGATING CORPORATE
# SOCIAL PERFORMANCE
# AND POLICY: A RESEARCH NOTE

Investigations of corporate response to social issues have
been characterized by numerous perspectives, indicators,
measurement techniques, and strategies of operationalization
and research design.[1] To a large extent, the result has been
a series of findings that are difficult to compare and contrast
with each other, and calls for more integration of work. Considering the variety of theoretical perspectives that have
spawned such a diversity of research questions that have then
been tested by many different techniques, of course, serious
criticism and reappraisal of these works were inevitable.[2]
As a point of departure for exploring these concerns, this
chapter briefly reviews a number of research issues that bear
on corporate social policy and performance. Given the complexity
and scope of this work, we will not attempt to do justice to the
rich business and society research literature in a brief concluding chapter. Rather, as others have argued, any attempt to
evaluate the current state of research in this area will tend to
be "preliminary, partial, and a bit presumptuous."[3] Nevertheless, the following discussion provides an essential foundation
for our proposed research strategy.


METHODOLOGICAL CONCERNS

Perhaps the greatest initial problem lies in the area of
conceptualization, for conceptual elements are arguably the
most important determinants of the entire research process.[4]
As Berrien has said, "it is only by erecting conceptual frame-

works that we discover where ignorance lies."[5] The same point has been forcefully argued by Kuhn in his analysis of science.[6] In fact, Kuhn goes so far as to contend that normal scientific scholarship is merely the working out of the specific puzzles posed by general views of the world or "paradigms." Applied to the area of corporate social responsibility, these considerations suggest that researchers must examine their models of the world, especially in regard to the social economy. What major assumptions are made about the nature and operation of business, the economy, government, or society as a whole? How do such premises affect the specific research questions which are, or perhaps are not, pursued?

Similar conceptual issues arise in connection with values and ideologies. According to Gouldner, value premises influence research in many important ways. Involving as they do beliefs about the nature of the world, "domain assumptions have implications about what it is possible to do, and change in the world."[7] In short, the ideals of researchers define what they see in their work, and determine how data will be interpreted.[8] Such difficulties have yet to be fully explored in the area of corporate behavior.

Along similar lines, the values and ideologies of those individuals being studied also seem to be an important consideration. While some investigators have focused on the social attitudes of executives and business students,[9] and the importance of values in relation to response to social needs,[10] values have received relatively little attention on the whole.[11] Even from such limited work, however, the importance of valuational factors can be clearly seen. Holmes, for instance, reports that executive perceptions of social responsibility were closely related to more general perspectives and value orientations.[12] Future research in the field should delve into these questions, and move on to related issues, such as the connection between expressed or unexpressed values and actual behavior, and policy decisions.

Measurement presents a second set of general research difficulties. Of particular significance within the field of business and society has been the problem of converting qualitative concepts like responsiveness into quantitative data. What, for example, would constitute a degree of "community mindedness" or a unit of "social performance?" If such units can be developed, is it possible to place a dollar value upon them?[13] Beyond these difficulties lies the treacherous problem of weighting the indicators of corporate performance.[14] In computing an equation of responsiveness, should energy conservation be considered as important

as, say, affirmative action programs? How do these two indicators in turn compare with community-oriented investments
or with contributions to charitable campaigns? Indeed, increasing awareness of such measurement puzzles has been a primary
reason underlying a lowering of expectations for social audit
possibilities.[15]

A third series of research difficulties result from the
general need for access to data sources.[16] Access depends
upon trust, which rests upon the perception by potential
respondents that proposed research will be helpful, or at least
nonthreatening. Finding themselves in such a dependent position,
researchers may tend from the outset to make strategic compromises on the purposes and focal points of their studies,
which may severely curtail their ability to discover abuses or
arrive at critical conclusions. One group of researchers, for
instance, saw an initial offer to inspect corporate records with-
drawn when it appeared that research results might not be
favorable to the organization.[17] Such general difficulties may
be greatly intensified in a polarized climate of opinion, where
public trust is declining and business has adopted a cautious,
defensive posture. This sort of situation can develop, for
example, in the wake of particularly well publicized attacks on
corporate practice.[18] Students of responsiveness policy thus
face a formidable dilemma: should they maximize access at the
cost of critical inquiry, or maximize free critical scholarship
at the cost of access to essential data sources? Of course,
sometimes it is necessary to admit defeat on both counts. Such
was the experience of one researcher who attempted to analyze
the impact of recent bank credit allocation policies on the larger
community and was given turn-of-the-century data.[19]

Despite these obstacles, investigators can and do collect
information that presents them with a new set of difficulties.
What is the overall quality of the gathered data? Are there
important biases that result from the world view of respondents—
including their view of researchers? What dominant values or
ideologies have influenced the data? Has there, for example,
been an attempt to present a certain self-image by providing
only socially acceptable answers?[20] Do the data include only
self-interested reports,[21] or does the researchers have a means
of checking responses through on-site observation or the
testimony of objective outside sources?[22]

Investigators must also assess other qualities of their
data, such as completeness and comparability. It may happen
that the data base of respondents is inadequate, that they are
not well informed on certain issues. There may also be specific

gaps in information which result from corporate secrecy or hidden policy agendas. Nonresponse to survey instruments, another well known problem of data incompleteness, has provoked considerable comment in the literature. Parket and Eilbert, for instance, used response and nonresponse rates as indicators of social responsibility, arguing that those who responded to their survey were probably more responsible than those who did not.[23] While such an interpretation may have some intuitive appeal, there is considerable debate on the issue. Buehler and Shetty, by contrast, reported that the social activity of an organization did not necessarily relate to its survey response rate.[24] In fact, they concluded that nonreporting firms tended to be more active in social programs than responding firms.

Where comparability of data sets is concerned, researchers often encounter a problem similar to the question of weighting discussed above. Data supplied by better informed respondents deserves to be taken more seriously than that provided by less knowledgeable sources. Annual reports, which have been widely used as data sources, provide a good illustration of other comparability problems. Bowman and Haire proposed that an organization's social responsiveness could be measured by the proportion of lines in the annual report devoted to social concerns.[25] Fry and Hock, however, disagreed, arguing that the extent of such reporting is a function of the size of the organization and of a perception that the firm suffers from a negative public image.[26] Thus, they suggest that it is often "the biggest and the worst" who present the most social data in annual reports. The acuteness of such problems is even more clearly highlighted when one considers what Loeb has termed "annual report doubletalk."[27]

Beyond these various issues loom the eternal research problems of reliability and validity. The former addresses the reproducibility of the findings, focusing on the extent to which another researcher utilizing the same methods would arrive at the same conclusions. The latter deals with the accuracy of the results: Do the research results correctly characterize the situation and capture what is really taking place? Reliability is more readily dealt with, since it can be improved by making research procedures stricter and more formalized, and by specifying the rules of procedure in greater detail. This is not to say, however, that it is easily managed. The variable of access, to cite just one example, can make it impossible for later researchers who enjoy less trust to replicate the findings of earlier, more favored investigators.

Validity is the great intangible in research. It is never possible to demonstrate conclusively that all relevant variables have been considered, that the data are complete and trustworthy, that communication has been successful, and that inferences are completely accurate. If the questions had been set up differently, if observations had been taken at a different point in time, if personal relationships had taken a different form, or if any of an unquantifiable number of details had been altered, the findings might have been different as well. More than any other factor, it is the issue of validity which excites and challenges the research imagination.

## THE PROBLEM OF MULTIPLE REALITIES

Participation in the life of human groups requires some sense of what is real, that is, of what exists, what is happening, and what matters. For ordinary purposes in everyday life, most of us maintain relatively stable and unexamined views of "the real." Pressures of family life, career, and personal involvements make it difficult for us to break away and reflect on large, philosophical issues such as the nature of the world. And yet, many of us know from experience that our picture of reality is fundamentally fragile or elusive, and never completely adequate.

Such realizations occur in many ways. Introductory psychology and organizational behavior courses, for instance, often raise very intriguing questions about perception. What do we see and not see, hear and not hear, and why? Many textbooks contain drawings which can be interpreted in two very different ways, as a vase or a human face, a group of ducks or antelopes, and so on. We may readily see one, but have difficulty identifying the other. Psychological experiments have made the same point, sometimes very dramatically, as when people will deny the strong evidence of their own senses under peer pressure. Clearly, the world could be perceived in different ways than those to which we are accustomed, and perhaps only some slight alteration in stimuli would be required to produce markedly altered perceptions.[28]

Cultural anthropology has developed the same issue of multiple realities from a slightly different angle. Ways of thinking and feeling about the world are collectively organized and socially transmitted, and the substantive differences are at times astonishing. A favorite illustration deals with such anomalies of language as the absence of a future tense for verbs in English. How do people go through the day without talking about the future, a concept that dominates our view of ourselves in the United States? The difficulties of comprehending the realities of other cultures are sometimes discussed in terms of the concept of ethnocentrism, which refers to the tendency to view everything within the definitions of one culture. Indeed, anthropologists raise the difficult and imponderable issue: Can we ever really understand a culture which is fundamentally different from our own?[29]

These cultural and psychological considerations are combined in sociology with factors of social choice and conditioning in an area called the "sociology of knowledge." The general emphasis here has been on the large role played by socialization in our processes of interpreting events in the world. As Sorokin has noted, contemporary persons in Western societies are taught to know reality by means of sensory perception, measurement, and the methods of natural science, while other peoples have been brought up to understand it through intuition, feeling, and mystical experience. What seems "sick" from the perspective of twentieth-century psychiatry, therefore, may have seemed saintly to Europeans in medieval times. Karl Mannheim went so far as to pose the question of whether social conditioning eliminated the possibility of valid knowledge. All socially transmitted perspectives, he suggested, were relative and inadequate in some way.[30] The same issue has been dealt with by Marxists in terms of "false consciousness," the idea that our view of the world is inculcated by the ruling class and may disguise its unjust domination. Middle-class persons, they argue, will fail to see the extent of suffering and exploitation in class-based societies because from their relatively prosperous position things look better than they truly are.

A further vantage point on the issue of multiple realities have been summarized in the phrase "the social construction of reality." This concept captures the collective process of building up and maintaining particular models of the world. Do we choose to view life in terms of "evolution" and "linear progress" based on natural science and technology? Or as an eternal circular motion in which particular phases occur in a predetermined sequence? Or perhaps as an increasingly intense, international struggle between social classes which will finally be resolved in a communist revolution? The shared adoption of a general model of reality will ultimately determine how we "frame" the flow of everyday events.[31]

The link to our central theme is, we hope, reasonably clear at this point. "Corporate social responsibility" is itself a multiple reality and, as such, confronts investigators with the array of problems just reviewed: perceptual variation, ethno-centrism, and relativity of knowledge. What, then, is the most appropriate methodology for anyone who wishes to do research in this area, to capture something of what Roethlisberger termed "the elusive phenomena?"[32]

Many people would undoubtedly respond to these issues by calling for a "scientific" method—the more scientific the better. Indeed, science is the touchstone or bedrock of truth from the modern point of view. Therefore nothing highlights the issue of multiple realities more clearly than the realization that science itself has become difficult to interpret, especially over the past six or seven decades. What is particularly intriguing about this development is the fact that much of the questioning began within natural science itself—indeed, within physics, which was considered the most fully developed and most reliable science. Here, quantum mechanics and the principle of uncertainty suddenly upset the established presumption of the nature and "knowability" of the universe, and the situation has become even more confused in the wake of such recent developments as subatomic physics which uncovered a mysterious reality, radically different from the hoped-for stable "building blocks."

It is perhaps appropriate to suggest, as a final comment, that the difficulties of knowing corporate social responsibility, and knowing it scientifically, are directly related to the difficulty of understanding the main trends of our age. For it may be that the phenomena we seek to interpret are themselves located in a context of profound change. In a philosophical critique of modern science, Berman has developed this theory as follows:

> The problem is that the whole constellation of factors—technological manipulation of the environment, capital accumulation based on it, notions of secular salvation that fueled it and were fueled by it—has apparently run its course. In particular, the modern scientific paradigm has become as difficult to maintain in the late twentieth century as was the religious paradigm in the seventeenth. The collapse of capitalism, the general dysfunction of institutions, the revulsion against ecological spoliation, the increasing inability of the scientific

world view to explain the things that really matter,
the loss of interest in work, and the statistical
rise in depression, anxiety, and outright psychosis
are all of a piece.[33]

The way out, Berman suggests, lies in the recovery of "some
type of holistics, or participating consciousness." This concept
leads us back to our central theme of building a strategy for
the investigation of corporate social responsiveness.

## THEORETICAL, SOCIAL AND EMPIRICAL TRIANGULATION

The essential idea of triangulation is quite simple and has
many familiar applications. We can most effectively estimate
an unknown position or quantity by relating it to several known
points of orientation or to several known quantities. The full
significance of triangulation for scholarly inquiry is suggested
by the following rhetorical question: "How can the social sciences
progress when they are relatively culture-bound, time-bound,
unreplicated, lacking in interest in macroscopic problems, un-
concerned with the correspondence between what is done and
what is said, and pay only lip service to reliability and validity?"[34]
Although the specific reference in this quote is to social science,
the applicability of the thought to the study of corporate social
policy should be readily apparent. We therefore propose that
future studies in the field employ the principle of triangulation
to the fullest possible extent. There are three major levels or
aspects of phenomena for which this can be done.

The nature and significance of theoretical (or perhaps
conceptual) triangulation can be best understood in the context
of the research problems associated with limited world views
and unexamined value systems. When issues are narrowly
framed and values unconsciously built into the research design,
the results will be affected in important ways. To overcome
such difficulties, we recommend that researchers draw upon
both the intellectual questions and the values articulated by
the most important social science traditions. We refer here in
particular to the concepts of conflict and consensus, continuity
and change. We have in mind such values as freedom and
accountability, equality and participation. At the conceptual
or theoretical level, methods can also be triangulated. Researchers can plan from the outset to complement the strengths
of the dominant survey method with other procedures such as

participant observation, content analysis, and historical inquiry. Each of these methods, in turn, can be triangulated internally by more refined techniques.[35]

In speaking of social triangulation we are thinking primarily of the participation of various types of groups in the research process. This can and should involve both investigators and respondents. In the former case, members of a research team can check and supplement one another's findings by making independent observations. Such a procedure might be particularly fruitful where one investigator has a special knowledge of one research strategy, while other team members have expertise in other techniques. Triangulation of respondents recalls our notion of relevant publics who are affected in various ways by corporate actions. They include subgroups within the corporation itself, as well as outside groups such as consumers and community residents.

By empirical triangulation we mean the cross-checking of data sets. This, in fact, is the sort of triangulation procedure most widely discussed in research texts, and the technique which most readily comes to mind when the term is mentioned. It is particularly important to check findings generated by one method with the data presented by another. Data produced in one cultural or subcultural context should be compared and contrasted with that gathered in others (for example, labor and management, producer and consumer, investor and resident). The same is true of data collected at different points in time, by qualitative and quantitative procedures, focused on verbal reports or actual behavior.

In an exploratory way, we have attempted to outline such a research approach in this book. Initially, this work began with a conceptualization of the meaning of social responsibility, which led to the construction of an ideal-typical model of corporate social policy variants. Based on the idea of theoretical triangulation, this conceptualization emerged from different philosophies or theories of social responsibility. When this conceptualization was used to examine the reinvestment policies of different banks, the research process delved into the positions and views of bank personnel, community groups, and the relevant bank agencies. At the same time, each of us made independent observations, and the resultant conclusions were based on a comparison and contrast of these findings (social triangulation). Finally, in terms of empirical triangulation, we drew upon archival information, self-reports put forth by the banks and the community advocacy group, interviews with key people representing the different groups involved, and an organizational survey (in one of the banks) which focused on employee views of the reinvestment policy. As a result, we were able to differentiate verbal reports from actual behaviors, and the views of the various groups involved from other relevant publics.

This strategy led into new and unanticipated directions. Each of the original types of corporate social policies, for instance, seemed more properly conceptualized as a range, with the research focused on the social process of dynamic assessment to ensure the original commitment to an interpretive sociology based on the meaning of interaction to its participants. It was also evident that the issue of conflict needed to be explicitly formulated in terms of specific disputing processes. Thus, the research experience has been one of a continual dialogic or dialectical relationship between theory building in the most formal and deductive sense, and the discovery of "grounded theory" in the fullest empirical sense. Although the empirical material is presented in an exploratory manner, our hope is that the triangulation strategy is clear and that its usefulness is underscored.

In summary, we believe that the research agenda we have proposed here will offer strong prospects for the development of a sound body of theoretical and empirical data in the realm of corporate social performance. Some might object that the process is too costly in terms of both time and effort. Given the scope of the field, however, nothing short of the type of integral strategy discussed throughout this book is necessary to capture the complex dynamics of corporate social policy and performance.

NOTES

1. For an overview of these differences see Robert J. DeFillippi, "Conceptual Frameworks and Strategies for Corporate Social Involvement Research," in Research in Corporate Social Performance and Policy, Vol. 4, ed. Lee E. Preston (Greenwich, Conn.: JAI Press, 1982), pp. 35-56; James E. Post and Patti N. Andrews, "Case Research in Corporation and Society Studies," in Research in Corporate Social Performance and Policy, Vol. 4, ed. Lee E. Preston (Greenwich, Conn.: JAI Press, 1982), pp. 1-34; and Liam Fahey and Richard E. Wokutch, "Business and Society Exchanges: A Framework for Analysis," California Management Review 25 (Summer 1983):128-142.

2. Post and Andrews, "Case Research," pp. 1-3.

3. Ramon J. Aldag and Kathryn M. Bartol, "Empirical Studies of Corporate Social Performance and Policy: A Survey of Problems and Results," in Research in Corporate Social Performance and Policy, Vol. 1, ed. Lee E. Preston (Greenwich, Conn.: JAI Press, 1978), p. 165.

4. Robert K. Merton, On Theoretical Sociology: Essays Old and New (New York: Free Press, 1967).

5. K. Berrien, "A General Systems Approach to Organization," in Handbook of Industrial and Organizational Psychology, ed. Marvin Dunnett (Chicago: Rand McNally, 1976), p. 60.

6. T. Kuhn, The Structure of Scientific Revolutions (Chicago: University of Chicago Press, 1967), pp. 24-25.

7. Alvin Gouldner, The Coming Crisis in Western Sociology (New York: Basic Books, 1970), pp. 47-48.

8. See A. Cicourel, "Basic and Normative Rules in the Negotiation of Status and Role," in Recent Sociology II, ed. H. P. Dreitzel (New York: Macmillan, 1970); and B. Glaser and A. Strauss, The Discovery of Grounded Theory (Chicago: Aldine, 1967).

9. See R. Aldag and D. Jackson, "A Managerial Framework for Social Decision Making," MSU Business Topics 23 (1975):23-40; R. Aldag and D. Jackson, "Some Properties and Correlates of the Social Attitudes Questionnaire," Proceedings of the Thirty-Seventh Annual Meeting of the Academy of Management, 1977; R. Aldag and D. Jackson, "Assessment of Attitudes Toward Social Responsibilities," Journal of Business Administration 8 (1977):65-80; and Frederick A. Sturdivant and James L. Ginter, "Corporate Social Responsiveness: Management Attitudes and Economic Performance," California Management Review 14 (Spring 1977):30-39.

10. See Gerald Cavanagh, American Business Values (Englewood Cliffs: Prentice-Hall, 1984); and Patrick E. Connor and Boris W. Becker, "Values and the Organization: Suggestions for Research," Academy of Management Journal 18 (1975):550-561.

11. See Aldag and Bartol, "Empirical Studies"; and Boris W. Becker and Patrick E. Connor, "A Course on Human Values for the Management Curriculum," Exchange: The Organizational Behavior Teaching Journal 8 (1983):10-16

12. Sandra Holmes, "Executive Perceptions of Corporate Social Responsibility," Business Horizons 19 (1976):34-40.

13. See E. Sheldon and K. C. Land, "Social Reporting for the 1970's: A Review and Programmatic Statement," Policy Sciences (July 1972):138-156; and Clark Abt, The Social Audit for Management (New York: AMACOM, 1977).

14. B. H. Spicer, "Accounting for Corporate Social Performance: Some Problems and Issues," Journal of Contemporary Business 7 (1978):151-170.

15. Kirk O. Hansen, "Measurement of Social Accountability," paper presented at the TIMS/ORSA Joint National Meeting, May 5, 1980, Washington, D.C.

16. R. Gold, "Roles in Sociological Field Observations," in Issues in Participant Observation, ed. G. McCall and J. Simmons (Reading, Mass.: Addison-Wesley, 1969); and I. Horowitz, The Rise and Fall of Project Camelot (Cambridge, Mass.: MIT Press, 1967).

17. R. Estes and N. Zenz, "Social Accounting in a Manufacturing Company: An Action Research Study," Journal of Contemporary Business 7 (1978):33-43.

18. For some focused criticism on the banking industry, see T. Cross and P. London, "It Makes a Difference Where You Bank Your Money," Business and Society Review (Winter 1975): 21-31; D. Leinsdorf and N. Etra, Citibank (New York: Grossman, 1973); and Carol Greenwald, Banks Are Dangerous to Your Wealth (Englewood Cliffs: Prentice-Hall, 1980).

19. Andrew Beveridge, Social Structure, Social Change and Credit Allocation (New York: Columbia University, 1977).

20. K. Thomas and R. Kilman, "The Social Desirability Variable in Organizational Research: An Alternative Explanation for Reported Findings," Academy of Management Journal 18 (1975):741-752; and J. Robertson, "Corporate Social Reporting by New Zealand Companies," Journal of Contemporary Business 7 (1978):113-133.

21. N. C. Churchill and A. B. Toan, "Reporting on Corporate Social Responsibility: A Progress Report," Journal of Contemporary Business 7 (1978):5-17.

22. See P. Rossi, "Testing for Success and Failure in Social Action," in Evaluating Social Programs, ed. P. Rossi and W. Williams (New York: Seminar Press, 1972); and C. Weiss, Evaluation Research (Englewood Cliffs: Prentice-Hall, 1972).

23. R. Parket and H. Eilbert, "Social Responsibility: The Underlying Factors," Business Horizons 18 (1975):5-10.

24. V. Buehler and V. Shetty, "Motivations for Corporate Social Action," Academy of Management Journal 17 (1974):767-771.

25. H. Bowman and M. Haire, "A Strategic Posture Toward Corporate Social Responsibility," California Management Review 18 (1975):49-58.

26. F. Fry and R. Hock, "Who Claims Corporate Responsibility? The Biggest and the Worst," Business and Society Review (Summer 1976):62-65.

27.  S. M. Loeb, "Annual Report Double Talk," Business and Society Review (Fall 1979):71.

28.  These issues are dealt with in most introductory texts in psychology and organizational behavior, especially in discussions of perception and influence. See, for example, F. L. Ruch and P. G. Zimbardo, Psychology and Life (Glenview, Ill.: Scott, Foresman, 1971); and James L. Bowditch and Anthony F. Buono, A Primer on Organizational Behavior (New York: John Wiley, 1985).

29.  See, for example, Maurice Natanson, ed., Phenomenology and the Social Sciences, Vol. 1 (Evanston, Ill.: Northwestern University Press, 1973).  The specific issue of language and reality is explored in John B. Carroll, ed., Language, Thought and Reality (Cambridge, Mass.: MIT Press, 1956).

30.  Karl Mannheim, Ideology and Utopia, trans. L. Wirth and E. Shils (New York: Harcourt Brace Jovanovich, 1957).

31.  See Peter Berger and Thomas Luckmann, The Social Construction of Reality (Garden City, N.Y.: Doubleday, 1966); also Erving Goffman, Frame Analysis (New York: Harper & Row, 1974).

32.  See F. J. Roethlisberger, The Elusive Phenomena (Cambridge, Mass.: Harvard University Press, 1977).

33.  Morris Berman, The Reenchantment of the World (Ithaca, N.Y.: Cornell University Press, 1981), pp. 22-23.

34.  H. Smith, Strategies of Social Research (Englewood Cliffs: Prentice-Hall, 1975), p. 272.

35.  Ibid., p. 290.

# INDEX

Ackerman, R., 14, 135

banks, as quasi-public
　institutions, 133-34
　(see also Community
　Reinvestment Act)
Bauer, R., 135
Bell, D., 55, 100
Benne, R., 85, 88-89
Bluestone, B., 93-95
Bowen, H., 9-10
Bruyn, S., 93
business and society, 1-29;
　integral conceptualization
　of, 30-65
Business Roundtable, 2,
　89-90

Carney, M., 95-96
Carroll, A., 15-17, 20
Collier, A., 100
Community Reinvestment Act:
　and Boston banks, 138-50;
　history of, 128-36; and
　MURAG challenges, 155-74
cooperative corporations,
　202-08; Mondragon model
　of, 206
corporations: macromanage-
　ment of, 34; social per-
　formance of, 15-19; social
　policy of, 19-22, 37-43;
　social responsibility of,
　9-12; social responsiveness
　of, 12-15; stakeholder view
　of, 4-9, 72-73, 130-33;
　stockholder view of, 3-4,
　72-73, 129-30

culture: general definition
　of, 67-68; and ideals,
　69; Sorokin's analysis of,
　67-68; and values, 68-69

dialectical thinking, 60
disputing, general model of,
　174-77 (see also Community
　Reinvestment Act)
Domhoff, W., 59-60
Durkheim, E., 51

ethical idealism, 90-104;
　Bluestone and Harrison
　on, 93-95; Bruyn on, 93;
　and Catholic social justice
　teaching, 98-99; Kavanaugh
　on, 100; Nader on, 92-93;
　political varieties of, 91-
　97; religious varieties of,
　96-104; Schumacher on,
　96-98
ethics: in business, 43-51;
　deontological theory of,
　47-48; and justice, 48;
　and relativism, 46; teleo-
　logical theory of, 47;
　utilitarian theory of, 47

Friedman, M., 10, 76-77
Frankfurt School, 59

Galbraith, J., 77, 92
Gouldner, A., 54-212
Greenwald, C., 132, 178

Harrison, B., 93-95
Hayek, F., 75-76

Hoffman, M., 44
Holmes, S., 19

ideal types: as method of
analysis, 70-72; of policy,
110-19; and social responsibility, 72-104
interpretive sociology, 127
(see also ideal types;
symbolic interactionism)

Jameson, K., 99
Jones, T., 19

Kavanaugh, J., 100
Keim, G., 11
Kolko, G., 60
Kristol, I., 78

Lindsell, H., 79-80, 84

MacIver, R., 127
Marx, K., 55-56
Massachusetts Urban Reinvest-
ment Advisory Group
(MURAG), 126, 157-63,
169, 173, 178
Mayo, E., 53-54
Mills, C. W., 58-59
Mulligan, G., 158-59, 163, 178

Nader Group, 92-93

Oates, J., 83
organizational responsibility,
119-23

Parsons, T., 54
philanthropy, 79-85; in Levi
Strauss, 80-81; Lindsell
on, 79-80; and marketing,
83-85
policy: and business, 37-43;
and corporate social
philosophies, 113-20; and

organizational philosophies,
120-23; and process of
interpretation, 126-51;
sociocultural view of,
110-11
Post, J., 18, 21-22, 35
Preston, L., 18, 35
productivism, 73-79; Friedman on, 76-77; Hayek on,
75-76; and supply-side
economics, 78-79
progressivism, 85-90; Benne
on, 85-89; Steckmest on,
89-90

Rawls, J., 88
research methods, 211-20;
and problem of multiple
realities, 215-16; triangulation of, 218-20 (see
also Community Reinvest-
ment Act; ideal types)
responsiveness of corporations, 12-15
Roethlisberger, F., 53
Ruder, W., 44

Schumacher, E., 96-97
self-management of corporations. See cooperative
corporations
Shearer, D., 95-96
Smelser, N., 54
social change, 187-208; and
Community Reinvestment
Act, 190-91; direction of,
197-98; integral model of,
188-90; problem of degree
of, 191-94; and problem
of persistence, 200-02;
and social issues life
cycle, 135-36; sources of,
190-96
social economy, as field of
sociology, 51-60; analytical

[social economy]
theories of, 51-55; critical
theories of, 55-60; Marx
on, 55-57; Parsons on, 54;
Sorokin on, 57-58; Weber
on, 52-53
social performance of corporations, 15-20
social policy of corporations,
20-22; Post's types of 21-
22 (see also policy)
social responsibility: ethical
idealist philosophy of,
90-104; philanthropic
philosophy of, 79-89;
productivist philosophy
of, 74-79; progressivist
philosophy of, 85-90;
subtypes of, 148-49; and
supply-side economics,
78-79

Sorokin, P., 57
Spencer, H., 51-52
stakeholder view of corporations. See corporations
Steckmest, F., 89-90
stockholder view of corporations. See corporations
Strauss, L., 80-81
symbolic interactionism, 127;
and reinvestment disputes,
170-78

Toennies, F., 56-57

Veblen, T., 56-57

Weber, M., 51-53, 127
Wilber, C., 99
Williams, H., 90
Wilson, J., 83
Wren, D., 81-82

# ABOUT THE AUTHORS

ANTHONY F. BUONO is Associate Professor of Management at Bentley College, Massachusetts where he teaches in the areas of organizational behavior and development, and problems of management in a changing environment. He is also on the faculty of the National Association of Bank Women's Management Institute at Simmons College and has previously taught at Boston College.

Dr. Buono is co-author of Quality of Work Life Assessment (Auburn House, 1982) and A Primer on Organizational Behavior (John Wiley, 1985). Widely published in the area of industrial and organizational sociology, he has recently published articles in Human Relations, Greek Review of Social Research, and Research on Corporate Social Performance and Policy.

Professor Buono holds a B.S. from the University of Maryland and an M.A. and Ph.D. from Boston College.

LAWRENCE T. NICHOLS is Assistant Professor of Sociology at Bridgewater State College, Massachusetts. He has taught at numerous colleges in the Boston area, including Suffolk University, Northeastern University, and the University of Massachusetts, Boston.

Professor Nichols is co-author of Beyond the Courtroom (Lexington Books, 1981), a study of current alternative methods for the resolution of interpersonal disputes. He has also done research on the intellectual and professional history of the discipline of sociology and has published in Encounter and Research on Corporate Social Performance and Policy.

**DATE DUE**

| | | | |
|---|---|---|---|
| APR 25 '88 | | | |
| SEP 29 1989 | AUG 09 2001 | | |
| DEC 08 1989 | DEC 05 2006 | | |
| DEC 19 1989 | | | |
| OCT 17 1990 | | | |
| OCT 23 1992 | | | |
| NOV 11 1992 | | | |
| DEC 28 1993 | | | |
| | | | |